Comments on *Canadian Garden Words* and other books by Bill Casselman

"Canadian Garden Words . . . vintage Casselman . . . This eclectic mix will have you taking a fresh and affectionate look at the humblest denizens of your garden."

Kate Harries, *Toronto Star*, Books, Jan. 3, 1998

"Bill Casselman . . . the master of Canadian words, usage and meanings . . . thoroughly entertaining and informative. A delight for anyone interested in words or gardening or both."

Canadian Geographic magazine's 1997 Winter Catalogue

"Amusing book . . . colourful, often hilarious, explanation of how Canadian garden and native plants got their names."

Wendy Warburton, *Ottawa Citizen*, Oct. 30, 1997

"Casselman loves righting word wrongs, even if it means ruffling a few feathers."

George Bentley, *Regina Leader-Post*, Feb. 1996

"A raconteur with wit and humour. Along this etymological odyssey, Casselman's enquiring mind showers us with myth, history, speculation, and pure trivia. If you have never had a desire to learn how plants got their names, this book may convince you otherwise."

Richard Aaron, *Toronto Field Naturalist*, Dec. 1997

"Bill Casselman was guest speaker in the Edwards Lecture Series at Toronto's Civic Garden Centre for a highly entertaining evening that explored the lore and history of plant names."

Trellis, Jan./Feb. 1998, newsletter of Civic Garden Centre

"What do you get when you cross a word scholar with an amateur gardener? Bill Casselman . . . his famous sense of fun and wordplay . . ."

Mary K. Nolan, *Hamilton Spectator*, Gift Books, Dec. 13 1997

"The best remedy for a case of the mid-winter blahs or cabin fever is a good dose of Casselmania."

Joanna Manning, *The Welland Tribune*

"For a full appreciation of how and why Canadians came by their unique linguistic heritage, there can be no better guide than Bill Casselman."

Moira Farr, *Equinox* magazine

"I have both of Bill Casselman's brilliant, funny, word books, and I'm planning to get to them soon."

Ken Finkleman, creator of CBC TV's *Newsroom* and *More Tears*

Canadian Food Words

The Juicy Lore & Tasty Origins
of Foods That Founded a Nation

Bill Casselman

McArthur & Company

CANADIAN CATALOGUING IN PUBLICATION DATA

Casselman, Bill, 1942 –
Canadian food words

ISBN   1-55278-018-X

1. Food - Terminology. 2. Canadianisms (English).* I. Title.

TX349.C37 1998   641.3'001'4   C98-931677-7

Cover, Design and Composition *by* Michael P. Callaghan
Typeset *at* Moons of Jupiter, Toronto
Printed and Bound in Canada *by* Transcontinental

McArthur & Company
322 King Street West, Suite 402
Toronto, Ontario, Canada, M5V 1J2

10 9 8 7 6 5 4 3 2 1

for JUDY BRAKE

Companion originally meant 'one with whom you share bread,'
hence 'frequent tablemate.'
This book is dedicated to my friend and companion,
Judy Brake, who has introduced
a sometimes reluctant me
to many exotic morsels
of national and international cuisine.

SETTING THE TABLE OF CONTENTS

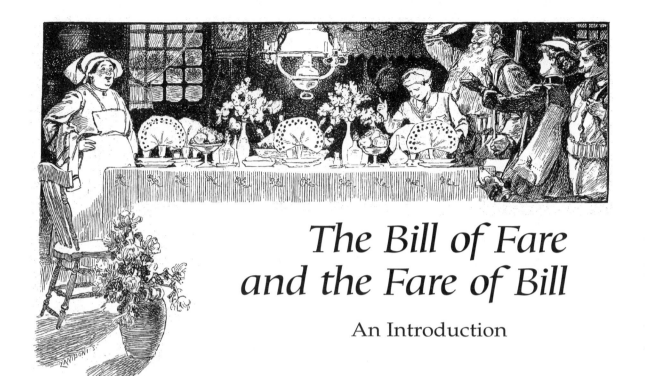

The Bill of Fare and the Fare of Bill

An Introduction

On this gustatory gallivanting across Canada, we learn about and enjoy some of the food words Canadians use and have used — many of these words as tangy and succulent as the foods they name. This book has some "new" old ideas and words for delicious Canadian fare. I wrote it for anyone interested in Canadian food and for chefs asked to prepare a "Canadian" menu who are perhaps weary of the *carte de la patrie* of fiddleheads, poached salmon, and maple syrup surprise. I wrote this book for cooking schools teaching Canadian cuisine, for food writers wanting a peek into historical kitchens, for any food lover and word nut curious about what our ancestors ate.

We aim to set the gastric juices flowing and to savour the etymological flavour of hearty Canadian edibles as well. Yes, the very terms for Canuck food and drink have word stories of their own to tell, tales spiced with the zest of our history, like lateer. Lateer is a term from the Canadian sugarbush. When maple sap has been boiled down to its proper stage, all slabby and ambrosial, you take a ladle and sling rills of hot maple syrup across an icy snowbank. As it cools, it solidifies; then you yank and stretch, seeing and feeling in your hands the pleasing metamorphosis of the sugary, fictile strands into maple taffy or lateer, from Québécois French *la tire*, toffee, itself from the French verb *tirer*, to pull. In Québec, maple taffy is usually twirled around a wooden stick, and even the festive get-together held to do this, a sugaring-off party, is called *une tire*.

To begin this gastronomic grand tour across the pasturelands of our Dominion, we hit the road in Newfoundland after a Jigg's dinner with scrunchins, washed down with a stain o' rum (a small portion), and then we light out for our West Coast, to lap up a foaming bowl of soapolallie ice cream.

Along the way, there are stops and mug-ups for Maritime fungy and bangbelly, bakeapple jam and blueberry grunt, fricko on Prince Edward Island, Labrador tea, bugger-in-a-bag pudding around Cascapedia Bay in the Gaspé region, rappie pie in New Brunswick, *gibelotte de Sorel* (perch stew) in Côte du Sud, a loaf of bread in Québec shaped like *fesses* 'buttocks' (but then English has *buns*), *viande boucanée,* which is salt pork smoked in the rafters of a maple sugar shack in la Beauce, some Finnish *pulla* bread in northern Ontario, some drepsley soup in southern Ontario, Red River bannock in Manitoba, Saskatoonberry turnovers along the Qu'Appelle River, paska bread and baked wind pills in Alberta, then up North where in early days, if a real woolly-whipper (northern blizzard) was blowing, we might have wolfed down rub-baboo and bannock buttered with buffalo marrow fat, or made do with "lean pickins" like spruce tea and rock tripe, or maybe moose-muffle soup followed by boiled quawk at Tuktoyaktuk. Our alimentary itinerary drops final anchor on British Columbia's Pacific coast, for a homey mess of geoducks at a Tofino eatery on Vancouver Island or a posh dainty like salmonberry charlotte at the Sooke Harbour House restaurant. And if no one has ever made a salmonberry charlotte, why then, perhaps some adventurous pastry chef may try?

A note about our lists and categories. Food words wander. Cooks trade recipes with friends and relatives in other provinces. If you see a culinary term listed under Nova Scotia and you used it as a child in Québec, don't freak. I have tried to place Canadian food words in the areas of the country where they originated or were first popular imports, but I shall be glad of any corrections or amendments readers wish to offer.

I wish to thank my Exacto™ knife of an editor, Pamela Erlichman, who vetted my prose, adding a gourmet dash here or semicolons *en aspic* there. Kim McArthur, the publisher who commissioned this and two other of my books, is an author's delight. She contracts for a book, and actually lets the author write it. Kim injects panache and a lovely light into all the sordid drearinesses of commerce. Scourge of sombre dolts in this politically correct, all-too-accountable world, she glows. Long may Kim McArthur shine, say I, and if a Methodist stern-heart ever attests that any of the more common-place saviours no longer want me for a sunbeam, then I'll be a sunbeam for Kim.

September, 1998
205 Helena Street,
Dunnville, Ontario, Canada N1A 2S6

CHAPTER 1

Newfoundland and Labrador

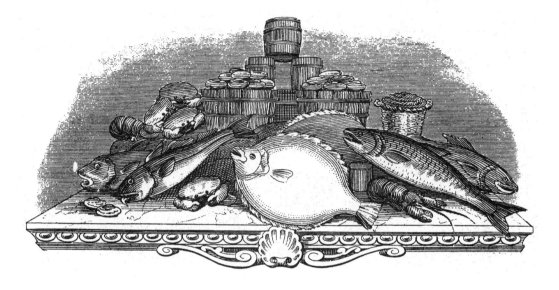

Stog Yer Gob with Prog

Or, stuff your mouth with food — the kindly order a guest might have heard from a rough-and-ready but hospitable bayman as he invited you to sit down to a Newfoundland outport meal, late in the last century. His wife might have added, "Make a long arm now." That is, help yourself. You can take a man out of the bay, but you can't take the bay out of the man, runs the island proverb. Maybe that's why, however far from home Newfoundlanders must roam to earn their daily bread, they never forget it: the daily bread their mothers baked, with the extra treat of damper dogs — wads of bread dough fried quickly on the lid (damper) of a hot woodstove, usually a treat for children, who were fed the damper dogs

or damper devils so they wouldn't gobble up all the fresh-baked bread.

This fondness for "The Rock" brings to a nostalgic conclusion the memoirs of John Crosbie, the controversial politician who was an adept Conservative cabinet minister. *No Holds Barred: My Life in Politics* has these curtain lines: "Someone once asked how you can tell which ones are Newfoundlanders when you visit heaven. The answer is, you can always tell the Newfoundlanders because they're the ones who want to go home."

Newfoundland has preserved its traditional cookery better than any other part of Canada and kept alive too the resonant food terms that label it. The isolation of island life accounts for some of the ease of preserving folksy dishes and for the unique, rich vocabulary of Newfoundland English — the oldest variety of English in the New World — amply reflected in wonderful culinary phrases like bitch and dogbody, flummy dum, lad-in-a-bag, lassy mogs, soaked sounds, partridge-berry squatum, toutins for breakfast, and a plate of fish and vang. Of course, there's no pain at all in a juicy slice of hurt pie.

Before 1949 few roads ran to outport villages. Sparse greens could be harvested during the short summer, but most food came to table by boat. Big supermarkets had no damn way to get to the outports. Most think that a blessing. The down side was scant fresh vegetables and meat, and a dependence by Newfoundlanders on fresh and dried fish and salted meat for basic protein, both of which feature naturally in their traditional recipes.

While it is true these food words, like scrunchins or fish and brewis, summon feelings as warm as home to many a Newfoundlander, their use arose from constraint and scarcity. Four hundred years of hard scrabble to jig a living from the sea have left their mark on the language and in the larders of

Newfoundland's cooks, in expressions like a bare-legged cup of tea, chaw and glutch, blind mush, baker's fog, dole bread, and whore's egg.

Early European Foodstuffs

The first Europeans, migratory fishermen who came in the summer to fish cod, naturally brought their own food with them, by necessity food that could endure the transatlantic crossing without spoiling — traditional European sailor's fare included ship's biscuit, beer, cider, peas, salt beef, and salt pork (usually as fat back, the strip of fat from the hog's back cured by dry salting). Imported foodstuffs were supplemented by fresh-caught fish. British victuallers supplied cheese, butter, vinegar, oatmeal, mustard seed, and spiritous liquors like aqua vitae as well. In these plain lists lie the origin of many Newfoundland dishes, like fish and brewis. Not surprisingly, given xenophobia, racism, and the conservative hesitancy of all humans to adopt new food staples, these migratory fishermen did not take much advantage of the local bounty on which the Aboriginal peoples of Newfoundland lived. Yet, early white explorers had fully reported on Beothuk and Inuit food sources, and later on noted what peoples of the interior of Labrador and Newfoundland ate. But Naskapi, Montagnais, and Mi'kmaq nutriments held little appeal to the white fishermen.

Aboriginal Foodways

The earliest First Peoples to settle the island probably came because of the abundance of fresh meat, including caribou (sometimes captured in Beothuk caribou fences), seals and whales (taken by the Thule and Inuit peoples using kayaks and umiaks), waterfowl, other birds, fish, and shellfish. Later Europeans exploring Labrador noted Inuit *pipshi*, dry-cured fish or meat, very similar to their beef jerky (compare Labrador Inuktitut *pitsik* 'dried fish'). The idea for seal-flipper pie must certainly have come from the Inuit dish of *utjak* ("seal flippers"). An Inuit pemmican called *sabalik* consisted of partly chewed blubber mixed with berries and trout roe. But most food of the Native Peoples did not appeal to whites, such as *uinastika*, caribou stomach dried, with some of its contents like moss still inside.

Eating Powdered Penis

Other food ideas, however wrong-headed, are remarkably persistent, for example, the small export trade between Newfoundland and the Far East, chiefly China and Japan, in powdered seal penis. The phallus of the hooded seal, *Cystophora cristata*, is used as an aphrodisiac by some, in spite of protests that the seal hunt is of scant economic benefit to Newfoundland, and in the face of biochemical evidence that seal penis extract has no organic effect whatsoever on the potency of human males. Of course, sex potions and aphrodisiacs throughout history have depended on psychological effect, on the power of mind over drooping matter. Primitive but apparently still compelling is the folk belief that, if one eats a big dick, one will have a big dick. Like the hunter seeking bravery who cuts out and eats the warm heart of the animal he has just killed, the person stirring seal-penis powder into his morning tea is engaged in semi-magical ritual, not scientific cure. Consuming penises, like eating animal legs to help one run faster, is an ancient nutritional fallacy — or should that be "phallacy"?

On the other hand, I see nothing evil in hunting a sustainable number of seals for fur and meat each spring. While the seal hunt may upset Toronto *artistes*, it is a natural, traditional source of income for some Newfoundlanders. Farther north, Inuit people use every part of a seal except its bark, and the protests of southern seal "experts" are the mere, distant honking of ignorant geese. I find quite unconvincing the protests by bourgeois city dwellers who have never had to live by nature, "red in tooth and claw" as Tennyson wrote.

In 1583, the navigator Sir Humphrey Gilbert landed at what became St. John's and claimed it for Elizabeth the First, thus founding England's first colony. He was lost at sea on the return voyage, but not before he had written that the country around St. John's was "very good and full of all sort of victuall, as fish both of the fresh water, and Sea fish, Deere, Pheasants, Partridges, Swannes, and divers Fowles."

By the mid-17th century, the American colonies were in full competition with England and Ireland to supply the main staples of the Newfoundland colony, hard tack and flour. Salt meat came chiefly from Ireland; rum, sugar, and molasses directly from the Caribbean islands or through New England colonial provisioning ships sailing north to trade.

As immigration increased, various European foods were added to the Newfoundland table. The

Immigrants Bring Their Cuisine

famines of the 1730s and 1740s in Ireland brought waves of Irish people, and with them, dishes like colcannon, crubeen, and pratie oatens. There is a Labrador haggis made with cod livers called Scotch dumpling.

The most influential Portuguese word in Canadian history is *bacalhao*, codfish. Cod and a possible western sea route to China were the magnets that first drew large numbers of Europeans to North America. Baccalaos was even an early name (1530) for Newfoundland itself. Variants in French, Spanish, and Portuguese lasted as names for the island for 150 years. Four Newfoundland place names still contain the word: Baccalieu (French 'codfish') Island, two Bacalhao Islands (Portuguese 'codfish'), and Baccalieu Tickle on Conception Bay. The Baccalieu bird is a local name for certain murres that nest on Baccalieu Island.

Newfoundlanders are not bashful about naming places after food either. Consider Cape Onion, Cheese Island, Doughfig Point, Mutton Bay, and Bacon Cove.

As they say in Newfoundland: when the rum is in the kag, the tongue doesn't wag. So, if you're reading this on a winter's day, when it's cold as a cod's nose, go ahead, take a sip. Maybe you'd drink it off dead Nelson — as they say when a tippler is a tad eager. What the heck! These lively food-and-drink words read better with a tot of screech. And if there are teetotalers hovering nearby, thicker than flies on a fish flake, be sly as a conner (an elusive wharf fish) and send them to the store. A teetotaler around these pungent words is liable to be as silly as a caplin. You have to make room for surprise and delight here, because, when you're dealing with Newfoundland English, everyway's likely! But, hey now, enough of my lip flap. Let's get into these expressions. I swear, some days I got a tongue like a miller's clapdish.

If you end up enjoying this scrumptious dish of words, all I can do is to echo that nifty nautical wish of Newfoundland: Long may your big jib draw!

ALEXANDERS

Also called Scotch Lovage or Sea Lovage, alexanders is an herb, eaten blanched as greens, raw in salad, or added as flavouring to a dumpling or duff (a flour-and-water pudding boiled in a cloth bag). As a Newfoundland food term, alexanders are large balls of boiled dough seasoned with Scotch Lovage and served with coady, a sweet sauce made of boiled molasses.

When it refers to the herb, the word appears as alexander, a singular, or alexanders, a collective noun, plural in form but singular grammatically. Thus one sees sentences like "alexander is an herb" and "alexanders is an herb."

The earliest scurvy-prone settlers and fishermen on Newfoundland were glad of an armful of alexander greens, especially in an area where there had been no time or proper season to put in a garden. Alexanders contains vitamin C and was eaten to prevent scurvy. A fisherman who had used up his ration of tobacco sometimes chewed the bitter root. The leaves and stalks of alexanders have a pungent taste, a tongue-rippling tang of strong celery or parsley. But if you were starved for greens, you developed a taste quickly, and young leaves and shoots are milder in flavour. One transatlantic use, however, gives a hint of how unpalatable alexanders may be to some. On the Isle of Skye in Scotland, alexander leaves are boiled in whey and used as a purgative for calves! In the Hebrides, outer islanders use the Gaelic word *shunis* to name the plant and consider it a vegetable for salads or for boiled greens. Their cooks tossed alexander leaves and peeled, blanched stalks into soups and stews to add an acrid celery zing.

But there was no damned romance in this wild weed. Alexanders, like so many of the old Newfoundland foods, was an herb of necessity, known to European sailors for two thousand years. Roman, Italian, French, Spanish, Portuguese, British, and

Scottish men of the sea learned to identify alexanders because it was antiscorbutic and could be obtained relatively easily during an outbreak of scurvy by putting ashore — if, of course, there was a shore handy. A widespread wild herb, it favours rocky coastlines and cliff meadows on both sides of the Atlantic. Growing one to three feet tall, and looking roughly similar to plants in the same umbelliferous family, like cow parsnip or Queen's Anne's Lace, alexanders blooms in midsummer in umbels of white or pinkish flowers. Early fishers in the New World found it along subarctic seashores from Rhode Island north, and up the coasts of Newfoundland and southern Labrador.

Word Lore and Botany

Alexanders, a member of the Umbelliferae plant family, bears the scientific name of *Ligusticum scoticum*. *Ligusticus* is the Latin meaning 'of Liguria,' ancient province of northern Italy whose chief city is Genoa. Medieval herbalists thought the plant of Genoese origin. *Scoticum* (of Scotland) is Linnaeus' specific, perhaps because his specimens were collected along the Scottish coast and sent to the founder of botanical nomenclature in his native Sweden.

The plant has been known as alexander(s) for a very long time. Pliny, ancient Rome's encyclopedist, mentions it. The form alexander (after Alexander the Great) is an example of a bit of Roman folk etymology. Originally in Latin, it was *holus atrum*, then *olus atrum*, then changed into forms like *olusandrum* and *alisandrum* and it was not too long before folk speech, including soldiers' Latin, heard this as *alexandrum*. The Latin *holus atrum* means 'black vegetable' and refers to the little ripe fruits of Horse Parsley that are almost black. Alexander did refer to a different plant than our

Newfoundland herb, but one in the same family. It labelled what we now call Black Lovage or Horse Parsley (*Smyrnium olisatrum*). Roman herbalists thought the plant was native to Smyrna, an ancient trading city on the Aegean coast of what is today Turkey, where its modern name is Izmir.

BACCALAO

One of the most important food words in Newfoundland history, this is a variant of standard Portuguese *bacalhau*, dried and salted codfish. Some form of this root is a word for cod in almost all the Romance languages. In fact, early European explorers once named Newfoundland and surrounding areas with the word. Here's Richard Eden in 1555 writing about the *Decades of the Newe Worlde*: "Cabot him selfe named those landes Baccallaos, bycause that in the seas ther about he found so great multitude of certayne bigge fysshes . . . which th' inhabitantes caule Baccallaos."

Caesar carries an ornamental staff or wand, called a scipio in Classical Latin, and later called a *baculum*. This is a possible origin for the common word codfish, *baccalo* or *bacalhao*.

A New Etymology

Such quotations fostered an early notion that Cabot had picked up the word from Aboriginal peoples of the North American East Coast. This linguistically dubious myth is still presented as fact in some dictionaries. Well then, explain a reference from 1504 to "dos bacalhas" (two cod), and — the clincher that puts the Cabot notion to rest — a reference in a Proto-Romance document to *bacallos* from the middle of the 10th century! Cabot certainly wasn't cruising Newfoundland waters in AD 950 now, was he? No, this word for cod is of Latin origin, and, while the *Oxford English Dictionary* may not deign to guess its roots, I shall. Naturally I'm donning flippers and scuba gear for such a plunge into the abyss of unattested etymology. I suggest two possible roots for baccalao. One natural fact that impressed ancient fishermen about the cod of cold North Atlantic waters was the remarkable number of roe produced by female cod. One female can contain five million eggs. *Baca* is an old Roman word for a berry or anything shaped like berries, for example, fish roe. Fish eggs certainly resemble little berries, suggesting a putative, diminutive form like *bacculus* (little berry) that could have become in early Spanish or Portuguese *baccalo* or *bacalhao*.

The other possible derivation of *bacalhao* is the Latin *baculum*, stick, staff, wand, wooden support, stay. The Romans would have come upon Atlantic coast peoples already drying cod on platforms made of wood with the filleted cod placed on parallel sticks, a version of the apparatus that every Newfoundlander knows as a flake. *Baculum* could have been Roman army slang for such racks, and, as has happened many times in word history before and since, the name of the rack came to be applied to the fish most commonly dried on the rack. "Hail, Brutus, let's boil up a few 'racks' for brekkie!"

Does any proof of such derivations exist? The same amount of proof that exists for Cabot borrowing *baccalhao* from a North American coastal language. To this date, no such word has ever been found in the languages of our maritime First Peoples. Page through wordlists of Beothuk (four very, very short vocabularies), Mi'Kmaq, Maliseet, Montagnais-Naskapi, Inuktitut. Page through until your eyes are like peach pits, and you will discover zilch, zero, *nada*. In the large Algonquian language family to which many of these eastern native tongues belong, there is no word for codfish even remotely similar to *bacalhao*. Call me flaky, but I challenge any linguist to hang me out to dry on this.

Just as salted cod has been the most important staple food in Newfoundland's long history, so *bacalhao* is today still the national dish of Portugal, prepared in dozens and dozens of recipes with as much dexterity and ingenuity as cooks on The Rock use in their salt cod dishes.

The word speckles the map of our Maritime provinces, too. Variants abound, such as Baccaro, Nova Scotia, and Baccalieu Island, Newfoundland, which are respectively Spanish and French versions of the word. And, just for authentic measure, it is sometimes spelled as Bacalhao Island. The Baccalao bird is a local name for murres or other birds that nest on Baccalieu Island.

My favourite such place name is at the mouth of Conception Bay in Newfoundland, Baccalieu Tickle — something I'd like to give to the hidebound, timid compilers of "authoritative" dictionaries.

BAKEAPPLE

Here's a one-hundred-percent Canadian word. In Canada, the bakeapple is a Maritime fruit, also called baked-apple berry, that thrives in soggy bogs on Cape Breton Island, and in Nova Scotia, Prince

Edward Island, and Newfoundland, and farther north in Labrador and the southern Arctic where they grow on the sparse skin of moss and lichen that covers swampy areas, often in company with partridgeberries. Caribou and ptarmigan compete with humans for these sweet berries rich in fibre and vitamin C. Some Inuit people collect bakeapples in the fall and preserve them for winter use by freezing. Newfoundlanders sometimes call the plant bog-apple. Prince Edward Islanders occasionally use the term *yellowberry*. Bakeapple pie is still a popular pastry in our Maritimes. In Gordon Pinsent's 1974 Newfoundland novel, *John & the Missus,* a couple enjoy tea-buns and bakeapple jam.

Word Lore

The Inuit word for this berry is *appik*. Late in the 18th century, says one cogent etymology, white traders borrowed the Inuit word, heard the *pp* as *b*, and combined it with the English word *apple,* to produce *abik-apple*, eventually further modified to bakeapple. Early German immigrants to Labrador called it *Apik-Beere* 'appik-berry.' Folksier origins say the raspberrylike fruit is amber and of wrinkled appearance, supposedly like a baked apple, but this was stretching metaphor a bit, as it resembles closely all the fruits of the *Rubus* genus. *Baie* is a French word for berry. One folk etymology of our Maritimes says that early French settlers first saw this berry new to them, and they inquired, in the improbable French of the folk story, "Baie, qu'appelle?" Berry, what's it called? English settlers who came afterward heard this as bakeapple, claims the tale. *Mais je pense que non.*

Rubus chamaemorus

Bakeapple is elsewhere called cloudberry and widely used in Scandinavian countries to make a sweet liqueur. Swedes ferment the berries to make a cloudberry vinegar. Lapps in Finland bury the collected berries in the snow for midwinter fruit. In Scotland it's cloudberry, and is the official badge of the clan McFarlane. One Slavic term for cloudberry is *molka*, a compressing of *malinka*, diminutive of the common Slavic word for raspberry *malina*. But standard Russian for cloudberry is *moroshka*, little berry of the *moroz* 'frost.' Even the Vikings ate the juicy, amber berries of this creeping shrub that belongs to the huge Rose family of plants and to the raspberry genus *Rubus*.

The botanical name of bakeapple is *Rubus chamaemorus*. It grows all over the northern temperate zone of the world and in some adjacent arctic climates. *Rubus* is a randy genus where species interbreed at the drop of a pollen grain, so that there are dozens of species worldwide. *Rubus* is one of the Latin words for red, and is an old botanical name for any bramble bush. The Latin root pops up in the English word *ruby* and in learned adjectives like rubefacient 'causing redness.' The single flower of each bakeapple is white. The specific part of its scientific name, *chamaemorus*, means 'ground mulberry,' describing its low habit of growth. *Chamai* in classical Greek means 'on the ground,' and *morus* is a Latin word for mulberry.

Canadian Place Names

Bakeapple Barren is an official toponym in Cape Breton Highlands National Park. Bakeapple Bay is an inlet of the larger Kolotulik Bay on the coast of Labrador, named to remind those sailing past in late summer that plentiful supplies of ripe berries awaited in bogs near shore. The Inuit word *appik* also appears in place names: Akpiksai Bay, Akpittok Island, and Akbik, all indicating areas where bakeapples are plentiful.

BAKER'S FOG

This is a comic label for store-bought bread, a feisty, culinary criticism of the spongy, glutinous white bread sold sliced in Maritime supermarkets. The staff of life has become the stuff of life. The implication by Newfoundlanders, Nova Scotians, and Prince Edward Islanders is clear: such commercially baked loaves have no substance and must be as nutritious as eating or chewing fog.

Bread as the staff of life first appears in the Old Testament in Leviticus when the anonymous compiler of the laws of ritual gets around to quoting God's curse upon those who would disobey Him. Basically, it's the same old bully palaver: *I'll smite you, and when I've smitten you, and you're well-smote, then maybe I'll smite you again.* Leviticus 26:26 adds "And when I have broken the staff of your bread, ten women shall bake your bread in one oven, and they shall deliver you your bread again by weight: and ye shall eat, and not be satisfied." So critical comments on bread are nothing new.

In this medieval woodcut, a baker ovens a round loaf of "the staff of life."

Baker's fog is also called cotton bread, ghost bread, and puff, as well as simply fog. This insipid glop is so despised — though still widely purchased and eaten by consumers — that *white-bread* has become a pejorative adjective to describe anything bland, bourgeois, and Waspy. Considering its mechanized manufacture, this is no surprise. Bleached flour and additives to swell insoluble portions are kneaded by electric beaters that pump more air into the dough and make it whiter. Giddy amounts of beer yeast make the dough ferment excessively, so that, at the end of the process, the consumer buys a cellophane-wrapped package of gas bubbles and wheat remnants. Baker's fog indeed! Sad to think there are adults who have never munched substantial, traditional breads: the chompable heft of pumpernickel (whose name means 'farting devil' in German); the crunch of brown satisfaction in a thick slab of buttered, week-old, dark rye; the meal-for-a-day in a two-inch plank of Russian black bread, easily sliced with a chainsaw.

BANGBELLY

Bangbelly is a pudding or pancake of Newfoundland, baked, or more usually fried over an outdoor fire by fishermen or hunters. It's made with flour, baking soda, molasses, and pork fat — fishermen used to substitute seal fat. Sometimes it was cut in strips and floated on top of thick pea soup. But a variety of recipes abound, including one that begins with blueberries, sugar, and hot water boiled into a bubbling mass, at which point balls of dough are dropped in until cooked. A belly-bang was low, coarse Elizabethan slang for a fart. Perhaps this noble provender takes its name from a mere reversal of the elements in belly-bang? Or, is it so heavy that it bangs the belly when eaten? But the origin may also lie in bang or *bain*, a hard-bread cake made by frying a batter of flour and water in tallow, from Québécois French *beigne* 'fritter.'

Supporting a transatlantic source is this next reference. In the best and best-selling book of Newfoundland recipes, Ivan Jesperson's *Fat-Back & Molasses*, Joan Andrews of George's Brook contributes a tasty recipe for Blackberry Bangbelly that originated in Dorset, and was brought over by early English immigrants to Cape Freels, Newfoundland.

Such was a cup of black tea served alone, without the side of a biscuit, sandwich, or bit of jam on bread. This is another example of food scarcity referred to not with bitterness, but humour.

A BARE-LEGGED CUP OF TEA

BARMY BREAD

Bread made with barm, which is yeast or some other leavening, was, of course, always clearly differentiated from unleavened hard tack. In Old English, *beorma* was the froth on fermenting beer which was scooped off, mixed with flour, and used to leaven breads. Barm is related to *fermentum*, the Latin word for yeast. Thus one who behaved as if he had consumed too much beer froth, or as if his head was full of the froth, was crazy or barmy.

Big Dipper™ is the trade name of a dark, Caribbean rum popular in Newfoundland and named after a bar at the airport in Gander.

BIG DIPPER™

Bitch is something like bangbelly, a cakelike concoction of flour, fat-back pork, and molasses. It's make-do fishermen's grub on an early sealing vessel, not fancy, hence the dismissive slang that implies one might as well be wolfing down steakettes of Lassie. Salty dogs also called it "pork bitch."

BITCH AND DOGBODY

This is cabbage soup, with other available vegetables but no meat.

BLIND MUSH

To blow the Christmas pudding is not to commit

BLOW THE CHRISTMAS PUDDING

culinary error, nor it is a bizarre sexual practice in which a person might wish to interfere with baked goods in an untoward manner. Picture instead a warm noon kitchen on a Christmas Day in Newfoundland. Wreathed in rummy steam, the cook proudly bears the pudding from the stove and prepares to sprinkle final splashings of the amber distillate on its thick-fruited and stout-nutted goodness. At the kitchen door a rifle shot rings clear across the cold air to honour deft cookery and add a festive sound. Blowing the Christmas pudding is a Newfoundland memory of more ancient noble feasts across the briny where hot puddings were piped to high table, or even saluted with cornet and drum as they were borne in upon high-held silver plates.

A Christmas pudding is wrapped and ready for steaming.

A traditional Sunday morning breakfast in New-foundland is fish and brewis. The "fish" in this dish is often salt cod. Brewis is hard bread or hard tack, also known as ship's biscuit or sea-biscuit, soaked in water and cooked with salt cod, and often served with scrunchins, which are cubes of fat-back pork fried golden brown and tossed over the brewis as a garnish or mixed right in with the cod and bread. Hard tack is a dry biscuit or bread made of flour and water with no salt, often baked in large ovals. It keeps for months. It must be soaked or dipped in hot liquids to be eaten easily.

Now here is a brief detour from our tour of New-foundland culinary words to quibble with the majority of dictionaries where the origin of the phrase *hard tack* is marked "unknown." But it looks like a shortening of the nautical term *tackle*, originally the fishing equipment and gear on board a boat. Fishermen's or sailors' humour might easily have invented a joking reference to this biscuit, claiming it was harder than the wood-en and metal tackle on the boat. English borrowed tackle from an early Dutch form like *takel*, itself related through a common Indo-European root to a Greek word of arrangement like *taxis*, so that tackle with its diminutive suffix was bits and pieces of equipment that had to be prepared and arranged on the boat before one set forth to fish.

Hard tack was cheap food first, then in England came to be applied to anything of low value or inferior quality. American English first applied the word *tacky* as a noun to name small, scruffy wild horses that roamed the Carolina colonies. Sometimes these tackies were captured and sold. By the 1830s, some poor whites or southern crackers were being put down with tags like "piney-woods Tackies." Around the turn of

BREWIS *or* FISH & BREWIS

Origin of the Term *Hard Tack*

the century, an American fad for costume parties where one came dressed as a hick or hillbilly produced the first common adjectival use in the phrase "tacky parties." Cartoonist Al Capp said that memories of these parties were partially responsible for the creation of his long- running cartoon strip, "Lil' Abner." Later in 20th-century American English, tacky gained wide popular use as a pejorative adjective meaning cheap, seedy, in poor taste, or vulgar.

Origin of Brewis

Now we return to what many islanders consider the best use of hard tack ever invented. Brewis has several spelling variants and pronunciations but is usually said as "broos." In the lyrics of four different Newfoundland songs, brewis is rhymed with *spruce* in one ditty, with *news* in another, with *lose* in a third, with *youse* in the fourth. Local folk etymology claims the word derives from breaking, that is bruising, the hard biscuit, before soaking it — a practice reflected in one complimentary catch phrase of Newfoundland: "as fine a b'y as ever broke a cake o' bread." The folk etymology is colourful but incorrect. Brewis existed as a word in Middle English, a period of development in our language usually dated from 1150 to 1450. The earliest printed reference in English occurs around 1300 in *The Lay of Havelok the Dane* as "make the broys in the led" which means "make the brewis in the lid," that is, remove the convex lid of a pot or cauldron, turn it upside down and use the hollow to make a sauce. In this case, it means to ladle broth from the pot into the lid, then put the lid, still upside down, back on top of the pot, and make sops by putting hunks of hard bread into the liquid.

Brewis or browis (or one of a dozen variant spellings) entered Middle English and Scots from a Norman French form of Old French *brouetz*, a soup made with meat broth, itself a diminutive of

Old French *bro* or *breu*. It caught on in English by popular association with an Old English cognate, *briw*, plural *briwas*, a word for soup. All of these words, including the English verb *brew*, hark back to the Indo-European mother tongue, where *bhereu* is a verbal root whose meanings include stirring, warming, and boiling. Distantly related words in English, fifth cousins of brewis, are braise, bread, breath, breeze, broil, broth, and imbrue. Latin cognates include the roots of English words like effervescent, ferment, fervent, and fry. The Bourbons who once ruled Naples, Spain, and France took their surname from a town in central France originally named after Borvo, a Celtic god of warmth.

Skin and debone the dried salt cod and cut into pieces. Soak overnight in cold water. Change the water in the morning and boil the cod about twenty minutes until tender. Some Newfoundland cooks soak the hard tack overnight too, then boil it in its soak water the next morning and mix it with the cod. Scrunchins can be sprinkled on top. Some add potato hunks and wild herbs. Others make brewis with bacon or ham. Coastal cooks from Maine to Massachusetts make fish and brewis too, and 16th-century Scottish recipe books mention the dish.

Making Brewis

Some Newfoundland kitchens stock a special implement called a brewis bag, a netlike pouch in which to soak the pieces of hard tack and boil them, after which the pieces are dumped in a colander to drain. Thus, one who does not retain imparted information, who is scatter-brained or forgetful, may be chastised in Newfoundland with the outport snub: "He have a head like a brewis bag."

The Brewis Bag

BRITCHES or BREECHES

The ovaries of the female codfish filled with eggs and with the enclosing ovarian membrane look like a pair of old-fashioned short pants, the breeches that were fastened just below the knees. Freshly caught cod roe is washed well and fried with scrunchins (see entry). There are a variety of food uses. Cod roe, pressed and smoked, can fill canapés, while some lovers of these fish eggs slather them on hot toast. Sturgeon roe is their upscale cousin, known as caviar. Other forms of the term heard in Newfoundland are britchins and britchets.

CALLIBOGUS

A prized quaff of the outports, this maritime tipple began in eastern North America, but nobody now seems to know the origin of the word. Although recipes vary, callibogus usually meant spruce beer fortified with rum or whisky, and the addition of a dollop of molasses. Native peoples taught white settlers to prevent scurvy by drinking spruce tea, an infusion rich in vitamin C, made by boiling tender, young spruce shoots in fresh water. Later, whites added yeast and molasses to ferment this mild antiscorbutic into the more potent spruce beer. Later still, some nautical scallywag, no doubt often seen "listing to starboard" or "stewed as a fresh-boiled owl," thought up callibogus, thus confecting a brew that would ding-swizzle a deckhand. But even admirals of the Canadian Navy have been persuaded to sluice their larynxes with callibogus, strictly, you understand, as a medical corrective to breathing in too much sea fog.

CAPILLAIRE TEA

In continental French, where this word began, it was an infusion made by pouring boiling water on the fronds of maidenhair ferns. *Capillaire*,

French for maidenhair fern, derived from the Latin of medieval herbalists where *herba capillaris* was the herb-garden name, itself from the Latin *capillus*, hair. But in early Newfoundland, Québec, and other Maritime regions, capillaire was a wintergreen tea made by pouring boiling water over the fresh or dried leaves of a little evergreen shrub named creeping snowberry, *Gaultheria hispidula*, and then letting it steep for several days in a closed container. Attend the warning that anything containing oil of wintergreen can be toxic to children with a hypersensitivity to aspirin. Capillaire is a wild tea to be enjoyed as a pleasant change from other teas, but in a small amount and infrequently. Wintergreen berries, white in this snowberry species, are edible, and have saved those lost in the winter woods who knew where to find the white berries under the snow. The rest of us must dial 911. Incidentally, the plant was named after an immigrant to early Canada, Dr. Jean-François Gaulthier (1708 – 1756) sent out to New France as a botanist and King's physician. Dr. Gaulthier popularized the use of local herbal teas and was rewarded when Linnaeus, the great founder of botanical nomenclature, named the wintergreen genus after him.

CHAW AND GLUTCH

This pair of old English dialect words for chew and swallow refers in Newfoundland to a modest meal of bread (the chaw) and tea (the glutch). In the hard times of the Great Depression in the 1930s, chaw and glutch were often the entire bill of fare at many a poor meal. This gave rise to a rueful Newfoundland prayer of the era: "For this bit of chaw and glutch, we thank Thee, Lord, so very much." Glutch does double duty in Newfoundland as a noun meaning a gulping, an act of difficult swallowing, or the throat or gullet itself, and also as a verb meaning to swallow with diffi-culty. Wilfred Grenfell, the British doctor who built hospitals and nursing stations at the turn of the cen-tury for people on the Labrador and Newfoundland coasts, wrote of a young patient who presented "with a kink in her glutch," something blocking her windpipe. Another doctor in a memoir speaks of "preparing gargles for kinkorns that would not glutch," illustrating the survival of wonderful old dialect words in Newfoundlandese that have large-ly disappeared from standard English. Kinkorn is early English dialect in Devonshire and Dorset for the windpipe, Adam's apple, larynx, or throat, also appearing in Newfoundland as keecorn and cacorne. Another dweller at a remote cove reported, "I have a pain in my kinkorn and it has gone to the wizen." Wizen here is the chest. The word, howev-er, is a variant of weasand, an older English word for gullet or throat.

CHIDDLES or CHITLINGS or CHISTLINGS

The English dialect word *chitterlings*, referring to animal intestines cooked as food, gets a special form and meaning in Newfoundland, where chid-dles or chistlings are cod roe or cod milt with or without their enclosing membranes. For style of preparation, see the *peas & melts* entry. Peas are fish spawn or roe.

COADY

A Newfoundland sauce, it is made by boiling mol-asses and butter for ten minutes, then pouring it over a pudding, for example, coady duff, or over flour dumplings in recipes like lassy coady dumplings. Lassy is an affectionate Newfoundland shortform for molasses. Later recipes for coady involve sugar, butter, water, and vinegar. Another coady calls for sugar, water, cornstarch, and one dash of vanilla extract. Some kitchens had a metal

Several fish from the cod family, counterclockwise from the top right: whiting, haddock, and two cod species

implement called a coady dipper in which the sauce was boiled and from which it was lovingly ladled on the steaming pudding or dumplings. The origin of coady may be a spelling variant of *coaty* or *coatie*, a little coating one puts on the food.

COD

When you say fish on The Rock, you mean cod. Other fish are specified by name. The now collapsed cod fishery was the mainstay of Newfoundland's economy for almost 500 years. As one local proverb puts it: no cod, no cash. The most important commercial species has always been the Atlantic cod, *Gadus morrhua*. The scientific name consists of the genus word *gadus*, medieval Latin for cod, and the general word for dried and salted cod in French, *morue*, possibly from a Celtic word for the sea, *mor*, cognate with other sea words in the Indo-European languages, like Latin *mare*, German *Meer*, Old Scandinavian *marr*, and Old Irish *muir*. Such a pivotal catch has naturally produced dozens of compound words in the vocabulary of Newfoundland fishing, words like cod-bag, cod banks, cod flake, cod-seine, cod-trap.

Origin of Cod

The word *cod* is marked "of unknown origin" in many dictionaries. I don't agree. Two verbal pathways are compelling to the questing etymologist. One suggests cod is simply a basic Indo-European word for the fish, related to the IE root **ku* 'hollow, bag-like' with a dental suffix (*d* or *t*), so that — contrary to what the *Oxford English Dictionary* states with such papal certainty — cod is indeed cognate with an ancient Greek word *gados*, which referred to one member of the cod family, the hake. The general idea behind this derivation is that a dried and salted codfish vaguely resembles an empty bag. Admittedly, the metaphor is tenuous, but, in the long history of nomenclature, that has never stopped far-fetched comparison from being the basis of new words. As we saw above, the medieval Latin version of this Greek word gives the genus name *Gadus*.

How to Stuff a Wild Cod piece

The second possible lineage of the word *cod* would begin with Old English *codd*, which around AD 1000 meant a small bag, a pouch, or the seed pod of a plant. By 1357, cod referred also to the fish, perhaps because the female cod produces so many eggs and the roe were eaten as a delicacy. By 1400, cod was also being used as a synonym for the human scrotum and testicles. By 1450, European males were covering the opening in the front of their breeches or hose with a padded flap of cloth called a codpiece, much like the bag of a modern jockstrap but worn on the outside. Later some of the more swaggering fops and fantasticos of Shakespeare's day, macho wannabes perhaps, were stuffing half of a dried gourd inside the cloth, both to cover and to emphasize their genitalia. The more hysterical foplings gussied up their codpieces with gathered ribbons, bits of lace, and tassels! In the history of human clothing this was already an old ploy: to put new emphasis on sexual parts by an exotic covering. But one must wonder whether or not this obsessive padding of their crotches by Elizabethan males had its psychological origin in the masculine fear that one was not of sufficient scrotal and phallic proportion to — what? — cause damsels to swoon upon glimpsing one's enormity? Men have been size queens for millennia. Every young male at least dreams of being outfitted like the hero of that coarse and funny 19th-century sea shanty "Ballocky Bill the Sailor." By the way, cod still means scrotum in the Ozark Mountains of the United States, so that an Ozark girl, new to a city high school, is reported to have blushed when the teacher asked her to go to the map and point out Cape Cod.

Codswallop

There is a folk etymology that this modern British slang for nonsensical talk or belief arose from the name of the fish and suggests a pile of fish guts. That's not likely. For three hundred years in British English, cod or cod's head commonly meant a stupid person. Although codswallop looks ancient, it is only in print from the 1960s and appears to be a modern coinage in which foolish speech is likened to a wallop of words by a fool. But codswallop may also stem from old British slang *cods* meaning testicles, and thus be similar to dismissive exclamations like "Balls!" or the British "Bollocks!"

The Choicest Cod Morsels

Sculps or jowls are the side parts or cheeks from a cod's head, tasty and fun if you enjoy picking fish bones out of every bite. Cod tongue is a dainty aptly defined in *The Dictionary of Newfoundland English*: "The tongue or hyoid apparatus of the cod-fish, much prized for its glutinous jellylike consistency and delicate flavour when lightly fried." And fit for a queen! At the 1998 banquet in London held to celebrate the completed renovation of Canada House, the Newfoundland chef served Her Majesty Queen Elizabeth and other guests these slender, lingual delicacies.

Cod Liver Oil's Canadian Connection

Early in this century, Norwegian cod supplied the world with most of its cod liver oil, rich in the vitamin A needed for growth of healthy bones, skin, and mucous membranes. But in 1924 a Canadian named William Harrison discovered that Grand Banks' cod livers had oodles more vitamin A than Norwegian cod livers. By 1929, he and others had founded a pharmaceutical company, Ayerst, and introduced Canadian cod liver oil in capsules, a form that conquered the world market and is still sold in our drugstores today as Alphamettes™.

COLCANNON

The famines of the 1730s and 1740s in Ireland brought waves of Irish immigrants to Newfoundland, and with them, dishes like colcannon, crubeen, and pratie oatens. Colcannon was first boiled cabbage and mashed potatoes topped with butter. This is clear from the original term in Irish Gaelic *cál ceannfionn*, literally 'cabbage fair-headed.' But it's a lively little Irish joking reference and was really like calling the dish in English "blonde cabbage," blonde because of the potatoes. As different cooks personalized the ancient recipe, colcannon came to be a boiled hash of as many as seven or eight vegetables, sometimes with bits of meat tossed in. Chopped chives, parsley, and a piquant hail of fresh-ground pepper can spice up the basic blandness of the recipe. Like its British sister dish, bubble and squeak, colcannon can also be fried into a kind of cake. In Ireland and parts of England it was traditional to serve colcannon on All Hallows' Eve.

Colcannon Night

Colcannon Night or Snap-Apple Night are still frequent synonyms for Halloween in many Newfoundland communities. To snap at apples is similar to bobbing for apples. Very ancient custom held this late October evening to be ghost-thick, ghoul-swarmed, ripe for magic and fit for prophesy. For a millennium or two, All Hallows' Eve has been an evening when properly performed rites might help one discover a lover or find out what marital fate awaited the young. Thus four objects were traditionally hidden in the large dish of colcannon served on Halloween: a ring, a coin, an old maid's thimble, and a bachelor's button. So, when spooks leave a broomy spoor across the night sky, one eats this cabbage-and-potato hash with care. Whoever finds the ring will marry soon. To the coin-holder, riches will accrue, while celibacy awaits both the thimble-getter and button-discoverer. Happily for eaters, one Newfoundland variation reduces the surprises in colcannon to several large buttons. If a girl finds a button, she will marry. If a young man finds a button, he will remain forever a bachelor.

The Folk Etymology

The spurious origin of colcannon says the word consists of cole, an old name of cabbage still seen in coleslaw, plus the military weapon, cannon. This compound "arose when Irish peasants turned cannon balls into kitchen implements by using them to pound vegetables into a paste." So runs a quotation from *Cupboard Love: A Dictionary of Culinary Curiosities* by Winnipegger Mark Morton. He does not bother to label this supposititious flapdoodle as just that: a wild guess by folk unacquainted with Irish Gaelic and even perhaps, most modern dictionaries.

The True Etymology

Irish Gaelic *cál* reflects an ancient Indo-European word for cabbage, literally vegetable on a stalk (IE * *kaul*, stalk). Related forms are: Old English *cal* (giving colewort 'cabbage plant,' an older name for one loose-leaved variety), Old Scandinavian *kal* (giving English *kale* and modern Norwegian *kaal*), German *Kohl* (giving *kohlrabi*), Latin *caulis* (think of cauliflower, a plant in the same botanical family as cabbage; think too of various words for cabbage, derivatives of *caulis* in the Romance languages, for example Spanish *col* and French *chou*), Greek *kaulos*, Medieval Dutch *kool* (in MD cabbage salad was *kool sla*, giving modern English *coleslaw*). Finally, showing the true spread of this cabbage word, a cognate appears in ancient Persian as *kelum*.

Perhaps the most appealing derivative is a French term of tender affection used by lovers and maybe by mothers speaking to small children, *mon petit chouchou*, a sweet intimacy one might translate as "my little cabbage-wabbage."

Irish Gaelic

Colcannon is an Anglo-Irish compression or slurring, a frequent habit in daily speech, of the Irish Gaelic name for this dish *cál ceannfionn*, literally 'cabbage fair-headed.' The adjective comes after the noun in Gaelic. *Ceann* means head; *fionn* means white or fair, when

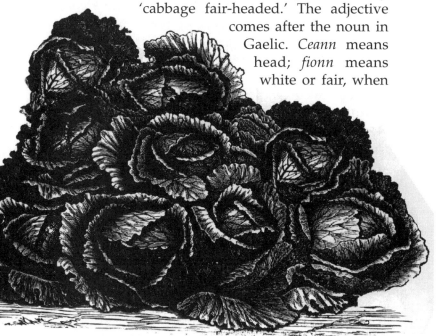

describing people it usually refers to a light complexion or to blonde hair. You will recognize the Gaelic word for white or fair in the common Gaelic female names like Fiona, and in less common but no less beautiful girl's names like Finola, Fionnula, or Fenella, all from the Gaelic *Fionghuala* "with white shoulders."

The initial part of the compound adjective *ceannfionn* is the Gaelic word for head, *ceann*, which appears in Gaelic surnames like the Irish O Cannan 'son of white head,' that is, son of a founding ancestor who was of fair complexion or blonde hair, and also in its Scottish cousin McCannan, with the same meaning.

CONVERSATION SWEET

Also called simply conversations, these are the little candy lozenges once popular among public school students on Valentine's Day, not just in Newfoundland but all across Canada. In different colours and often shaped like little hearts, conversation sweets had short phrases printed on the upper surface of the lozenge, usually endearments like "I Love You," "Be Mine," "My Buddy," and "Let's Be Friends." Such candies did not begin in the 20th century, having been manufactured in Europe throughout the 1800s. In Britain they were called "conversation lozenges." One imagines Queen Victoria placing a special order for regal lozenges which she briskly handed to Prince Albert when he asked for sex too frequently, sweets stamped with the words: "We are not amused."

CRACKER

In Newfoundland, crackers are the ripe, red berries of a dwarf member of the dogwood family, *Cornus canadensis*. Because the fruit appears in tight clusters, another common name is bunchberry, and there is a colloquial name of American origin: crackerberry. Crackers are edible but not very palatable, sometimes serving as emergency rations for those in the bush. The fruit does have vitamin C. The folk name, *cracker*, arises because they crack when eaten raw. The berries also pop and crack when boiled in sugar syrup to make a compote. A more sober common name is northern dwarf cornel. In Québécois French the plant is *quatre-temps*, four times because bunchberry often has four leaves; each flower has four petals and in some cases four berries in the autumn. Algonquian peoples used cracker roots to brew a tea for colicky babies and to make an infusion for coughs and fevers.

Crackers carpet moist, shady woodlands and logged-over areas all across Canada. In the fall, the leaves turn a deep bronzed-plum colour, and fruits appear in shining clusters of orange-red drupes. The prim symmetry of massed cracker-berry plants makes it one of Newfoundland's most attractive spring wild flowers. An involucre of creamy-white bracts surrounds each flower-head like the starched and fluted ruff of an Elizabethan collar, giving the little plant the air of a modest courtier awaiting regal attention in some verdant chamber of nature.

Swine shows off some fine trotters, hocks, or crubeens.

CRUBEEN

Another pure Gaelic word gift from Irish immigrants to Newfoundland, *crúibin* is the diminutive of *crúb* (hoof) and means a pig's trotter, usually pickled in salt and boiled. Crubeen is the hock of a pig's foot, the joint between the tibia and the little bones of the foot. Variations in crubeen recipes include boiling pig's trotters then battering them in egg and breadcrumbs and grilling. They can also be cooked in a spicy stock or braised.

DAMPER DOGS & FLACOONS

Damper dogs are quick bread — wads of bread dough fried quickly on the lid (damper) of a hot woodstove, usually a treat for children, who were fed the damper dogs so they wouldn't gobble up all the fresh-baked bread. Although *damper dogs* is pure Newfoundlandese, damper appears in 18th-century British slang as any little, between-meal nibble that takes the edge off or dampens the appetite. By 1833 damper is Australian slang for an outback bannock, Australian bush-bread, an unleavened bread of flour and water baked in hot ashes, if no stove were handy. Newfoundland synonyms include damper boys, damper cakes, damper devils, or joanies. The verb *to damp* meaning 'to dull, to check the force of' and its later extension *to dampen* appear to have been borrowed into Middle and Early Modern English from German *dämpfen* 'to dim, to wet down, to lessen.'

Flacoons

When the hunk of dough cut off to make a damper dog is flattened into a pancake shape, these little breads were sometimes called flacoons in Newfoundland. I suggest flacoon may stem from the fact that the dough was rolled flat by using a bottle, in Old French *flacon*, which gives a more familar English bottle word, *flagon*. The process of verbal transformation in the borrowing was much like one Anglo-Irish word for boy or youth, *gossoon*, from French *garçon*.

DUMB CAKE

In some other parts of Canada, a bake-over was and is a pleasant, social get-together at which women made pies and baked goods, perhaps for sale at a church bazaar, together at one house. Newfoundland has preserved an old Irish spin on such an occasion: the making of a dumb cake. Unmarried young women and even still hopeful spinsters gathered to bake and eat one cake. During the making, baking, and consumption of the cake, no talking was permitted. In the relative silence of the proceedings, said the old superstition, fate would grant a maiden a prophetic vision of the man who would marry her. Until they consumed the last crumb of the dumb cake, be they virgins or old maids, not a whisper could escape their lips.

In stories that seem as old as night, the wise traveller, venturing through dark woods or sailing a skiff into churlish waters, has taken along some gift to placate "the little people." For elves, trolls, pixies, brownies, imps and goblins, sylphs and gnomes, yes, whole platoons of fairyfolk lurk out there, waiting to play tricks, simple or fatal, on any wayfarer foolish enough to deny their existence. A forest elf could blow leaves across the path after one passed, disguising the trail and making one lost forever in dense bush. A water kelpie might ease up alongside a little dory bobbing in the fog and, while you were turned away jigging a line, the kelpie might pull your only boatmate into the sea, and you could search for him far as ever a puffin flew and never find so much as the cork from his bottle of rum. Many an unfortunate returned from a trip into deep woods fairy-struck: physically harmed, sometimes partially paralysed. Fishermen from the British Isles brought to Newfoundland several folk beliefs about such malignant sprites. One involved stuffing a fairy bun or piece of bread into one's pocket to ward off such water spirits. If you met a nixie, you offered the bun and hoped the bad fairy would take

FAIRY BUN

BREAD FOR THE ROAD

COMPANY BREAD

it and vamoose. If the trip was by land, one took "bread for the road" or "company bread," company being a euphemism for spooks, much as some people called fairies "the good folk" when they plainly were not.

Do you chuckle in condescension at such quaint superstition? If so, consider modern-day, middle-class joggers in New York City's Central Park, going out for an early-morning trot, who make certain they carry a twenty-dollar bill in case a mugger waylays them. NYC muggers reportedly get very angry if, having taken the trouble to accost you, they find you without funds. I know one television producer of a very popular NBC news-magazine program who lived for years on Central Park West and who never left the apartment to jog without stuffing a twenty into a pocket. The producer was never mugged, but the twenty was always there.

FIGGY DUFF

Newfoundland balladeer John Burke (1894 – 1929) sang of the island "where the figgy duffs are seen, that would sink a brigantine." This is a Newfoundland boiled pudding with raisins. In some British dialects, fig was a synonym for raisin as early as the 16th century.

A lad awaits
a steamed pudding.

A common recipe involves moistening stale bread crumbs, squeezing the water out, then adding raisins, brown sugar, molasses, butter, flour, spices like ginger, cinnamon, and allspice, and a teaspoon of soda dissolved in hot water. Mix this well, put into a dampened pudding bag made of cloth, and steam for two hours. Or stick the bag in the oven with a Jigg's dinner (see entry) for one hour, and cook a main course and a dessert at the same time. Serve with coady sauce (see entry). Variations abound in the recipe and in the spelling of this treat: figged duff, figgedy duff, figgity duff, figgy pudding, figgity pudden. In British culinary history, figgy duff is related to a very old recipe, suet pudding, in which a bit of hard fat was tossed into the mix for flavour.

Even centuries after immigrants brought the word and the food to Newfoundland, it was still heard in England, for example, in 1846 a Cornish writer extols "a thoomping figgy pudden." In Cornwall and Devonshire, fishermen took to sea with figgie-dowdie, a West-Country raisin pudding. In the popular Christmas carol "We Wish You a Merry Christmas," you are also wished "a figgey pudding." But this is the medieval European *figee*, a dish of true figs (fruits of the common Mediterranean cultivated tree *Ficus carica*). Figgey pudding consisted of dried figs stewed in wine.

Fig = Raisin?

How did fig come to mean raisin as well as true fig? Well, it was a little gefuffel that happened when raisin entered English right after the Norman Conquest in 1066. Raisin had two meanings in French, and in early English, too. *Raisin* stemmed from Latin *racemus* 'a cluster of grapes, a raceme of grapes.' Raisins of the sun were grapes partially dried on platforms under Old

Sol. In the English language, as the word *grape* came to mean the unprocessed fruit itself, raisin came to mean the dried fruit. Interestingly, grape also came from a French word *grappe* that first meant 'a cluster of grapes,' itself from another noun *grape* which was the hook that vineyard workers sometimes used to harvest grape clusters. It is related to English words like grapnel and grappling hook, both referring to an anchor with sharp claws.

Now the true fig, when first introduced to England, was a relatively expensive imported luxury. Figs appeared on the tables of the rich in London, at court, and on groaning country boards at the feasts of wealthy nobles. But most of the Anglo-Saxon peasantry would never see, let alone eat, a fig. They heard the word though, perhaps from fellow Anglo-Saxons who were servants at the tables of the high and mighty. Well, underlings could have figs too, but they would be the less expensive and more available raisins. So, raisins replaced figs in culinary treats.

On Your Duff

Duff is just a northern British pronunciation of dough, on the analogy of other similarly spoken spellings like *enough* and *tough*. "Get off your duff" displays a metaphor in which the human buttocks are compared to plump rolls of dough. On The Rock, a humungous duff, a pudding fit for Paul Bunyan, was sometimes called a stogger, because you could stog your gob (stuff your mouth) with it, and because the cook had to stog a large pudding bag to make it. Often a Newfoundland cook set aside a particular day or days of the week on which to make this pudding. Such happy apppointments were "duff days." Another name in Newfoundland for this boiled pudding is lad-in-a-bag.

FLIPPER PIE

The *locus classicus* on seal-flipper pie appears in *Newfoundland*, a 1969 book by feisty Newfoundland writer, Harold Horwood: "Canadians (and other foreigners) often make the mistake of supposing that this famous Newfoundland delicacy consists of the animals' paws. Not at all. The paws are called pads, and are usually discarded. The flipper is the front shoulder, corresponding to a shoulder of lamb or a shoulder of pork, except that it is much tastier than either. It is heavy with rich, lean meat, the colour of red mahogany, so tender that you can cut it with a fork, and of a hearty, gamy flavour like that of wild duck." Horwood is quoted thus in the second edition of the *Dictionary of Newfoundland English*.

Note the difference between a seal's flipper and its "pad."

Flipper dinners and flipper suppers, often put on by service clubs as fund-raisers, are a feature of April on the island. Sealing ships returning from the spring harvest on the ice floes of Labrador or the Gulf come back to harbour with barrels of flippers, so awaited in St. John's that they sell out quickly. One folk saying speaks of those who are peckish as "hungry as dogs at a flipper barrel."

Flipper pie is an ancient recipe with roots in Scandinavian countries and the Outer Hebrides off Scotland. But the earliest fishermen who crossed the Atlantic for Grand Banks cod and who eventually tested the coast of Labrador saw Inuit people eating *utjak* 'seal flippers,' raw and cooked.

One simple recipe comes from cooks at Happy Valley and Goose Bay in Labrador. A difference of opinion exists about parboiling the flippers first. Some say this produces a horrible, oily smell that gets back into the meat, doubling its "sealiness." Most cooks soak the flippers in cold water and baking soda for thirty minutes, then trim off the fat. Next dredge the flippers with flour and brown with pork fat, onions, and bacon in a frying pan. Then cover and bake two or three hours until tender. Finally, cover with a biscuit pastry and bake for twenty or thirty minutes more. Serve with lemon wedges. A gravy is sometimes added before the pastry is applied.

FLUMMY DUMM

This is a quick trappers' bread in which the hunter-cook makes a fast dough of flour, baking soda, butter or lard, sugar, and water. Then he wraps the dough around a thick stick and toasts it over an open fire. One variant saw flummy dumm made early in the morning into a long, rolled string of dough which was then wrapped around a stovepipe (funnel), and left to bake until done, its progress dependent on the strength of the fire in the stove. Flummy dumm looks like a comic alteration of another name for such a bread, funnel bun. This baking-powder bread was also called stove cake or funnel cake.

A gandy is a pancake made of bread dough fried in pork fat and topped with coady (molasses sauce). The name probably derives from gander, whose prime meaning is a male goose, but with slang extensions that refer to men without women, or husbands without their wives. In early American slang, a gander was a grass-widower, a man living apart from his wife often because his employment took him some distance from his home, like a fisherman at sea for a time or a trapper or hunter off in the woods for weeks on end. In British slang, a gander-moon referred to the husband's banishment from the nuptial bed during the last months of a wife's confinement before childbirth. So gandies may have been the first quick grub that men at work made for themselves.

GANDY

Hurt, with a welter of spellings like eart, heurt, hirt, hort, hurt, whort, and several diminutives like hurtle and whortle, is a very old English berry name. *Hurtes* appear in print by 1542, but its cousin *hurtleberry* appears by 1450. The word has disappeared from standard English, but is still common in many British county dialects. In Newfoundland it refers to a number of species of the *Vaccinium* genus including blueberries, blackberries, bilberries, and huckleberries. In fact, Mark Twain's eponymous Huckleberry Finn takes his nickname from an American alteration of hurtleberry. Newfoundland has ground hurts, stone hurts, and black hurts. This abundant berry ended up early on in hurt pie and other dishes like hurt cake, hurty pudding, and in a delicious

HURT PIE

brew of fermented blueberries called hurt wine, still offered with Christmas cake to lucky mummers who come calling during the holidays.

JIGG'S DINNER

This is a boiled dinner of salt beef and vegetable dish, although salt pork can be used, too. The salted meat is soaked overnight in cold water, then boiled for three-quarters of an hour, at which time the cook adds turnip, carrots, cabbage, and potatoes, boiling until the potatoes are done. This makes a hearty repast for a fisher who's been jigging, that is, using a weighted hook with a line and no bait to catch squid or cod by jigging the line, jerking it up sharply. A jigger line often has two or more hooks attached. Is this the origin of the name *Jigg's dinner*? The verb *to jig* is also used in Newfoundland to mean "to hook a husband." As a noun, a jig can mean a romantic date. Could a Jigg's dinner have been an honest way to convince a potential husband that the female cook preparing the meal knew how to feed a hungry man? In any case, it's a word woven into the tough fabric of island life. Even official Newfoundland place names refer to this method of fishing, spots like Jigging Cove, Jigging Head, and Jigging Point.

KEDGEREE

Boiled rice, eggs, and salt cod feature in this savoury dish brought to Newfoundland by British immigrants. But the first recipe came to London tables during the days of the Raj in India. The word begins to appear in English during the 1750s. In Hindi, it's *khicri* from the even older Sanskrit term *khicca*, then as now, a boiled rice with lentils, onions, and eggs, often with a curry. The British added the smoked fish, usually haddock, and by Victorian times, kedgeree was one of the staple foods of the large English breakfast. In

Newfoundland, for example, in some kitchens on Fogo Island, kedgeree is often presented with a garnish of chopped egg yolks.

LABRADOR TEA

This is a labradorable little evergreen shrub of the heath family, *Ledum groenlandicum*, which has been a staple infusion of northern peoples since the first humans crossed from Asia to America some 12,000 to 20,000 years ago, give or take a day. One Ledum species is circumpolar, so anthropologists posit that First Peoples might have brought with them knowledge of its refreshing

After the hunt, a pause for a hot drink

and medicinal properties . Labrador tea is made by lightly steeping cleaned, crushed, dried leaves. Arctic explorer Sir John Franklin in his 1823 *Narrative of a Journey* reported that the tea smelled like rhubarb. It acted as a mild digestive and perked up one's appetite. The Hudson's Bay Company for a time imported the leaves into England where they enjoyed popularity under the peppy name of Weesukapuka. Canadians spelled it in a variety of ways, usually referring to the plant as wishakapucka, their attempt at the Cree term, *wesukipukosu* 'bitter herbs.' The leaves might also be added to kinnikinick as part of the standard native smoking mixture. Both the plant and the refreshing infusion made from its leaves were also called simply "country tea" by many pioneers. Farther inland, the drink was known as Hudson Bay tea.

Labrador: Origin of the Place Name

There is some dispute about which misty wisp of history produced the name. What we do know is the first record in print. In the journals of John Cabot written about 1516 is this passage: *terra noua de pescaria inuenta de laboradore de re de anglitera tera frigida* 'new land good for fishing found by a worker of the King of England, and a very cold place indeed.' But no one knows the precise origin of the name. British etymologist Eric Partridge in his *Origins* likes the tale of the explorer Gaspar Corte-Real who touched shore in 1500 on a voyage of piscatorial quest and sailed back to Portugal carrying a shipload of Inuit slaves! Historical proof of this particular atrocity is scant. In 16th-century Portuguese, the euphemism for "slaves" was "workers" spelled *labradores.* Modern Portuguese is *lavradores,* but the word now means farm workers. One of the names for Newfoundland on early Italian maps is *Terra del Laboratore* 'land of the worker.' Then into the lexical fray enter scholars who say another Portuguese, one João Fernandes, a rich *lavrador* or landowner in the Azores came north through the Atlantic in his own ships looking for the fabled cod fishery. Some historians give Fernandes credit for discovery of the coast of Greenland and some of the coast of North America.

An interesting folk alteration of the very word *Labrador* occurs among early Acadians in Nova Scotia who heard Labrador as *la bras d'or*, the arm of gold. And so they gave the name to Bras d'Or Lake.

LASSY MOGS

Lassy and lasses are common short forms for molasses on the island. Mogs are small cakes made of flour, baking powder, butter, salt, etc. When sweetened with molasses instead of sugar, they are, of course, lassy mogs. Mog may derive from a British dialect verb that meant "to go slowly" because the little cakes rose slowly when baked. But Mog and Moggy were also dialect nicknames for Margaret in certain rural areas of the British Isles, so these cakes may simply be lassy Margarets. Or — the origin I think most likely — mogs may have been made at first by stamping out the dough with a cutter consisting of an empty mug turned upside down.

LIVE JAM

Jam made to be eaten immediately and not preserved with pectin is live jam, just as live tea is made by pouring boiling water on tea leaves in the cup and drinking the tea "right off the leaves."

MUG UP

A mug up is a quick snack, maybe tea and a biscuit, between meals, late at night, or as a pause during work. The term is widespread in early

English dialects for a fast bite and a cup of tea, and it came across the Atlantic to be used extensively along the Atlantic seaboard of North America and all across the northern regions of what would become Canada. Sailors and fishermen have enjoyed mug ups for at least three hundred years.

NEWFIE BANANA

A Newfie banana is the crunchy root of the cinnamon fern, *Osmunda cinnamomea*, which children sometimes dug up and ate.

NUNCH & NUNNNY-BAG

From a portmanteau word in which noon and lunch are blended comes nunch, any snack between meals by hunters, trappers, sealers, or fishermen, who might carry the provisions for such a quick meal in a nunny-bag (from a British dialect term *noony* 'lunch'). Made of canvas, sealskin, or burlap, with or without a drawstring, this knapsack was called a nunny-bag, a ninny-bag, and a nonny-bag, and might also contain some of the fisherman's personal effects, perhaps his pipe and tobacco, matches, or in olden days, a tinderbox with flint and steel to make fire. Another term sealers used for such portable storage was scrawn-bag.

OLD SCRIPTURE CAKE

Pious Christians often used the Scriptures as a recipe to make a Christmas cake. To show one's acquaintance with many passages of Holy Writ, one used only ingredients mentioned in the Bible, and, of course, one had to quote a Biblical passage beside the ingredient in this manner: 1 cup milk — Exodus 3:8, where the devout and learned would remember the reference to "a land flowing with milk and honey." This flurry of quotations did show praiseworthy knowledge of the Bible, or at least knowledge of how to use a good Biblical concordance, a book which lists alphabetically every occurrence of every word used in the Bible. Hallelujah! Praise the index!

PEAS & MELTS

Peas are the eggs of any fish, in Newfoundland usually herring roe. Melts is the milt — herring testes filled with sperm and the milky spermatic fluid. Using only freshly caught herring, the cook washes the peas and melts thoroughly and separates them in cold water and pats them dry. There are many recipes, but a familiar one is to dredge them lightly with flour and fry them in pork fat until crisp. Serve with fried onion rings, mashed potatoes, and bacon.

PRATIE OATENS

The Irish word for potato is *práta*, and immigrants from Ireland brought this dish to Newfoundland. Pratie oatens were mashed potatoes mixed with oatmeal, formed into little cakes, and fried in bacon or sausage fat.

SCOTCH DUMPLINGS

A kind of haggis once popular among Labrador fishermen, a Scotch dumpling was the stomach of a big cod crammed with chopped cod livers and cornmeal. Any baked fish liver was considered a good cure for night blindness.

SCREECH

Newfie screech began as a drinker's derisive term for any cheap rum, usually a dark Demerera, that might render the quaffer somewhat vociferous after too frequent a tipple. Now it's also a trademarked brand name of a dark Caribbean rum bottled on the island.

SCRUNCHINS

A juicy, salivant, lip-licker of a word, scrunchings or scruncheons or cruncheons are fried cubes of fat-back pork, sprinkled over fish and brewis, or served as accompaniments to many other dishes. Scrunchins also refer to pieces of any fish or animal fat after the oil has been extracted from them.

SLUT

A slut is a whopper of a copper kettle, the big four-gallon kind with a broad bottom and a taper to the top, used on sealing ships. A bubbling slut sat always on the galley stove, and members of the sealing crew poured smaller kettles full of the hot water from the slut, so they could brew a cup of tea by their bunks.

SOLOMON GOSSE'S BIRTHDAY

Solomon Gosse was an early Newfoundland settler who was a cheapskate. He may have been a real person or the mythical embodiment of a skinflint ship owner who fed his fishermen on mighty slim pickings. In any case, Solomon Gosse's birthday was the playful excuse used on any day of the week when a boiled dinner was served, maybe salt pork, cabbage, and duff (pudding), especially if the day was not usually a "pot day," a day for a hot meal of meat and vegetables as opposed to salt cod and hard tack.

SOUNDS

Sounds are the air bladders of a cod that regulate the buoyancy of the fish, permitting it to swim up to the surface or to sound, to go deep. These hydrostatic organs lie along the inside of the cod's backbone, which some fishermen call the sound-bone. The air bladders are removed when splitting cod, dry salted and stored in a wooden tub, sometimes for months. To make a dish of cod sounds, the coarse salt is washed off and the sounds are soaked in cold water for a day. Then their black lining is scraped off, and they are boiled and simmered until the cook decides they are "done." Sounds are then fried in pork fat with chopped onions and homefried potatoes. Some say cod sounds make the zingiest breakfast on The Rock.

SQUATUM

A term invented by Newfoundlanders, squatum is homemade berry wine, made by crushing wild fruit like blueberries or partridgeberries, adding sugar, and letting it ferment. The word arose from a verb no longer used in standard English, a dialect verb, to squat, that meant to squeeze, crush, or flatten. The verb disappeared from standard English early in the 18th century, but not before immigrants using it had come to Newfoundland, where it has been kept alive and useful as part of islanders' unique vocabulary. If the squatum made from local berries does not seem potent enough after fermenting, there is no harm in adding a splash of grain alcohol to the mix, no harm until one attempts to get up the morning after.

TOUTIN

Toutins, toutans, toutens, toutons, or towtents, are still on the home breakfast menu of some Newfoundlanders. Bread dough is made and set to rise with yeast at night. The next morning the dough is cut into small pieces and fried in pork fat. Hot molasses with a pad of butter melted in it might top the toutins that are served at breakfast to children off to school on a frosty winter morning. There are many varieties. Bits of bacon can be sprinkled on top. One toutin is flattened into a pancake form and wrapped around a sausage or a slice of bologna. Toutin may also refer to a pork cake, a bun made by mixing diced pork with flour, water, baking powder, and molasses. Toutins were common fare from a sealing ship's galley or done over a wood fire in a hunting camp. Sometimes molasses toutins and fat-back toutins would both be served at the same away-from-home meal.

VANG

Fish and vang fed many a fisherman. It was cod dished up with melted pork fat. Vang is a Newfoundland dialect version of the older British dialect word *fang* meaning a slice or piece cut off.

WHORE'S EGG

This spiny, prickly sea urchin clings to coastal rocks, wharves, and anything set in ocean water. Newfoundlanders have a politer name for it too, ose's egg (or cosy-egg or oar's egg), a name which is a blending of another more formal name, urse-na, and sea-egg. English-speaking islanders picked up ursena from French-speaking fisher-men. Because of its bristliness the French called it *oursin* 'little bear.' Early sealers may have watched seals breaking sea urchins and eating them, because there are still folks who find cosy-eggs a treat. Children can collect ose's eggs and dry them until the spines fall off, then they make nifty little round toy boats, miniature versions of the old-fashioned coracle. And, on the pleasant image of kids safely at play in a tide pool, we leave Newfoundland, and continue our quest for authentic Canadian food words on another island nearby.

An underwater habitat with thriving echinoderms like the sea urchins called whore's egg (opposite page)

CHAPTER 2

Prince Edward Island

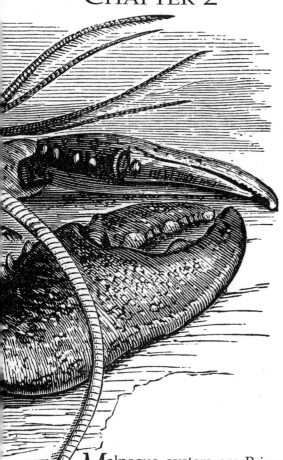

Oysters from Abegweit

Malpeque oysters are Prince Edward Island's most internationally renowned food, and it is fitting that the phrase contains a place name in Mi'kmaq, the language of its earliest named settlers. Malpeque is a French try at *mak paak* 'big bay,' an apt descriptive for the large body of water cutting deep into the north coast of the island, rich in oysters and other foods from the sea.

The Mi'kmaq trace their ancestry back to aboriginal hunters and fishers whom anthropologists call "the Shellfish People," and whose sites on P.E.I. have been dated as old as 10,000 years. Those ancient people, probably seasonal visitors from the mainland, drawn by good catches and abundant wildlife, could have walked to the island across a

flat lowland now covered by the waters of Northumberland Strait. Geologists suggest that as glaciers melted some 5,000 years ago, this plain was covered by rising ocean levels. Nowadays, visitors to P.E.I. can speed across Confederation Bridge.

Mi'kmaq people have lived on the island for almost 2,000 years, and Abegweit has been the affectionate way they refer to Prince Edward Island. Loosely translated from their language, Abegweit means 'cradled on the waves.' The word is pronounced EPP-eh-kwit, all syllables short. More precisely, the Mi'kmaq root is *epegweit*, 'lying in the water,' or *abahquit* 'lying parallel with the waves.' The first Mi'kmaq hunters paddled to Abegweit even in the wintertime by canoe to fish and take wildfowl; and after drying their catch along the shores of Bedeque Bay, they would return to permanent winter camp on the nearby mainland. The Mi'kmaq divided their ancestral lands into seven parts, which still bear the ancient names, as attested in the Mi-kmak Grand Council for the District of Epekwitk (Abegweit).

Most people who have called the island home have been more than fond of Abegweit, a lovely, watery name. Here is Lucy Maud Montgomery, author of *Anne of Green Gables*, writing in 1939 in *Prince Edward Island*, "You never know what peace is until you walk on the shores or in the fields or along the winding red roads of Abegweit on a summer twilight when the dew is falling and the old, old stars are peeping out and the sea keeps its nightly tryst with the little land it loves." The island's deep, fertile, reddish-brown soil, now sandy, now clayey, holds abundant deposits of iron oxides that produce the famous redness.

Ships, too, have proudly borne the name of Abegweit. A CNR automobile ferry that used to ply the waters of the Northumberland Strait between New Brunswick and P.E.I. was christened M.V.

Abegweit. Then in 1962, the body of water crossed by the ferry was officially named the Abegweit Passage.

Samuel de Champlain called Prince Edward Island *Île de Saint Jean* in 1604. The British possession of the island in 1759 caused a simple translation to St. John's Island. Then in 1798 the British garrison at Halifax was being commanded by Prince Edward, Duke of Kent, and some local royalist, some cringing, lickspittle toady, thought it might show a pleasing deference to name yet another piece of colonial real estate after yet another imperial poobah. That Prince Edward, the island's namesake, was the father of Queen Victoria.

As they did everywhere in the Americas, invading Europeans noted what native peoples ate. The logbooks of explorers and the diaries of early settlers pay close attention to local food supplies. In *Abegweit Was Their Home*, a pamphlet published by the Micmac Village Encampment at Rocky Point, P.E.I., early Mi'kmaq foods are enumerated: seal in winter; beaver, rabbit, moose, bear, deer in early spring, then ducks and geese and their eggs harvested after their spring migration north; fish from island streams, lobsters, clams, and oysters. Bone marrow was a treat. Moose and caribou intestines made casings for sausages. The sap of yellow birch trees and maples sweetened Mi'kmaq foods. For vegetable greens Mi'kmaq cooks prized among many wild plants the unfurled fronds of the ostrich fern, now called fiddleheads, and several tubers called wild potatoes, probably tubers of the arrowhead plant, *Sagittaria latifolia*, and especially *sequbbun* 'groundnuts' (*see* entry for *Mi'kmaq potato*). Wild mint leaves were one of many seasonings. Summer and fall brought the bounty of wild berries, some being dried and stored for winter. Autumn's gift was the harvest of beech and hazel nuts. Plump eels could be speared as they squirmed into the cool muck of autumn rivers, and later in the year, tom cod were fished up through ice-holes.

What became Prince Edward Island was just one of the Mi'kmaq living places, but they revered it and called it *Minegoo* 'the island.' In this word we see the common Algonquian root for water *mine*, which appears in numerous North American place names like Minesing in Ontario (derived from the Ojibwa word for island) and the American state of Minnesota, a Siouan descriptive referring to the river and meaning 'cloudy water.' Minnehaha does not mean 'laughing water' but simply 'waterfalls.'

The food words peculiar to Prince Edward Island reflect its ethnic composition, chiefly Highland Scots, Irish, English, and Lowland Scots. About 12 percent of the population are of Acadian origin, but only 4 percent say French is their mother tongue. Acadian foods and dishes are listed separately in their own chapter, since many of these recipes are found wherever in our Maritime provinces Acadians live. People of Mi'kmaq, Dutch, Lebanese, and Scandinavian origin make up a small but vital 2 percent of the island population, while some families had Loyalist ancestors who came north after the American Revolution.

Several Prince Edward Island places were named after foods. There's the hamlet of Oyster Bed Bridge, as well as Gaspereaux on P.E.I.'s east coast. *Gasperot* or *gaspereau* is the Canadian French word for alewife, a local species of herring. Both Nova Scotia and New Brunswick have Gaspereau Rivers. The town of Crapaud (French for toad) took its name from Rivière aux Crapauds, an older French name for the Westmoreland River. But it was not a river full of toads. The term reflects an early Acadian phrase for an eel, *crapaud de mer*. The local river slithered and roiled with fat eels in the fall of the year.

BAR CLAM

A local name for an edible bivalve mollusc also called horse clam, the bar clam burrows into underwater sandbars. "Happy as a clam at high tide" is a colloquial expression of carefree gaiety.

The Bar clam is large, coarse, heavy, with a ridged shell, and is not of great commercial importance on our east coast. The word *clam* stems from the same ancient Germanic root as the English verb *to clamp*. New Englanders fishing in our waters or migrating north added distinct recipes for clam chowder to our Maritime provinces. Also imported from the New England states was the cheery fun of a clambake where the molluscs are steamed on hot rocks over which layers of seaweed are placed. Certain persnickety gourmets claim that clams on the half-shell should never be spritzed with fresh lemon juice, since the tartness of the lemon actually overrides and masks the delicate savour of moist clam meat. However one seasons this sea treat, daintiness has no place during its ingestion. Clams should be sucked down in a lascivious, sybaritic slurping, much as Tom Jones and his mistress devoured oysters before they devoured each other in Tony Richardson's 1963 film version of the Fielding novel.

BEDLUNCH

This appears to be a term exclusive to Prince Edward Island to denote a little snack taken before retiring for the night.

BLUE POTATO

Although never an important commercial variety on Spud Island (P.E.I.), blue potatoes can still be purchased from individual growers and at some farmers' markets. Some Maritimers swear that the distinctive taste of blue potatoes, always cooked in their dark-blue skins, makes them the gustatory pinnacle of potatodom. Potatoes appear to have been cultivated first by the Inca peoples of Chile and Peru. Among the varieties found by Spanish *conquistadores* were potatoes with blue-violet skins and even one with black skin and black flesh. Potato varieties have been cultivated in Ireland since 1585, and one of the Irish potatoes was a "blue." Therefore, it is unclear whether the blue potato of our Atlantic provinces came from Ireland or was introduced into North America by traders directly from native Chilean or Peruvian stock. One of the old varieties of blue potato in our Maritimes was the MacIntyre, sometimes known in Prince Edward Island by the offensive, racist slang term, "nigger toes."

BLUEBERRY GRUNT

This dessert and its name are general throughout our Maritimes, and appear to have been borrowed or brought up to Canada by Loyalists from New England. It's a steamed pudding that makes grunting noises while it is being steamed. Sometimes it is shortened simply to *grunt*. Blueberries were one of the wild fruits that Mi'kmaq cooks dried like raisins and then used through the winter. The general recipe for grunt consists of boiling blueberries in water and sugar until juicy, then making a biscuit dough and dropping tablespoons of the dough over the blueberry compote, covering the saucepan and cooking for a quarter of an hour or thereabouts. Grunt is delicious served with any thick cream. For a similar dish, see the *fungy* entry under Nova

Scotia, where grunt is sometimes called blueberry slump.

BOXTY

Irish immigrants to our Maritimes brought this "poor man's bread," made from grated raw potatoes and flour, a sort of potato bannock. Boxty bread was one of the traditional Halloween foods for some people from the north of Ireland. The first part of the word probably contains the Irish adjective *bocht* 'poor,' so-called because it was made of potatoes not wheat.

CENTRE CAKE

At church socials and fund-raising suppers in P.E.I., outdoors or indoors, a fancy fruit cake often reposed in glory atop a pedestal plate in the centre of the long tables at which parishioners ate. At the end of the meal, this centre cake was auctioned off to raise money for some church cause

CLOUTIE

Scottish settlers brought this name for a pudding (usually plum) steamed in a bag. Cloutie is Scots for a wee bit of cloth, being a diminutive of clout, from Old English *clut* 'rag, piece of cloth, diaper.' Clout has a compound in the old synonym for loincloth, breechclout. Bagged puddings have many colourful names in Canadian cookery. See the entries for *bugger-in-a-bag* in the Gaspé section of the chapter on Québec, for Newfoundland's *figgy duff*, and for the Alberta treat, *Son-of-a-Gun-in-a-Sack*.

DOUGH DOLLY

Bread dough is set to rise at night. In the morning, slices of the risen dough are cut off and fried for breakfast. The phrase *dough dolly* seems to be unique to Prince Edward Island. Dough dollies are roughly similar to Newfoundland's damper dogs.

EEL PIE

Eels can be speared through a hole in the spring ice, or caught in late fall when they are fat and sluggish and just beginning to burrow into bottom muck. They can be fried or broiled, or even chopped up into an eel pie and put into a dish lined with stuffing. Add lemon juice, mild onions, seasonings; top with puff pastry. Make béchamel sauce and add it to the pie after it has baked for an hour and a bit. Keep some of the béchamel aside to serve with the pie — béchamel is a white sauce made by adding boiling milk to a cold roux (flour and butter cooked to a blonde colour). Louis de Béchameil (1630 – 1703) was a wealthy French gourmet who became head steward to the Sun King, Louis XIV. He claimed — some say unjustly — to have invented the sauce that bears his name, minus the letter *i*.

Eel is a lovely, slithery slip of a word, Germanic in origin. Compare German *Aal*. And yet its legitimate adjective *eely* never became widely used in English. The eely connivings of Ottawa lobbyists would seem a most apt use. More obscure still is a splendid English word that names a place where these snakelike fishes are caught, an eelery.

FINNAN HADDIE

This is a smoked fish brought to North America by Scottish settlers. Long popular in the Maritimes, *Findon haddock* was originally made in Scotland in the fishing village of Findon near Aberdeen by smoking haddock over a peat fire, a turf fire, or a fire made from green wood. A rival claimant for the name is the Scottish village of Findhorn on a river of the same name.

Not as widespread as the term *finnan haddie*, but still heard now and then in a Gaelic kitchen is the name of a Scottish soup made from finnan haddie. It's called cullen skink, where the first word is a dialect variant of Cologne, and where *skink* is a beef or haddock soup, the word probably deriving from German *Schinke* 'ham,' so that the original phrase *Cologne ham* was a comic put-down, implying that Germans in Cologne had to use smoked fish in their soup because they could not obtain ham. Or perhaps the joke is even more obscure and utterly lost to history.

FOOSY

A foosy was any little, out-of-the-ordinary morsel of food set aside for a special occasion — perhaps a cake just for visitors, dainties for auntie's tea, or a candy treat as a reward for children. The word sounds like one of several British dialect pronunciations of the adjective *fussy*.

FRICKO

This is an anglicizing of the Acadian French *fricot* 'stew, food.' On Prince Edward Island, fricko or frickle is usually chicken stew with dumplings, but some recipes add onions, potatoes, and pork. For more details, see the *fricot* entry in the chapter on Acadian foods.

FRIENDSHIP CAKE

To make a friendship cake, the cook ferments fruit (peaches, pineapples, cherries, pears, apples, etc.) for thirty days (hence, the other name, *thirty-day cake*). One makes enough of the fermented fruit to pour off a few cups of its juice to give to friends as starter. This fermented base is thus passed around a community from friend to friend, just as sourdough starter was shared among pioneer breadmakers.

A Scottish term for a *wee dram* of any alcoholic

GILLOCK & OTHER BOOZE TERMS

drink, gillock is also seen in spellings that mimic its pronunciation: jillic, jillock, jullic. There are several terms on the island for a quick drink of booze, such as a snap, a snapper, and — one that is most apt — a smile o' rum. A little snort of hootch might also be offered by saying, "Would you have a dish now?" A pup was a little bottle of moonshine, whereas a teddy of shine was often a beer bottle filled with bootleggers' illicitly made alcohol. A teddy of shine was sometimes offered to potential voters as a bribe at election time.

The opposite, a big drink, a voluminous quaff indeed, was a riveter, often of rum or moonshine.

GULCH

This is a Prince Edward Island version of what is called in Newfoundland *chaw and glutch*. Gulch, ultimately from a British dialect verb meaning 'to swallow,' is junk food with low nutritional value or food that looks revolting and not very appetizing. See the *chaw and glutch* entry in the chapter on Newfoundland food.

GUT PUDDING

This is a poor man's sausage, usually with no meat rather made from a stuffing of cornmeal and hard fatlike suet.

IRISH MOSS PUDDING

Also called sea-moss pudding, this Maritime dessert is similar to a blancmange, but an edible seaweed is the jelling agent instead of gelatine, and whipped egg whites replace the more usual cornstarch. One old recipe was thought especially helpful for invalids or anyone with "a delicate digestion" and this was Irish moss jelly, in which a small handful of cleaned, dried Irish moss was boiled in two cups of water, then cooled. A cup of milk was then stirred in and a little sugar added. Highly restorative, according to many an Island grandmother!

Irish moss, Canada's most valuable commercial seaweed, is one of the red algae, usually *Chondrus crispus*, but several other seaweeds are sometimes called Irish moss. It is called carrageen in Scotland and Ireland, and was named after a town near Waterford in Ireland, Carragheen. But the town may also owe its moniker to an Irish term for the moss, *cosáinín carraige*, literally in Erse 'little foot of the rock.' *Chondrus crispus* is related to another popular edible seaweed called dulse. See the entry for *dulse* in the chapter on New Brunswick food words. Irish moss is exported from Prince Edward Island and processed to yield a hydrocolloid, carrageenin. All of us use products every day that contain carrageenin as an emulsifying and stabilizing agent. For example, it holds together the ingredients in many toothpastes, shampoos, cosmetics, pharmaceuticals, and prepared foods like chocolate milk, ice cream, and commercial salad dressings. Check the list of ingredients on any commercial food product that might qualify as 'goopy.' Carrageenin is also used to clarify liquids like beer, wine, coffee, and honey. In many frozen foods, carrageenin helps retard the formation of ice crystals in products that can be kept cold for long periods.

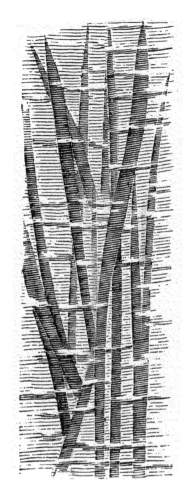

Gathered as well along the coasts of Nova Scotia and New Brunswick, Irish moss has been an important commercial crop on Prince Edward Island for so long that some unique Island terms have grown up around its collection, notably the noun *mosser*, referring to one who harvests the seaweed. A mosser is also a high, stormy wind that wafts Irish moss toward the shore. Such winds help produce the underwater waves of turbulence that rip Irish moss fronds from their holdfasts on

Irish Moss Industry on P.E.I.

seabed rocks in the lower tidal and subtidal zones.

Water-plumped and tempest-rolled, rows of green strands festoon shores in the north of Prince Edward Island near Tignish, Miminegash, Cape Tryon, North Rustico, and Covehead. Moss that reaches a beach is forked into piles by *combers* using hand rakes. *Horse mossers* collect Irish moss near shore by rakes and wire-mesh scoops pulled through the water by a *moss horse*. Such horses are usually large and fearless, for they sometimes have to haul moss in water right up to their necks and work among several dozen other horses when twenty or thirty horse mossers all harvest one stretch of shore after an especially bountiful storm. A former term for profit from such a sea-gift was *moss money*. In olden days, children often had the job of cleaning freshly harvested moss of pebbles, shells, sea wrack, and other unwanted seaweeds. On Prince Edward Island one such impurity is called *monkey fur*, being the seaweed genus *Halopteris*, whose thick brown strands are matted through the Irish moss and make it hard to dry. Another tangly intruder has the P.E.I. nickname, *shoe-string*. It's a green, eelgrasslike seaweed of the *Chondra* genus and must be plucked from a mosser's haul if the harvester wants top price from processors.

Popular Canadian balladeer Stompin' Tom Connors who wrote the rollicking "Bud The Spud" about P.E.I.'s potato industry also celebrated seaweed in his "Song of the Irish Moss" where he wrote "You can hear them roar from the Tignish Shore / There's moss on Skinner's Pond . . . "

JOLLOP

A jollop on P.E.I. is any big mess of food made from kitchen leftovers. Spelled like dollop, this is probably from mid-17th-century English farm slang where a jollop was the wattle of a turkey or rooster, the implication being that when you wolfed down such goopy leftovers, you really had to move your jowls, that is, your wattles. Jollop appears to be a compound of jowl + lap, analogous to dewlap.

The succulent, slurpable viscera of this noble mollusc grow to juicy, shuckable maturity in the waters of Malpeque Bay where they provide Prince Edward Island's most internationally renowned food, highly prized as the world's most flavoursome oyster on the half-shell. Malpeque is an Acadian French rendering of *Mak Paak* 'big bay,' a place name in Mi'kmaq, the language of the island's earliest named settlers. It is an apt descriptive for the large body of water cutting deep into the north coast of the island, rich in oysters and other foods from the sea. Malpeque is also the official name of a federal electoral riding of the province. But the name is often used for any high-quality oysters from Prince Edward Island waters. On Malpeque Bay and at several other island localities, commercial oyster farms abound. Here seed oysters are "sown" into the muddy bottom of the bay and when mature the oysters are removed by long, scissorlike tongs.

MALPEQUE OYSTER

Groundnut, *Apios americana* or *Apios tuberosa*, is a member of the pea family, and its dark-red or brown flowers resemble those of sweet pea. These climbing plants thrive in damp ground from Prince Edward Island to Ontario. Mi'kmaq people prized the sweet tubers of this plant which has a chestnut flavour, and they call it *sequbbun*. Early white settlers in the Maritimes shared the taste, sometimes by necessity — a report from Port Royal in 1613 tells of Biencourt and his followers scattering through the woods around the fortifications searching and digging for groundnuts. The

MI'KMAQ POTATO *or* GROUNDNUT

Nova Scotia town and river, Shubenacadie, is an Acadian French attempt at a Mi'kmaq phrase that means 'sequbbun (groundnuts) grow here.' The plant is also called Mi'kmaq potato, bog potato, and travellers' delight. The botanical genus name is Greek *apios* 'a pair,' because the tubers on an individual rhizome seem to grow in pairs. One healthy plant may have ten or twelve tubers.

PORK & JERK

Here is some P.E.I. humour that arose during times when food was scarce. Pork and jerk was a poor meal, at which the pickings were so slim that a small piece of pork was tied with a long string and passed around the table. If any of the hungry became too greedy and tried to eat the whole piece of pork, it could be jerked away from the too-eager eater and passed on to the next starveling. It was also said that one fish was sometimes tied with a long string and passed about a poor man's table in a similar fashion.

POTATOES & POINT

Here's another jokey reference to the poverty and bad times. Potatoes and point as a phrase was brought to P.E.I. and Cape Breton by Irish immigrants. The gist of the jest is that all one has to eat at a particular meal are potatoes, and that one may point at other

richer foods, such as steak or ham. A similar phrase is *bread and think*. The bread is on the table; the hapless diner can think about other foods. An older English phrase is *bread and skip*, as in "there's bread and bacon, and skip the bacon."

RAGGED ROBINS

This is an old meringue dessert, for which egg whites are beaten until stiff. Then a dash of vanilla extract and a sprinkle of salt are added. Chopped dates, glazed cherries, walnuts, corn flakes, and some sugar are added to the egg white mixture which is then dropped on a greased cookie sheet and baked until light brown.

RUM RUNNERS' BLACK BOTTOM PIE

Melted chocolate is poured over a graham cracker pie crust. The filling is an egg-yolk-milk-gelatin mixture cooked in a double boiler. A few snorts of brandy are added to the filling after it cools. The topping is whipped cream with bounteous splashings of rum stirred in — strictly for flavour, you understand.

SMELT STORM

An old Canadian term in our Atlantic provinces, a smelt storm is a snow- or windstorm, toward the end of April, heralding the spawning run of smelts into tidal estuaries and harbours. It is also called a black storm, a sheep storm, or a robin snow. In spring, smelts are fished using a broad landing net. But much Maritime smelt fishing happens in early winter when rivers are frozen, and homemade smelt shacks are pushed out onto the ice, a hole is bored, and a smaller net fastened to wooden poles is dropped through the hole. Those with quick reflexes sometimes spear smelts, but this takes great patience. Being a small fish, the smelt is often not filleted. Most just lop off their heads, and fry them.

More fastidious eaters pull the guts out through the gills after decapitation, and snip off the fins and tail with kitchen scissors. Some Acadians like to poach smelt by simmering in herbed water.

Etymology of Smelt Words

Smelt came into Old English from a word for small fish in Old Scandinavian, the language spoken by the Vikings. Compare modern Norwegian *smelta*, itself sprung from an Indo-European root like (s)*mel* 'soft, slimy, smooth.'

Acadian French for smelt is *éplan* or *épelan*, dialect variants of standard French *éperlan*, borrowed into early French from Middle Dutch *spierlinc*. Québec has its very own *Rivière Éperlan* 'Smelt River,' a little stream near Forestville on the north shore on the St. Lawrence. Compare *Spierling* in German, an old synonym for the standard German word for smelt, *Stint*. *Spierling* probably means 'little spear,' referring either to the shape of the fish or its method of capture. Scottish and northern English dialects still have a synonym for smelt that was also borrowed from the Dutch word, sparling or spirling. This is the source of *some* of the English surnames in the Sparling-Sperling-Spurling group.

SPRUCE GUM

Before commercial chewing gums like Wrigley's were available, Canadian pioneer kids peeled off the slightly bitter gum that oozed from spruce trees and had a good 'chaw.' Guess what? Modern scientific analysis has revealed that most gums of conifers have chemicals that are fungicidal and antibacterial!

STENCHEL

An old-timey breakfast might have been stenchel on porridge. Stenchel was a glutinous melange of molasses, water, and ground ginger. It was also a restorative drink for farm labourers working in the summer fields. That stenchel was a cup or two of molasses, vinegar, and ginger dissolved in a gallon of cold water (!).

From Scottish Gaelic *strupag* 'wee dram of spiritous liquor' comes this word, now rare in our Atlantic provinces, for a little tea break, perhaps a cup of tea and cookies in the afternoon or just before bedtime.

STRUPAC

Visitors arrive just in time for strupac.

CHAPTER 3

Nova Scotia

As in other provinces of Canada, the foods that Nova Scotians or Bluenoses cherish most were brought to the "wharf of North America" by immigrants. The original inhabitants were a people speaking an Algonquian language, the Mi'kmaq, who arrived, based on archaeological evidence, at least 10,000 years ago. They've been in the neighbourhood quite a while then — long enough even to make place names from some of their food words, for example, Shubenacadie.

The Nova Scotia town, lake, and river of Shubenacadie is a French and English attempt at a Mi'kmaq phrase signifying the presence of 'sequbbun' (groundnuts). The tasty groundnut, *Apios americana*, is a member of the pea family, and its dark-red or

Bluenose Places Named After Foods

brown flowers resemble those of the sweet pea. They thrive in damp ground from Nova Scotia to Ontario. Mi'kmaq people prize the sweet tubers of this plant which has a chestnut flavour, and they call it *sequbbun*. *Sequbbunakade* is Mi'kmaq for 'groundnut-place.' Groudnut is also called Micmac potato, bog potato, and travellers' delight. The botanical genus name is Greek *apios* 'a pair' because the tubers on an individual rhizome seem to grow in pairs. One healthy plant may have ten or twelve tubers. Mi'kmaq people taught white settlers that these tubers were a good source of starch. As early as 1613, Biencourt and his followers at Port Royal went on foraging trips around the colony and along the nearby shores digging for groundnuts.

The Mi'kmaq locative suffix *-akadi, -akwadik* shows up in other regional place names like Quoddy Harbour, from Mi'kmaq *nooda-akwade* 'seal-hunting place,' and Tracadie, from *tul-akadik* 'camping place.' A bit south, Maine's Passama-quoddy Bay is from a Mi'kmaq phrase that means 'pollock place,' referring to a marine food fish called pollock in English. Other Nova Scotia places indicating food location include Antigonish, from Mi'kmaq *n'alegihooneech* 'broken-branches,' a reference to a place where bears came to forage for beechnuts. Baccaro, east of Cape Sable Island, is from a Basque word for codfish. Bakeapple Barren, named after the delicious little berries, is in Cape Breton Highlands National Park. Bass River explains itself. The Canard River was just ducky for hunters of wildfowl. Framboise abounded in wild raspberries. Big clams lurked in tidal flats offshore at Grosses Coques. Ostrea Lake once had oyster beds. The Latin word for oyster and its zoological genus name is *ostrea*. Later and more playful English place names based on food words in Nova Scotia include Pickle Bay, The Beefsteak, and Cheese Factory Corner.

Later immigrants, who came long after the Mi'kmaq, included John Cabot who made landfall at Cape Breton Island in 1497, and more than a century later, de Monts and Champlain who founded Port Royal in 1605, the first farm settlement by Europeans on land that eventually became part of Canada. The French named it Acadia. In 1621, King James I granted Sir William Alexander land officially dubbed New Scotland or, in Latin, *Nova Scotia*. Governor Cornwallis founded Halifax in 1749 and arranged an influx of German Protestants, more than 2,000 of whom were settled near Lunenburg. In the years that followed, pre-Loyalist New Englanders came to Nova Scotia, along with Irish and Yorkshiremen. Significantly, the first Scots reached Pictou in 1773. The outbreak of the American Revolution began a flow of more than 20,000 Loyalists. African-Americans came first as slaves of some Loyalists, as free people from Jamaica, and as free citizens after the war of 1812. Today, people from England, Ireland, Wales, and Scotland make up 70 percent of the population of Nova Scotia, while roughly 8 percent are of Acadian and French origin. Ninety-four percent list their mother tongue as English, 3 percent as French. Naturally, the food words that have endured in Nova Scotia reflect the ethnic composition of the province.

Many foods once eaten by and some still enjoyed by *les Acadiens* living in Nova Scotia are listed in

ACADIAN BOILED HAM

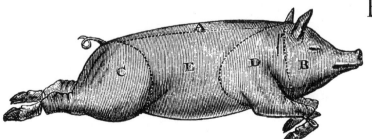

their own chapter in this book. But this recipe was borrowed by other Nova Scotians from their Acadian neighbours. A big ham is cleaned, trimmed, encased in a thin, floured cloth, tied up, and simmered for five hours in cold water and cider. A special Acadian touch was to wrap the ham before bagging in a few strands of fresh-mown hay.

BARLEY BREAD

This Lunenburg favourite was once made completely from barley flour and mixed like a cake. The modern recipe, however, calls for five parts of wheat flour and three parts of barley flour. The early German settlers in Nova Scotia also made porridge from barley. This gruel was called *Gerstengrütze*. Note that *grütze* has the same, ultimate Germanic root as the American *grits* and the British *groats*.

BLUENOSE POTATO

A maritime potato once had a tip that was bluish, hence Bluenose potatoes. Folklore claims this as the origin of the common nickname for residents of the province. But there seem to be as many derivations of bluenose as there are Nova Scotians. Said also to be the source of the phrase are the blue noses of fishermen coming into harbour after the cold Atlantic winds have frosted them. In the war of 1812, there was supposedly a Nova Scotia privateer with a cannon in her bow painted bright blue. She preyed on Yankee ships, and they called her The Bluenose. And now we have the famous symbol of Nova Scotia, Canada's most famous ship, the Bluenose schooner, which appeared in 1927/28 on a stamp, and has adorned the obverse of the Canadian dime since 1937. In

1898, a monthly called the *New Brunswick Magazine* reported that Bluenose "originated with the Loyalists of Annapolis county, who applied it to the pre-Loyalist settlers as a term of 'derision' during the bitter struggle to pre-eminence in public affairs between the two sections of the population in the provincial election of 1785." Over the years, many supposititious origins have surfaced and

sunk in the Bay of Improbability. Truth is, nobody truly knows the origin of this nickname. See also the *blue potato* entry in the chapter on Prince Edward Island food words.

BRAWN

Here's a word used with a meaning now obsolete in modern English, but preserved in an old Nova Scotia recipe, probably brought to North America early in the 18th century. Of course we still use brawn today to mean physical strength or muscularity. And in the specialized culinary vocabulary of the boar's-head dinner, brawn is a rare term for the flesh of the pig's head that has been boiled, chopped, and moulded. But from 1400 to about 1650, brawn could mean the meat of any animal used as food. And this is the old meaning in the Nova Scotia recipe for English brawn, a veal-shank and pork-hock stew made by boiling the meat off the bones in seasoned water, then making a stock from that water after the meat has been removed.

BROWN-SUGAR HOUSE

This is a long-obsolete insult among travellers concerning accommodations in 19th-century Nova Scotia. A brown-sugar house was a low-class inn or cheap hotel, mentioned, for example, in an 1830 letter as being so ill-supplied that it did not have "all the requisites for refreshment [including] the best loaf-sugar." Nineteenth-century refined white sugar was often sold in conical loaves of various sizes, hence the many peaks in North and South America called Sugarloaf Mountain.

These little date tarts contain no pork, but perhaps the pastry shells were made long ago with pork fat instead of butter. The filling is chopped dates simmered in brown sugar and water until "just gooey." Yum! Sometimes a sinful mantle of butter icing tops the tart.

CAPE BRETON PORK PIES

Here's an old Scottish and Anglo-Irish dialect verb preserved in a Nova Scotia dish. To champ once meant to mash and also to munch and chew food

CHAMP

noisily. Think of horses champing at the bit. In our Maritimes, champ is a mashed potato dish, sometimes known by its Irish name of *chappit tatties* where chappit is chapped, that is, cracked or fissured because a hole is made in the centre of the mashed potato serving and a large pad of butter is put into the hole to melt. As one chomps the champ, one dips each forkful into the melted butter.

CHOWDER

This English word may have been born in Acadia, first borrowed into English from the French kitchens at Port Royal or from French fishermen early in the history of Newfoundland. Chowder was adopted from *chaudière* 'heater, kettle,' an early and still much-used French word for a large iron pot or cauldron. French fishermen netting along our Atlantic coast had big kettles on board into which some of the day's catch, often cod, was tossed to make a kind of continuing fish stew. *Faire la chaudière* meant 'to make the kettle of fish stew.' Like another famous French-Canadian dish, *tourtière*, the receptacle in which the food was made came to be used to name the food itself. Like *chaudière*, a number of words in regional continental French that mean fish soup (*chaudrée, caudière,*

caudrée) derive from the Late Latin *caldaria* 'boiler, heating kettle.' So does our English word caldron or cauldron, through an old Norman French form, *cauderon*. Nitpicking English scholars added the *l* back into the word during the 15th century. The related Spanish word for cauldron gives a term in geology for a wide volcanic crater, caldera. The ultimate Latin root is *caldus* 'warm.' The hot tank in a Roman bath was the *calidarium*. The common adjective for warm in Romance languages usually derives from *caldus*, for example, French *chaud*, Italian *caldo*, and even Rumanian *cald*.

COOKY-SHINE

This wonderful Scotch dialect phrase for a tea party used to be heard quite frequently in Nova Scotia among those of Gaelic ilk. This use of the noun *shine* to mean a party or convivial gathering appears related to the early Victorian English term *shindy* meaning 'spree, bit of merrymaking' and to its slightly later American variant *shindig* meaning 'a country party with dancing' or 'a noisy get-together.' Tea-shine was a colloquial term for a tea-party in 19th-century Britain.

DEACON'S NOSE

I first encountered this term in the now somewhat-dated satire of the Nova Scotia humorist and judge, Thomas Chandler Haliburton, creator of Sam Slick, in his series of comic books about *The Clockmaker* (1836 – 1853). Though Haliburton's barbs against his fellow Nova Scotians are those of a condescending Tory and were written first as newspaper columns, there are still good laughs in Haliburton's crude diatribes against the foibles of human nature. Those foibles have not changed much in 150 years. In Haliburton's *Nature and Human Nature*, published in 1855, is this passage about the food served at a mid-19th-century supper in Nova

Scotia, during which the host says, "Mr. Slick, what part shall I help you to — a slice of the breast, a wing, a side-bone, or the deacon's nose, or what?"

This humorous bit of slang for the derrière of a cooked bird, usually a chicken or turkey, has variants like the parson's nose and the pope's nose. None of these comic metaphors is Canadian in origin, but all are used here. Sometimes such terms are offensive. I would like to offer a Canadian compromise, a term that lessens any possible offence and yet maintains a little humour. Just use the technical word in ornithology for the fleshy protuberance on a bird's butt that supports the tail feathers. The parson's nose is the uropygium, from Greek *ouropygion* literally 'tail-rump-let,' little tail-rump. A uropygial gland opens dorsally at the base of the tail feathers on the uropygium and secretes an oil used by the bird in preening its feathers. The bird transfers oil from this gland to its bill and then coats and waterproofs each feather as needed. "A slice of white meat, dear? A drumstick? How about the uropygium?" The pope's nose has a *locus classicus* in modern literature, and mentioning this will raise the tone of any discussion about the phrase. Use of the expression begins a family argument in the first scene of James Joyce's seminal 1914 novel *Portrait of the Artist as a Young Man*.

DIGBY CHICKEN

A bit of Nova Scotian self-mockery is present in the gently satiric phrase *Digby chicken*, which refers to a tiny herring that is smoked, salted, and stored for winter use. Some Nova Scotians also call fillets of the little fish, Digby chips, both named after the Nova Scotia fishing port that commemorates Admiral Robert Digby, commander of HMS Atlanta, one of the ships that conveyed the Loyalist founders of the town to the shores of Nova Scotia in 1783. Herring were gutted, scaled, cleaned, and then plunged into a barrel of brine for two days. Then a hardwood fire was started in the smokehouse. When it was roaring merrily, damp sawdust was tossed on to make dense smoke. Sometimes the sawdust was made from aromatic wood like spruce. The herring could then be placed on a grid made of greenwood saplings that was put over the smouldering billows to smoke for two or three hours.

DULSE

Dulse is an edible seaweed, a red alga, also called salt-leaf. Although it is described as tough and flavourless by those who dislike it, dried crisps of purply dulse are chewed by themselves and added to soups and stews as salty thickeners. Along the coasts of our Canadian Maritimes, dulse grows in the intertidal zone at the low-water mark, attached to rocks or other seaweeds by a holdfast shaped like a disc. Many Canadians say the best dulse in the world is harvested along the rocky shoreline near Dark Harbour, on the west side of Grand Manan Island, New Brunswick. But some Nova Scotians who go out collecting would argue vigorously about that contention.

Word Lore of Dulse

Dulse was borrowed directly into English at a rather late date, circa 1698, from Scots Gaelic *duileasg* < *duil* Gaelic, leaf + *iasc* Gaelic, fish, hence in origin it is a playful, Celtic nickname, leaf-fish, because it came from the sea like fish and was an edible leaf. In Welsh, it's *delysg* or *dylusg*, in modern Irish (Erse) *duileasc*. Sometimes in Scotland, it's spelled *dilse*.

Dulse is *Palmaria palmata*, which grows on both shores of the North Atlantic Ocean. Longfellow wrote that "the tide is low, and the purple dulse is lovely." The genus name *Palmaria*, is botanical

Latin from *palmaris* Latin 'the width of a hand,' also influenced by *palmatus* Latin, 'with lobes that resemble a human hand with the fingers stretched out.' Dulse has dark-red, palmately divided fronds. It belongs to the family *Rhodophyta*, the red algae family, whose name is made up of two Greek word elements, *rhodo* 'rose-coloured, red' plus *phyton* Greek 'plant.'

The Rhodophytes

The Canadian coast has about 175 arctic, 350 Atlantic, and 500 Pacific species of seaweed, many of them algal. Algae are divided into greens, browns, and reds. Most seaweeds are red and brown algae. Rhodophytes are a division of the algae, which store floridean starch, a compound that makes them sweet, mucilaginous, and sticky. Many commercial products of a glue-like consistency are made from red seaweeds, for example agar-agar, algin, and carragheen. They are hydrocolloids used to thicken, stabilize, or emulsify products like ice cream and toothpaste.

DUTCHMESS

Dutchmess is the pride of local cooking in Lunenburg, Nova Scotia. Dutch is *Deutsch*, German. And mess is not a mess meaning an untidy jumble. It's mess meaning a serving of food. Lunenburg Dutchmess, sometimes called *Hausküchen*, is salted cod and potatoes dressed with bacon bits or salt pork scraps and onions. By the way, all meanings of mess stem from Old French *mes* 'a portion of food put in front of the eater' from the verb *mettre* 'put' or 'place.' Latin had *missus* to mean one of several courses during a meal.

FISHSTICK

This is an oblong fillet of frozen fish that is breaded, often pre-cooked and sold in cartons. The term may have been coined in Nova Scotia by marketing executives at one of the large fish-processing plants. Indeed the first long "fingers" of breaded fish may be the idea of some Nova Scotian fisherman's wife, but I could find no printed reference to a specific individual or company as the inventor of fish sticks. If you know the originator, reader, please write me at the address given at the end of the preface to this book.

In the days before fish sticks

FRUMETY

The standard spelling is frumenty, with a heavy stress on the first syllable, hence the folk spelling. Frumenty is hulled wheat boiled in water until the wheat kernels burst, and then left to cool and slowly turn to a jellylike consistency, often overnight. The next day this wheaten mush is heated in a saucepan with some milk, then sweetened and seasoned with brown sugar, cinnamon, shaved almonds, and perhaps nutmeg. This peasant food first appears as a word in the 14th-century French term, *fourmentée*, from Latin *frumentum* 'grain.' Derived from the same Latin word, the term *froment* is still used — in place of the standard word *blé* — in French cookery for various types of wheat.

FUNGY

Fungy or fungee (pronounced FUN-jee) as a noun is of Nova Scotian origin. It's a deep-dish blueberry pie, perhaps first named in Yarmouth County. The *Dictionary of Canadianisms on Historical Principles* states that the word is of unknown origin. Not really. It is an extension of the 16th-century adjective *fungy* 'full of air holes, spongy like a fungus.' In Newfoundland, fungy bread was poorly baked with too much yeast or other riser and consequently had big holes. The watery component of blueberries is driven off the fruit when it bakes, and bubbles of steamy vapour often make little holes in deep-dish blueberry pastries, so that some early cook probably referred to this concoction as a fungy sort of pie. And the name, like blueberry stain to dental enamel, stuck. See the entry below for *grunt*.

GOOSE TONGUES

This edible beach plant is also called seashore plantain, *Plantago juncoides.* The specific means 'like a rush,' and indeed the grassy tufts look somewhat like rushes of the *Juncus* genus. But the long, lingual leaves appeared to Nova Scotia and New England fishermen to resemble the tongues of geese. This edible marsh green, harvested in midsummer, has a spicy saltiness that makes it an Acadian favourite picked fresh in salads or pickled in brine for winter use. Early French sailors added goose-tongue greens to boiling broth. The plant thrives on sandy or shingle beaches washed by salt water, in salt marshes, and in rock crevices of our Pacific and Atlantic coasts. It is also found along the shores of Hudson Bay, James Bay, and Ungava Bay in northern Québec. Tender young leaves are best for salads, while older leaves can be boiled in soups, stews, or chowders. The adventurous cook may like to pickle goose tongues in vinegar. If you are going to pick it for the first time while tromping along a beach, make sure you can identify the plant accurately. Ask a local for help, because there is another beach plant called arrow-grass that looks like goose tongues but is toxic. See also the entry on *passe-pierre* in the chapter on Acadia.

GRUNT

Grunt or slump or fudge is a steamed pudding or dumpling made with blueberries or huckleberries. But one can also enjoy in a Nova Scotia kitchen rhubarb grunt, raspberry grunt, and even apple grunt. In *Folklore of Lunenburg County, Nova Scotia*, the great Canadian folklorist Helen Creighton gives one definitive recipe: "Put berries in a pot, cover well with water and cook. Cool and add sugar. Drop baking powder dough in it." Maritimers enjoy many variations, including one made from the little red cranberrylike fruits of foxberry or cowberry, *Vaccinium vitis-idaea.* Grunt is the toadish plorp! sound made as baking drives pockets of heated water vapour out of the gelatinous mass of the cooking berries. Grunt can be a main course as well as a dessert.

KIACK

Kiack is a rough-scaled, bony little fish called the alewive in English, and *ki'ak* in the Mi'kmaq language. It is often fished during the spring salmon run when it comes up maritime rivers. Its zoological name is the daunting *Pomolobus pseudoharengus* or apple-bellied false herring. The little fish does have a naturally big belly, and this gave the English common name too, an alewife being just what it looks like, a woman who kept an alehouse, sampled her brew copiously, and had a fat stomach. In Nova Scotia, kiack became an insult, too. Kiack was a term of derision in early Nova Scotia for anyone who ate alewives, implying that they were poor, rustic, and could not afford to indulge in civilized "town" food.

LUNENBURGER KARTOFFEL-SUPPE

This robust potato-and-sauerkraut chowder was a reliable staple of the poorest table. Diced potatoes are added to sauerkraut cooked in water. Fried salt pork scraps are tossed in, and then some flour is browned in the salt pork fat left in the fry pan. This browned flour is stirred into the mixture to make a real Lunenburg potato "soup."

LUNENBURG PUDDING

This pudding is actually a pork sausage, and — as they say — every part of the pig goes in except the squeal. Sausage casings are now usually bought at a butcher shop or meat packers. Note the original meaning of pudding in English was 'sausage,' which sense survives in terms like blood pudding, black pudding, white pudding. British English still uses a French borrowing, *boudin*, to name a black pudding. It is a curiosity that Canadian French borrowed pudding from English back into the food language of Québec as *poutine*. Remember, too, what Robert Burns called that obscene Scottish nightmare-parody of sausage known as haggis: "great chieftain o' the puddin'-race." Och! Pudding is an English mangling of the Old French *boudin*, from Latin *botellus* 'pudding.' Or it may be that French *boudin* is of Gaulish provenance and is a diminutive form of the Celtic root *bot* 'penis,' which as *bod* is still the word for penis in Irish Gaelic or Erse. Thus *boudin* would first be a joking reference to a sausage as a 'little penis.' That Celtic root *bot* may have been borrowed into early Latin also, to give *botellus* 'little penis, sausage.'

The eventual association of sweet pudding and sausage occurred because early dessert puddings were stuffed in a bag and boiled or steamed, the stuffing in the bag reminding cooks of stuffing sausage meat in casings, often made of sheep or pig intestines. Elizabethan cooks began to adapt some of the sweet pudding recipes so that they did not have to be boiled or cooked in a cloth or bag. In 20th-century British English, pudding evolved to mean any dessert: "What's for pudding, luv? Month-old treacle again?"

Production line in a 19th-century sausage factory

Caution: Bowels Ahead

Now here is a small detour to discuss another French derivative from the Latin *botellus*, which gives us the English word *bowel*. The etymology looks like this: *Botellus* Latin, little sausage > *boel* Old French > *bouel* Middle English > *bowel* Modern English. Yes, your bowels are your sausages. Bowels, the plain English word for intestines, go all the way back to a Roman battlefield. Roman physicians who were trying to find out how the human body worked and how it was made, were hampered by religious taboos and superstitions. For example, early studiers of the human body were not allowed to dissect a corpse. Cutting up a dead body was not legal in ancient Rome and Greece. It was thought to be a horrible sin. So those ancient scientists studying anatomy had to rely on looking at the dead bodies of humans who had suffered fatal, body-ripping injuries. One of the places these early anatomists could see cut-open bodies was on the battlefield after a bloody fight in a war. Exposed coils of intestines stuck out from the corpses of slain soldiers. Perhaps these soldiers had fallen when their bellies or abdomens had been slashed open with a sword. Their intestines or bowels, exposed in a wide-open wound, looked like little sausages. So the Roman word for bowels was *botelli* 'little sausages.' More common use of such a word in Latin may have come from soldiers' rough slang: "Got a bellyache, Brutus? Guess your sausages are upset today."

Another word from the same root word as bowel is — botulism, from another diminutive relative of *botellus*, this time spelled *botulus* 'sausage.' Botulism is a severe food poisoning, first observed in early 19th-century Germany in carelessly prepared sausages, which lay around uncooked for too long after they were made and so germs grew in the raw meat. The toxins in the poisoned food can be fatal if ingested in great quantity. The cause is excessive growth of a poison-making bacterium called *Clostridium botulinum*.

PIKELETS

Brought to Nova Scotia and elsewhere in Canada from England and Scotland, pikelets are drop-scones or thin crumpets, made following a standard scone recipe. A beaten egg is added to a cup of milk. Flour, salt, a pinch of sugar, baking soda and cream of tartar are combined and stirred into the egg and milk. To make each pikelet, a generous spoonful of the batter is plopped into a hot frying pan or on a griddle. The pikelet is flipped when the batter bubbles. As always with quick breads, the precise heat of the griddle or pan must be determined by testing. These little crumpetty breakfast quickies are very popular in Australia and New Zealand, where the term *pikelet* enjoys much broader use than in Canada.

Pikelet entered English from the Welsh term for this scone, *bara pyglyd*, literally 'bread pitchy,' that is, bread that is sticky like pitch or viscid as pitch, but — the cook trusts — never as black as pitch.

POCKET SOUP

This was the ancestor of today's powdered soups and dried cubes of bouillon and stock like Bovril™. Also called "portable soup" and even "glue," the preparation of pocket soup involved boiling then simmering stock for a whole day, being attentive to frequent stirrings, until the solid residue could be formed into little balls or cakelets. Fishermen and lumberjacks took the little cakes in a pocket or grub pack and tossed them into a pot of water boiling in a galley or over a campfire.

RICHIBUCTO GOOSE

Richibucto goose is salted shad (a fish) as prepared in Richibucto, Kent County, Nova Scotia. It's a comic reference to common use of this food; compare Digby chicken.

SALMON ON A PLANK

Planking salmon is a cooking method taught to early white settlers by indigenous peoples. The fish is cleaned, boned, beheaded, befinned and betailed, then salted and set aside while the fire is built. A special hardwood plank about twenty centimetres thick and forty centimetres wide and about one metre long should be kept solely for planking salmon. It must be thoroughly cleaned after each use. Several stones or a couple of bricks hold the plank upright on one end near the fire. The salmon, skin against the wood, is tied on to the plank with cooking twine or — if the chef wishes to be *très* outdoorsy — the fish may be attached to the plank with strips of greenwood from a sapling. This, of course, will do the sapling no good at all. Finally, sprinkling a little flour over the moist flesh of the fresh salmon, one positions the fish-bearing board appropriately near the blazing fire until done, about ten minutes per inch of salmon flesh. A similar method of cooking by Cree peoples is ponasking. To ponask even became a verb in Canadian English. See the entry in the chapter about Manitoba food words.

SANDFIRE GREENS

This edible plant of Atlantic and Pacific coastal beaches, mudflats, and salt marshes is a glasswort, *Salicornia europaea*. The genus name means 'salt-horn,' because it prefers saltwater and grows in little horns of many branches. The stems of older plants are red and succulent, hence the common name sandfire.

False Samphire

But the word *sandfire* is also a folk variant of samphire, and another name for this plant is false samphire. It is also called pickleweed, because the tender young tips of the branches make a dandy relish. These tips of young sandfire greens can be tossed fresh into a salad, or eaten as an emergency vegetable if you are lost along some unknown saline shoreline.

Glasswort

As for the old English name glasswort, *wort* was the first word for plant in Anglo-Saxon, before it was displaced after the Norman Conquest by the French *plante*. The stems of sandfire greens are succulent and, after a frost, semitransparent and glasslike. Some authorities say the whole plant was once burned for its ash and used in making glass and soap.

Glassworts were collected, pickled, and sold as food in many parts of the European Atlantic coast, often under the name samphire. But glasswort is really a false samphire, for the word *samphire* correctly refers to a totally different beach plant, true samphire.

True Samphire

The botanical name of true samphire is *Crithmum maritimum*, a member of the large plant family of Umbelliferae to which belong other herb and food plants like carrots, celery, parsley, fennel, dill, and common wild plants like Queen Anne's Lace. This plant grows about twenty centimetres high in fertile tidal muck. It resembles other umbelliferous plants and this physical similarity resulted in an old English common name, sea-fennel. As a plant of the tidal seashore, with a bounty of water at high tide and then relative scarcity of water at low tide, one of its survival modifications has been the development of succulent tissues that hold plenty of salt water and add to the warm spiciness of the plant's taste. The botanical name in French, *crithme*, also produced a less-used name *christe maritime* 'Sea Jesus.' This is not sacrilegious naming. On the contrary, it reflects thankfulness to Christ because these sea greens could be eaten as emergency food in times of hunger. Compare a different little seashore plant of the glasswort genus *Salicornia* called *christe-marine* in Canadian French.

For a look at how confusing common names can be in any language, see the entry for *passe-pierre* in the chapter on Acadian food words.

SOLOMON GUNDY

This Lunenburg favourite is chopped fillets of salted herring marinated in vinegar, pickling spices, and onions. The name is a Nova Scotian attempt at the German name, *Salmagundi*, influenced by the old English nursery rhyme about Solomon Grundy, a gruesome rhyme — in the best tradition of British *sang-froid* — about death, hardly fit to be associated with food, and so worth quoting:

> *Solomon Grundy,*
> *Born on Monday,*
> *Christened on Tuesday,*
> *Married on Wednesday,*
> *Took ill on Thursday,*
> *Worse on Friday,*
> *Died on Saturday,*
> *Buried on Sunday.*
> *This is the end*
> *of Solomon Grundy.*

Charming ditty. Only the British could imagine that wee toddlers need early lessons in the nanosecond span of human mortality, so that — what? — they may retire from kindergarten to a childhood of

Prozac™ cookies? A mother reading this rhyme at twilight to a little sleepyhead surely holds unusual views about how best to prepare children for the joy of being alive.

In some form or other, *salmagundi* was in widespread, multilingual use in 18th-century Europe, to name a dish of chopped meat, anchovies, eggs, onions, etc., served cold. It also came to refer to any pot of kitchen leftovers, or culinary hotchpotch. The first occurrence of the word is in the works of that mighty giant of early French satire and an ebullient coiner of new French words, Rabelais, who wrote it as *salmigondin*. British etymologist Eric Partridge suggests Rabelais coined the term. Other word-ferrets posit an Italian origin from *salame* 'salted meat' plus the verb *condire* 'to pickle' (compare condiments). But the true origin may be — how it irks the questing etymologist to type the word — unknown. The term was shortened later in 17th-century French to *salmi*, to name a richly sauced ragout of game meat.

CHAPTER 4

Acadia

A Brief History of Acadia

Acadia was the name of the first permanent colony that France founded in North America, roughly comprising parts of what became the Canadian provinces of Nova Scotia, New Brunswick, and Prince Edward Island. Acadians are descended from French colonists who homesteaded first in 1604 on St. Croix Island and then in 1605 at Port Royal. For most of the next 150 years, Acadia was a political pingpong ball, batted back and forth between warring enemies, England and France. Most Acadian pioneers who arrived from France throughout the 17th century trace their ancestry to French emigrants who came from areas in France south of the Loire River. More than half of Canada's present Acadian population of approximately 400,000 have forebears who came from the historic French provinces of Poitou, Aunis, Santonge, and Guyenne.

Present-day Acadians speak a lively dialect of French which contains many archaic vocabulary items that arose in the provincial dialects of old France and that long ago disappeared from standard French. Acadian French also boasts words and usages that differ from the other chief dialect of the language in Canada, namely Québécois French. For example, Québec French uses a Huron word *atoca* for 'cranberry.' Standard French is *canneberge.* Acadian French is *pomme de prée* 'meadow apple.' Note another common kind of difference here in which the form of words alters slightly between a dialect and a literary language. Here the old Acadian word for meadow, *la prée*, is feminine, but in standard French it is masculine, *le pré.* As well as distinctive phonetic features, words like *charette* 'cart' and *coquemar* 'kettle' adorn Acadian speech. A wild herb of the Maritimes that tastes like coriander and can be used to replace it in recipes has the delightful Acadian name of *poivre des pauvres gens* 'poor people's pepper.' On the predominantly Acadian Îles de la Madeleine in the Gulf of St. Lawrence, one still hears *bargou*, an old Acadian word for oatmeal porridge, distinct from the standard French for porridge, *gruau*, related to the Old French word *gruel*, which was borrowed into Middle English. Old French *gruel* was a diminutive form of Old French *gru* 'coarse-ground grain.' Bargou seems to have been borrowed into Acadian French from 17th-century English nautical slang where the word burgoo meant 'thick oatmeal porridge.' For its ultimate root in Persian, see the entry later in this chapter.

Like all dialects, Acadian has its own slang, and its own word for this argot, *chiac*, based on a local pronunciation of Shédiac, an Acadian town in New Brunswick, also famous for its Shediac oysters. *Chiac* has plenty of Acadian words from old French dialects, and some North American English borrowings transformed by Acadian French spellings and pronunciations.

By 1755, Acadia was again British and called Nova Scotia, and the British wished to secure the colony against all further French "trouble," first by bringing colonists loyal to Britain into Nova Scotia. In the decade from 1750 to 1760, more than 10,000 emigrants arrived from New England and from parts of Germany like Hanover and Brunswick. The defining catastrophe of Acadian history began in 1755 when England, fed up with Acadians who staunchly refused to swear oaths of allegiance to Britain but also wanting to rid Nova Scotia of anyone with French ties, ordered mass deportation of the Acadians by imperial fiat. This expulsion of the Acadians, which lasted until 1762, forced more than 10,000 people out of their homes. Families were broken asunder. Acadians who did not cooperate in their own deportation were jailed or sent back to France, in some cases by way of prison camps in England. Acadians were also shipped unwillingly down the eastern seaboard to New England to British colonies that did not want them but were forced by London to take them. Some Acadians — famously — were expelled as far as the swampy bayous of southern Louisiana where they formed their own culture, and where the word *Acadien* was shortened and Americanized to *Cajun*. Cajun folk music is still alive and distinct in Louisiana, as are Cajun dishes like jambalaya and the spicy filé gumbo in which powdered sassafras leaves are used to thicken the gumbo. Some Acadians did not wait to be deported but fled into hiding in parts of what would become Québec. Other exiled Acadians died of

hunger, shipwreck, disease, and forced marches out of their homeland.

Only after France gave up all claims to her Atlantic holdings and to all of New France in the Treaty of Paris in 1763, did England grudgingly permit sporadic resettlement of the Acadian people. Fugitives came out of their hiding places inland; Acadian prisoners were released from custody; other Acadian exiles returned from British colonies in the south. They had to swear unconditional loyalty to Britain, of course. To their great dismay, returning Acadians found that the very farmlands they had themselves cleared had been given during their exile to British and German immigrants. Acadians were not welcome where fields were fertile. Poor and kept poor, they were forced to settle on remote and rocky shorelines, and to take up a new way of making a living, subsistence fishing. As Roman Catholics, they had no civil rights and did not exist politically. Until 1789, Acadians could not vote in Nova Scotia. They couldn't vote in Prince Edward Island until 1830. During the period of the expulsions from1758 to 1763, Acadians could not own land in the colony.

By grit and slow perseverance Acadians today in Canada have left behind their exile, but not forgotten it. Memories of poverty and subsistence remain, however, in the kinds of foods that are traditional among them, in the simplicity of make-do recipes, which ingenious cooks have fashioned over four centuries into a tasty cuisine that, as much as any part of their heritage, still calls forth Acadian joy and memories of the warm comfort of home cooking.

I could not list every food word that is exclusively Acadian in this popular survey, but I hope you will see in the notes and dishes offered here something of the remarkable resilience of Acadians, who now abound in every important profession of

Canadian life, from the Governor-General's house of Rideau Hall where the genial Acadian Roméo LeBlanc welcomes the world on behalf of his people and his country, all the way to the Supreme Court of Canada where another Acadian adorns our highest legal office, Mr. Justice Michel Bastarache. In folklore and folk music, Acadians have always been strong and proud. One thinks, also, of contemporary Acadian singer-composers like Edith Butler and Angèle Arsenault. The mid-20th century has seen the rise of several talented Acadian writers, perhaps of most renown the dramatist and novelist Antonine Maillet whose dramatic monologue of an old Acadian washer-woman, *La Sagouine* (1971), is one of the masterpieces of Canadian literature. Among the wry memories of this seventy-two-year-old scrub lady are recollections of how the poor eat: flapjacks reheated for three meals and the only Sunday treat a serving of beans. Maillet's work gives a voice — many voices — to the personal history of her people. My own favourite Maillet is the chorus of voices of returning Acadians in her novel *Pélagie-La-Charette* (1979), available in an English translation as *Pélagie: The Return to a Homeland* (1982). This unepic epic sold a million copies in France and won the prestigious Prix Goncourt. In this saga, a young Acadian widow performs a laborious ten-year trek in an oxcart from exile in Georgia up the eastern seaboard of America and on back to her home in Acadia. Maillet's French is a unique mélange of Acadian dialect and literary French, but her characters and their humour

Une charette, a two-wheeled oxcart

and their tribulations sound gongs in any human heart that is open to fellow beings.

Acadian French

Acadien, Acadian French, is spoken along our east coast in Québec, New Brunswick, Nova Scotia, Prince Edward Island, Cape Breton Island, and is also heard in some communities on the north shore of the St. Lawrence and the islands in the Gulf of St. Lawrence. Acadian settlers came chiefly from the French provinces of Aunis, Poitou, and Saintonge, and this historical fact accounts for the wonderful, burly clout of *Acadien*, for the stock of old French vocabulary items and bits of ancient syntax preserved in the amber of this robust dialect. Standard French for wheelbarrow may be *brancard*, but in *L'Acadie* it's *boyart*. The mailman might be a *facteur* in France, a *postier* in most of Québec, but in purest *Acadien* the name of his occupation recalls the days of coach and four, because he's a *postillon*. English borrowed this to get postillion, one who rides a post-horse or one who rides the near horse of a team when there is no coachman. Another Acadianism is *bec* for any high ground, instead of the Standard French *élévation*. Fence in SF is *clôture*, but in Acadian French it's a mouthful, *bouchure*.

Barachois is an Acadian French word that is used in English on Cape Breton Island, and in Nova Scotia, New Brunswick, and sixty-six times in Newfoundland place names. *Barachoix* was Norman French for sandbar. Early Basque fishermen used it too, referring to a sandbar or gravel bar in front of a saltwater pond, where they could haul up their boats. In Canada's Atlantic provinces it means a saline pond near a larger body of water that is cut off from it by a sandbar or narrow strip of land. Sometimes one sees it Englished as barrisway or barrasway. Newfoundland has Barasway de Cerf (a pond where you might see a deer), and the delightful mouthful L'Anse au Loup Barasway (Wolf Bay Cove). Also on The Rock the diligent toponymist finds Rocky Barachois Bight. Barachois is a very frequent element in maritime place names. Almost at the tip of the Gaspé peninsula is the Québec village of Barachois-de-Malbaie. Near Shediac in New Brunswick is another big B, while Newfoundland's south coast claims Barachois Bay and Barachois Point. In Nova Scotia, there's MacLean Barachois, pleasantly combining the memories of two of the province's founding linguistic forces: Gaelic and *Acadien.*

Origin of the Name Acadia

Nova Scotia means 'New Scotland' in Latin. So stated the royal grant of land issued to Sir William Alexander in 1621. But, until 1713 the area was officially called Acadia, which at the time included parts of Québec and New England. Now Acadia is generally used to mean the area of original French settlement in our maritime provinces. The Italian navigator Giovanni da Verrazano first named it *Archadia* in 1524, while he explored the east coast of America as commander of a French expedition. He also discovered what became New York Bay, and the Verrazano Bridge to New York City is named after him. He misspelled the Latin word *Arcadia* — possibly because of its pronunciation in his particular Italian dialect. But that was not the only slip of the pen affecting this place name. In the diary of his voyage to the New World, Verrazano stated that he named a stretch of the coast along what came to be called Chesapeake Bay *Archadia* because of "the beauty of its trees." Later in the 16th century, mapmakers applied the name Arcadia to land to the north around Cape Cod. Slightly later yet another cartographer pasted the label on the coast of Maine; still later,

Arcadia was applied to the Atlantic regions of New France, particularly to present-day Nova Scotia. The letter *r* began to disappear from the name on early maps — probably at first through a single copyist's error — so that eventually the region was known as Acadia and in French *Acadie*.

The First Arcadia

The Romans borrowed the word from the ancient Greeks who used it to denote a geographic area of mountainous forest in the centre of the Peloponnese. For the Greek pastoral poets like Theocritus, Arcadia was a symbol of rural simplicity and the joys of the shepherd's life, tending flocks and making music all day long with flute and pipes. It is probably the source of one of the oldest jokes in the European tradition: What do you call an Arcadian with forty mistresses? A shepherd. The god Pan haunted the caves and streams of Arcady. Sportive nymphs bounded happily through upland pastures and centaurs frisked in the clover. Arcadia was such an evocative token of pastoral ease that it entered all the later languages of Europe. Although the precise origin of the word is lost, a study of classical Greek makes clear the reverberations that Arcadia set off in the Greek mind. Ancient Greeks heard similarities in its sound to *arkys*, a hunter's snare or net. Arcadia was the stomping grounds of the goddess Artemis, the virgin huntress known to the Romans as Diana. It reminded them also of the verb *arkein* 'to be strong, to endure, to be sufficient,' and its impersonal form, *arkei moi* 'it's enough for me; I'm happy, content.'

And now, from frisky nymphs to the beckoning aromas of Acadian kitchens! Some of the Acadian food words presented in this chapter, like *bargou*, are exclusive to the Acadian dialect and are not common in Québec French. *Acadien* shares other words, like *fricot*, with Québec and continental French.

ANGUILLE À PETITE-EAU (SIMMERED EEL)

In the recipe for this Acadian treat, the eels (*anguilles*) are skinned, cleaned, cut in short pieces, floured, and fried in butter first. Then, the fried eels are seasoned with salted herbs, salt and pepper, and simmered (*à petite-eau*) in water in a covered skillet for just under an hour.

Like Aboriginal peoples and some other Maritimers, Acadians fished eels in the winter through a hole in the ice by spearing eels with a tridentlike spear called a *fouine* (from Latin *fuscina*, trident, harpoon; standard French *foène*). At low tide in the summer, eels can be taken using an implement invented by Mi'kmaq people and called in Acadian French by its Mi'kmaq name, *nigog*. There is even an Acadian verb, *nigoguer*. The Mi'kmaq *nigog* is a kind of fishgig, consisting of a single long spike with many smaller hooks attached to it. This totally Canadian word *nigog* has no precise equivalent in continental French, but was sometimes translated by the standard French word *digon* which properly refers only to a barbed hook used by European fishers to take deepsea flatfish such as halibut, flounder, turbot, and sole. See the entry for *eel pie* in the chapter on Prince Edward Island.

Most dramatically, Acadian eel fishing was done at night from a canoe using torchlight to lure eels up within spearing distance. One evocative early description of fire-fishing comes from the diaries of Sir Richard Henry Bonnycastle (1791 – 1847), commandant of the Royal Engineers in Upper Canada, and then in Newfoundland. Off duty, he travelled British North America and wrote personal observations of life in the colonies, like the passage below from his *The Canadas in 1841*, quoted in *'And Some Brought Flowers': Plants in a New World* by Mary Alice Downie, Mary Hamilton, and E.J. Revell (1980):

> We went to see two of the *voyageurs* launch the canoe for the purpose of fire-fishing. This sport is pursued by placing over the bow a bundle of bark, pine-knots full of turpentine, or other combustible wood, and then paddling slowly over the water. [Among Mi'kmaq and Maliseet fishermen, birch-bark torches were used.] One man paddles, whilst the other kneels near the fire, and watching the fish as they rise to scan the strange appearance which attracts them, he, with unerring aim, darts his fish-spear into the 'victim of curiosity.'
>
> The sight of the canoes fishing by fire light is very beautiful on a dark summer night. Large sparkles are continually falling, and floating like meteors on the placid bosom of the dark lake; while the fitful blazing of the fire, the strong reflections on the dark figures in the canoe, and the stream of pencilled light which follows its wake between the observer and the shore, heighten truly the picturesque scene.

BARGOU (OATMEAL PORRIDGE)

This Acadian word for oatmeal porridge is still heard on the Îles de la Madeleine. It is not in standard French and is infrequent in Québec French. It appears to have been borrowed into *Acadien* directly from 18th-century British naval slang where burgoo was oatmeal gruel eaten by sailors.

Canadian and American English also grabbed the term from British traders who used burgoo to name any unappetizing food, especially a thick stew made from camp or kitchen scraps of meat and vegetables. In the United States, a burgoo was a stew or meal eaten outside at a picnic or gathering, then burgoo came to be applied to such a gathering itself.

The word was first borrowed into English late in the 17th century by travellers who encountered a wheaten porridge in the Middle East called *burgul*, which in Arabic and Persian was 'bruised grain' or what we would call cracked wheat. Later on in the 20th century, English borrowed the word again in its Turkish form *burghal*. Bulgur or bulghur or bulgar wheat is still popular among vegetarians. It is basically coarse-ground dry porridge, made by boiling whole wheat grains, drying them, and then grinding them up. Lovers of Lebanese cuisine will know the use of bulghur wheat in the minty treat of tabbouleh salad.

Adding to the hop, skip, and jump of this word's voyages through history, we suggest that this wheat dish may bear the name of the people who first invented it, the Bulgars, an ancient Turkic people from grain-rich steppelands of central Asia who migrated and conquered indigenous Slavs of the lower Danube region during the 7th century and founded what became Bulgaria.

BAUME (WILD MINT)

This Acadian word for any of several wild mints used as flavourings is a shortening of the standard French *menthe baume*, which as a garden subject is called *baume des jardins* in Québec. *Baume* stems from the same root that gives balm in English.

BEIGNE (DOUGHNUT)

But how about a doughnut fried in seal blubber oil? You might still be able to nibble on such an Acadian *beigne* on the Îles de la Madeleine. *Beignes à la mélasse* or molasses doughnuts are another Acadian treat, often made for special occasions like a wedding or at Christmas.

Beigne harks back to a non-Indo-European, pre-Roman word like **bunnia*, directly related to Gaelic *bun* and Catalan *bony* 'bump on the head.' The asterisk preceding a root citation labels the form as hypothetical, a root based on comparative research and conjecture as opposed to printed proof. Since the earliest speakers of languages had no writing system, no inscriptions survive. When *beigne* first shows up in 17th-century French, it meant: 'bump on the head' and also 'tree stump.' The present meaning of *beigne* today in France is slap or clout or blow, in other words, what might cause a bump on the head. English borrowed its word *bun* for a little form of leavened bread from a French dialectic offshoot of the same root, *bugne*, that denoted a slightly raised pancake. But all the food references obviously began as jokes in which a bump of bread (a bun) was compared to a bump on the head. After all, after one has received a clout on the noggin, the goose-egg bump grows in size, just as a little bread bun rises as it bakes.

Beigne is a Canadian French usage showing how ancient meanings of words can remain in a dialect while disappearing from a standard language. The word for doughnut today in France is a later, diminutive form, *beignet*. It means 'fritter' as well in France. Among *les Québécois et les Acadiens*, *un beignet* is also a fritter or a pancake. A familar Acadian dish is *beignets râpés* 'potato fritters,' while *beignets à la râpure* are potato pancakes made by blending finely grated potatoes in an egg-and-flour batter, forming them into palm-sized pancakes, patting them thin, and frying until crispy brown.

In current Québec slang there is the joual put-down, *bégnet* 'dummy, stupid person,' which is very close to the Ontario expression, "Don't be such a doughnut."

BLÉ D'INDE LESSIVÉ

Basic hominy is husked, coarse-ground corn kernels boiled in water or milk. Ground to a finer consistency, it is called hominy grits in the southern United States. A southern breakfast order might be "ham and eggs and a mess o' grits." France uses *maïs* to denote what North American English calls corn. The British call it maize or Indian corn. The French in Canada, learning about it from Aboriginal Peoples called it *blé d'Inde* with the sense of 'cereal crop from the West Indies.'

Paleobotanists have found the earliest traces of maize in the Tehuacán Valley of Mexico and dated it to 5500 BC. The botanical name of our modern corn is *Zea mays*. The specific, like maize and *maïs*, comes from *mahiz*, the word for corn in Taino, the extinct language of an Arawakan people who lived on certain islands of the Caribbean and who first demonstrated the uses of corn to Spanish explorers; thus the earliest appearance of the word in a European language was as *maíz* in Spanish.

Because it takes a long time to prepare, Acadians made hominy only for large public events or for a cooperative get-together such as *une corvée* where neighbours might get together for a barn-raising or to build a needed public road or put a dike along a friend's seaside field. Hulling corn has always been the tedious part of preparing this food. One Acadian way was to soak the kernels for a night, then boil them next day in a cauldron of water to which has been added baking soda and potash. Even after the kernels burst, it takes many changes of water to leach all the potassium out of the corn.

Incidentally, the French verb *lessiver* 'to leach, to clean by washing with ashes or lye' stems from the same Latin root as a fancy chemical verb in English, to lixiviate 'to extract solid matter from a solution by washing.' Both hark back to *lixivium*, a Roman washing solution containing lye [potassium carbonate] made from wood ashes. The authors of learned tomes about Roman history — and there are several — who opine that the Romans knew nothing about making soap need to have their Latin wordlists washed.

BONDINETTE

These are made from minced chicken or rabbit meat mixed with mashed potatoes and seasoned with a salty gravy, then tapped into the slots in a greased muffin tin and baked for twenty minutes. When taken to table, a sprig of parsley may adorn each bondinette. I can't find the origin of this Acadian word, and would be glad of help from any reader who knows it.

BOUCANIÈRE (SMOKE-HOUSE)

Some Acadians still smoke herring (*hareng boucané*) in little shacks with fires made of spruce sawdust. Salted herring (*hareng salé*) is hung above the smokey fire for two or three weeks. Smoked herring is eaten hot, cold, and even sometimes flaked and put into soups and stews.

Those nasty old pirates, the buccaneers, took their name from the same root that gives *boucané* 'smoked.' At the end of the 16th century and throughout the following century, *boucaniers* were, first, rough French hunters on the Caribbean island of Santo Domingo who hunted the large herds of wild cattle sprung from escaped domestic stock brought earlier by Spanish explorers. These lawless ruffians dried and smoked their beef on a wooden grid called a *boucan*. The word could also refer to the little cabin in which the smoking was done. The French freebooters and criminals who infested the island and preyed on Spanish ships had borrowed the word and the technique from local Tupi people, in whose language *mokaém* or *bokaem* meant 'wooden grill on which meat or fish was smoked.' Soon *boucanier* came to refer to any Caribbean pirate. And it entered English quickly. By 1719, novelist Daniel Defoe had his most famous character, Robinson Crusoe, declare that he had "been an old Planter at Maryland, and a *Buccaneer* into the bargain." Even earlier, in 1700, Defoe referred in print to "Buccaneering Danes."

In Québec French *boucane* is a slang word for bootleg hootch or homemade whisky, presumably because one needs smokey fires to make a good homebrew. One Québec phrase for sunglasses is *lunettes boucanées.*

BOUILLIE

In Old French *la bouillie* was a thick soup made from milk and flour primarily as a food for babies and invalids. In Acadia and Québec, one finds descendants of this basic dish in a thick corn soup called *bouillie simple* in which hulled corn is added to the milk-and-flour stock.

BOUILLON

In the classic cuisine of France, bouillon is the stock or broth made from boiling vegetables or meat. Bouillon is the liquid part of the French meat-and-vegetable stew, *pot-au-feu*. Bouillon is the liquid beginning of many a soup and sauce. A spiced stock used mainly for boiling fish and shellfish is *court-bouillon*. But in Acadian cuisine, *bouillon* is a heartier affair, and can often be translated into English as stew. Among many *Acadiens* in New Brunswick, for example, *bouillon* is a synonym for *fricot* 'stew.' *Bouillon au maquereau* is a stick-to-the-ribs mackerel-and-potato stew eaten as a meal by itself, and with a big spoon!

From French-Canadian fur-trappers and voyageurs, Canadian English borrowed bouillon also. Until well past the turn of the century in our north, a bouillon was a thick stew of potatoes, salt pork pieces, edible roots, and anything else available in a camp larder.

BOUILLOTTE (A FISH AND POTATO STEW)

Bouillotte began its noun's life as the old French word for hot-water kettle, later to be replaced by *bouilloire*. In North America, particularly among *les Acadiens*, *bouillotte* named a dish of simmered fish and potatoes, the fish often being cod. Around Chéticamp in Nova Scotia, this fish stew was also called *morue en cabane*, the 'cod-in-a-cabin' referring to the little fishing shacks beside the docks where fishers prepared their voyages and where they boiled the cod upon returning from a successful catch. This noun use derives from the old and now rarely used verb *bouillotter* 'to simmer' made up of *bouillir* 'to boil' with a diminutive verbal ending *-otter* added to modify the meaning, hence 'to boil gently.'

Now in standard French *bouillotte* is the word for hot-water bottle or bag. In older French it was a long metal pan into which hot water was poured and then the pan was used to heat a pioneer bed. A *bouillotte* was even carried outside and put on the seat of a sleigh or cutter to facilitate at least a warm start to a winter trip. In the 1920s and 1930s in Québec, a metal *bouillotte* was employed to heat up the car seats of wealthy persons. Just think of some rich *derrière* suffering the cold leather of a limousine seat. *Quel dommage!*

CAMBUSE (SIMMERED WHOLE COD)

This is an old Acadian whole-cod dish, where, head and all, a big cod is simmered with little pieces of salt pork fat (*lardons*) and veggies.

In Québécois French a *cambuse* was an open fireplace in the living quarters of a lumber camp. Smoke escaped from a hole in the roof over the fireplace. Earlier, *cambuse* referred to a small, portable stove used by voyageurs and explorers < Old French *cambuse*, store, hut, ship's galley, then galley stove < *kabuis* Dutch nautical term for ship's larder and galley hut < *kab-huis* < *kaban-huis* 'tiny, cabin-like house.' *Cambuse* also became camboose in Canadian English, referring to the open fireplace in a logging camp's living quarters, and also to the cook's shanty when it was in a separate building. In the early, free-for-all English of northern Canada, camboose in turn became confused with caboose, also borrowed from the Dutch nautical word *kabuis*.

CISELETTE (PORK & MOLASSES DESSERT SAUCE)

Literally the word means 'little chisel,' but I have no idea why it was applied by Acadians to this old-timey sauce made by frying diced pork or salt pork in its own fat. After the pork dice has browned, it is removed, and molasses is added to the remnant pork fat in the pan. The molasses is heated gently to boiling and then the fried pork dice goes back in. *Ciselette* is offered with crêpes, fresh bread, or toast. It was widely popular throughout Acadia, and different communities had different pet names for this molasses sauce. It was called *bagosse*, an old French dialect word that could mean 'deceptive blather, homemade liquor, or shoddy merchandise.' Other terms for this sauce were *bourgaille*, *bourdomme* (from *bourdonner* 'to hum like a bumblebee or cicada,' based on the sound of the ingredients as they fry in the pan), *mousseline* (*sauce mousseline* is usually based on whipped cream, with the original implication that it was like fine muslin cloth), and *tamarin aux grillades* (this is possibly an Acadian kitchen joke that means basically 'monkey cutlets,' the tamarin being a South American monkey related to marmosets). *Tamarin* in French also refers to the tropical fruit of the tamarind tree, whose acidic pulp is used for perserves. Tamarind juice is still made into a laxative drink. Take your pick, but, somewhere in this phrase, there's a little jest.

COQUE (CLAM)

Acadian and Canadian French use this old word for shell to refer to the short-necked clam. In standard French *coque* is a cockle, and *palourde* is any clam. In Québec and Acadia, *palourde* designates *une grosse coque*, a big, thick-shelled clam called a quahog in English. Among the dishes popular in Acadian cuisine are *coques à la vapeur* 'steamed clams' in which, after cleaning, one pops the clams by heating them in a big covered pot with no water until, after about a quarter of an hour, the shells open. *Fricot aux coques* 'clam stew' and *pâté aux coques* 'clam and potato pie' are also Acadian yummies.

CORVÉE

By the middle of the last century a *corvée* was like a bee in English. A whole community would get together and offer free labour to help build a neighbour's barn or put up a little church or build a needed local road. Canadian French even borrowed the English word in phrases like *faire un bi* and *faire un bee*. In Acadia and Québec, *corvées* were always occasions for a big spread of food, especially many pots of *fricots* to feed the hungry workers.

Medieval workers perform a corvée, building a seigneur's barn.

Feudal Tenure in Québec under the Seigneurial System

But the word *corvée* began in the days of feudalism, as the Late Latin feudal term *opera corrogata* 'solicited works,' referring to a form of peasant exploitation in which a land owner, *un seigneur*, or the Church, forced serfs or tenant farmers to perform a certain amount of compulsory, free, manual labour in return for subsistence farming on seigneurial land. This forced labour typically involved road repair, building stone bridges, clearing land, or supplying stone and wood. These conditions of feudal tenure lasted in French Canada until 1854 when the government of United Canada passed the Seignorial Tenure Bill abolishing such exploitation and offering some monetary compensation to those who had been tenants. Early habitant farmers in old Québec also owed duty to the authorities as militiamen and this, too, involved corvées of enforced labour on fortifications, bridges, and roads, sometimes performed instead of paying local taxes. In the latter part of the 19th century, the term came to be used more happily for volunteer work in a community, for example, *faire une corvée pour lever une grange* 'to hold a barn-building bee.'

CRÊPES À LA NEIGE

When eggs were in short supply, Acadians made these crêpes with hard-packed snow. Fried for a few minutes on each side, they were served with pieces of maple sugar. Each year on February the second, at the feast of *la Chandeleur*, Candlemas in English, Catholic priests bless the candles to commemorate the purification of the Virgin Mary and the presentation of Jesus in the temple. In Québec and Acadia, *crêpes à la neige* used to be served at home for this feast, often with little surprises hidden inside each crêpe. If one found a penny, one would be rich. If one discovered a ring within, one would be lucky in early marriage. Two buttons in a crêpe might signify that one would have many children.

FAYOTS (DRIED BEANS)

Standard French would be *haricot sec*. Fayot is an older French term for this bean, preserved in ancient French dialects and persisting in *français acadien* long after it disappeared from contemporary French speech. Traditional Acadian pork 'n' beans, *fayots au lard*, are prepared in a large iron cauldron after the beans are soaked overnight, then put into the pot in alternate layers with salt pork fat. After cold water is added, the vat is simmered for four hours or oven-baked. Sugar or molasses are put on as a sauce when the beans are served, never — in a true Acadian recipe — when the beans are cooking. *Jamais! Je vous en prie!*

FRICOT

Fricot is *the* Acadian food dish, so common that "Come and Get it!" can be translated into *Acadien* as "*Au fricot!*" It's a thick, hearty soup of potatoes with meat or fish or seafood, always eaten with a spoon. Acadian clam chowder is *fricot aux coques.* Acadien fricots often have dumplings too, called *grands-pères* 'grandfathers' or *poutines* (but see *poutine* entry in Québec chapter).

Fricot à la poule 'chicken stew' is part of every Acadian cook's repertoire. Note the constant Acadian use of *poule* 'hen' when chicken as a food is meant. One seldom sees the standard French *poulet* 'young chicken' in old Acadian recipes for the practical reason that one did not kill a laying hen. Eggs were too important to have their production cut short by slaughtering the hen at too young an age. Since older hens were used in most chicken dishes, such recipes often called for long simmering.

At Christmas and New Year's, rabbit stew was an Acadian favourite. For *fricot au lapin des bois,* rabbits were often snared so that they would retain more blood, making them tastier than if the rabbit was shot and then bled copiously. If no meat at all was available for a stew, an Acadian mother might prepare, with a wink, *fricot à la belette* 'weasel stew.' This meatless, onion-and-potato dish was tricky and sly like a weasel, and really only pretended to be a stew. Another jokey name for this recipe among Acadians on Prince Edward Island is *fricot à la bezette* 'stupid cook's stew,' implying that the inclusion of the meat or fish was forgotten.

In standard French, Acadian stew would be *un ragoût acadien.* But the word *fricot* was in continental French by 1767 meaning a feast. By 1800, it was in use in France to denote a meat stew and then prepared food in general (*faire le fricot = faire la cuisine*).

FROLIC
(A BEE)

Acadian pioneer neighbours rallied around one another to help put up a barn, make quilts, dry apples, finish a road to the farm. What might be a quilting bee in Upper Canada was a quilting frolic in New Brunswick's early days. A stick-to-your-ribs meal, dancing, and several cups of good cheer might follow all the communal hard work. British immigrants brought the term to our Maritimes early on, where it was borrowed directly into Canadian French and Acadien. See the entry for *épluchette* in the chapter on Québec.

Frolic came into English from Dutch *vroolijk* 'happy, joyous.' Compare its cognate synonym in German *fröhlich*, as in the German for Merry Christmas, *Fröhliche Weihnachten*. The Indo-European root **fro* means 'hop.' It has descendants like German *Freude* 'joy' and even English *frog* whose root meaning is 'the hopper.' Classical Sanskrit, ancient tongue of India and sacred language of Hinduism, has the related *pravate* 'it hops.'

GALETTE AU PETIT-LARD DE LOUP MARIN
(SEAL BLUBBER COOKIE)

Galette is the usual word for cookie in *français acadien*, for example, *galette au sucre* 'sugar cookie' and *galette à la mélasse* 'molasses cookie.' It also means hot bread roll or *petit pain* in the phrase *galette blanche*.

Un loup-marin 'sea wolf' is an old French-Canadian term for a harp seal. It certainly sounds less alarming to English ears than the correct term in standard French, *un phoque*, from which interlingual confusions might arise to affront the modesty of any embryonic bilingualist. The term was common in several European languages by the middle of the 16th century. Obsolete in modern English, sea-wolf once meant 'seal' or 'sea-elephant,' while sea-lion to denote a large, eared seal, has been splashing about in English since 1697. Both English and Canadian French or some early French dialect may have borrowed the term, as a loan-translation, from 15th-century nautical Dutch where *zeewolf* was a sea monster, then a seal.

To make this cookie, the seal fat is chopped up and boiled for a good hour in hot water. After the fat has been drained, the usual suspects — cookie-ingredientwise — are mixed in, namely, flour, milk, eggs, baking soda, salt, and, to cut the greasy taste a bit, a splash of vinegar. Patting, rolling, kneading follow, and then half an hour in a 200° centigrade oven. *Petit-lard* is merely blubber from little seals.

GALETTE DES ROIS (TWELFTH NIGHT COOKIE)

Three Kings' Biscuit is a treat baked on the church feast of Epiphany, January 6, commemorating the coming of the three wisemen or Magi to worship the baby Jesus. The feast of Epiphany is also called Twelfth Night in English. Acadian forebears and other Roman Catholic immigrants to North America brought this traditional confection from France. Each little cookie usually contains one bean, *la fève des Rois*, the bean of the Magi. For more on the etymology of *galette*, see the entry for it in the chapter on Québec food words.

GRAINAGE (EDIBLE WILD BERRIES)

Here is another word that has — with this meaning — disappeared from current continental French, but has been kept alive in *français acadien*. Grainage is a collective term for edible wild berries like strawberries, raspberries, blueberries, etc. It is also used to denote a wild berry patch: *je vais aux grainages aujourd'hui.*

GRANDS-PÈRES

These "grandfathers" are the flour-and-baking powder dumplings often plopped into stews like Acadian *fricots* and *pots-en-pot*. They are usually dropped into the stew at the last to simmer for a final seven or eight minutes. Other names for these dumplings are *poutines blanches* or *pâtes*.

MIOCHE

More fully, *mioche au naveau* (old French dialect word for turnip; compare with modern French *navet*). The turnips and potatoes are simmered until tender, then mixed with seasonings and maybe a few onions fried with pieces of salt pork fat.

In some parts of Acadia, *mioche* by itself denotes mashed potatoes. In Quebec and France, *mioche* is a term of endearment for a little boy, that meant literally 'a crumb of bread,' like the current French word for breadcrumb, *mie*. *Moche*, *mioche*, and *mie* all stem from the Latin *mica* 'small bit, little portion.' *Meuche* is a local Acadian pronunciation from the Îles de la Madeleine. As a modern French adjective, *moche* developed the meaning 'ugly' or 'of little value.'

Mailloche is a big wooden mallet, with which various foods were pounded into a mush, the French word borrowed from an Italian dialectic form like *maglioccio* 'big mallet.' In Canadian French, *une mailloche* can denote a bump on the head (originally from a mallet) or a ball of butter or wax.

MOUQUE (MUSSEL)

In Acadian, *mouque* is a general word for a mussel, like its counterpart in standard French, *moule*. *Pâté aux mouques* is a mussel-and-potato pie still popular with Acadian cooks. Many of the seafood sauces, *fricots*, and other other recipes for molluscs feature mussels with clams, quahogs, and oysters.

In Québec French, *mouque* refers to the inedible crow's-bill mussel (also called *bec de corneille*).

Mussel, *moule*, and *mouque* all stem ultimately from Latin *musculus* 'muscle.' Mouque was a dialectic variant of *moule*, a back formation of *moucle* 'mussel' in the regional French of Aunis. Some of the original Acadian immigrants came from the old French Atlantic province of Aunis.

NAULET

A *naulet* was a little cookie, sometimes made of gingerbread, shaped like a baby, to represent the baby Jesus, given to Acadian children as a Christmas treat. Or perhaps it was merely a little early training in the doctrine of transubstantiation which the children would encounter later during Roman Catholic mass. In any case, it's a dialect spelling of what began as *noëlet*, itself an alternate diminutive for the phrase *le petit noël* 'Christmas gift given to a child.' Note that the food terms are not capitalized in French as the word for Christmas itself is, *Noël*. An Acadian Christmas cake was *un nolet, un gâteau de Noël*.

PASSE-PIERRE

Passe-pierre is an edible marsh green picked in midsummer, a tidal maritime plant whose spicy saltiness makes it an Acadian favourite picked fresh for salads or pickled in brine for winter use. Briefly, after the expulsion of the Acadians, *passe-pierre* was one of many subsistence greens for some Acadians who escaped deportation by hiding in remote areas of the Maritimes. *Passe-pierre* is a seaside plantain, *Plantago juncoides*. The specific means 'like a rush,' and indeed the grassy tufts of *passe-pierre* look somewhat like rushes of the *Juncus* genus. See the entry on *goose tongues* in the chapter on Nova Scotia.

The origin of the term *passe-pierre* is complex and interesting. *Passe-pierre* is an Acadian variant of the old continental French name, *perce-pierre*, itself a variant of an even older plant name *l'herbe de Saint-Pierre* 'Saint Peter's herb.' Several maritime plants and creatures have been named after Saint Peter, including in French a fish. Peter, of course, was a fisherman on the Sea of Galilee when Jesus called him to be a disciple and to become 'a fisher of men.'

His Hebrew name was Simon or Shimon. Jesus or earlier companions nicknamed him *Kephas* 'rock' in Aramaic. In the Greek of the New Testament, he became *Petros* 'rock, stone,' subject of the most egregious pun in the New Testament, where Matthew reports Jesus saying to Peter (*Petros* in the Koine Greek of the New Testament): "Thou art Peter, and upon this rock (Greek: *epi tautei tei petrai*) I will build my church." The herbalist monks and priests who collected plants and often named them were well aware of this rock/Saint Peter connection. In 17th-century botany, this plant is listed as *herba divi Petri* 'herb of the divine Peter,' and one of its names in German is *Meerpeterlein* 'Little Sea Peter.'

St. Pete gets hot tips from angel dude.

All that said, however, there is another twist to this ropey old tale. *Perce-pierre*, *passe-pierre*, and *l'herbe de Saint-Pierre* originally referred to a totally different plant, not to seaside plantain at all, but to a plant called sea-fennel or true samphire, *Crithmum maritimum*. For a discussion of true samphire, please see the entry on sandfire greens in the chapter on Nova Scotia food words. Sorry, the confusion does not end there. Very early in Acadian history, sailors who knew about *l'herbe de Saint-Pierre* or *perce-pierre* or *passe-pierre* also discovered that the seaside plant they knew from France did not grow along North American ocean shores. So they transferred the name to an edible plant that was common on our maritime beaches, a plant of the glasswort clan, *Salicornia europaea*, still called marsh samphire in New England, and called false samphire or pickleweed or sandfire greens in Canada. For a discussion of true samphire and false samphire and sandfire greens, I will repeat my request that you see the entry on sandfire greens in the chapter on Nova Scotia food words.

But the seaside plantain's similar habitat does account for two of its old names, *passe-pierre* and *perce-pierre*. All along the northern coast of Atlantic Europe, this plant prefers to grow in rich, tidal flats, but it struggles up also through the rocky shingle of sea beaches. As *perce-pierre* and *passe-pierre*, it may be said to pierce through shore rocks.

PETS DE SOEUR (NUN'S FARTS)

There is a hefty dollop of anticlerical humour in all dialects of French, and *le français acadien* is no exception. The stranglehold that the church once kept firmly about the neck of even secular affairs in small Acadian and Canadian French communities in olden days caused occasional resentment among people of the parishes, and one of the relatively innocent ways ordinary folk could get a *soupçon* of revenge against dictatorial priests and strap-armed teaching nuns was in the sacrilegious, off-colour satire of folk names for daily things. Nun's farts are little dessert pastries that look like cinnamon rolls. The *t* in *pet* is pronounced in Canadian French, but not always in continental French. These wee confections are also called *bourriques de soeurs* 'nuns' belly buttons,' or more politely *rondelles* 'slices' or *hirondelles* 'swallows.'

Inching a little higher up the obscenity scale, one finds a doughnutlike roll made from leftover homemade bread dough called *trous de soeur* 'nun's holes.' They are usually eaten with molasses — to sweeten the experience.

POT-EN-POT

Usually a stew or casserole, the phrase *pot-en-pot* arises because two pots are used, and part of the contents of one pot are poured into a second pot at some point during preparation. In Old French, *en pot* meant 'boiled' as opposed to *rôti* 'roasted.' In many recipes named *pot-en-pot* a pastry lining and crust encloses the final stage before baking. Other Acadian *pot-en-pot* dishes feature layers of meat or fish alternating with dumplings (*pâtes*). Seafood casseroles are common in Acadian kitchens too, such as *pot-en-pot à l'éplan*, a delicious smelt and dumpling affair in a casserole dish. An Acadian eel pie is *pot-en-pot à l'anguille* with a pastry crust on top.

POUTINE

Pronounced [poo-TSIN] in Canadian French, perhaps first borrowed — with the spelling *poutine* — from the English word *pudding* by the Acadians, this food term has acquired many meanings in Québec and Acadia. Here are discussed only Acadian uses of the word. For a more detailed history of *la poutine* with its modern meanings and its other borrowed relative *le pouding*, please see the *poutine* entry in the chapter on Québec.

Poutines râpées are the famous Acadian potato dumplings made from two parts of grated raw potatoes squeezed dry in a cotton bag, and from one part plain mashed potatoes mixed together with the grated potatoes and formed into a ball about — as one Acadian cook told me — "the size of the fist of my *petite tante* Yvonne." In parts of New Brunswick, a hole in the centre of each poutine is stuffed with diced salt pork. To cook these poutines, drop two or three into water at a rolling boil then simmer for two and a half hours. *Poutines râpées* may also be plunked into a gently bubbling *fricot*.

Poutine en sac is another of the old European puddings steamed in a cloth bag, so many of which have made their way to Canada with names like son-of-a-gun-in-a-sack, bugger-in-a-bag, cloutie from Scotland, and figgy duff from Newfoundland. Also called *poutine à la vapeur*, the pudding is some variant of a lard-sugar-eggs-flour-milk-baking-powder mixture to which is added raisins and perhaps blueberries, apples, cranberries — whatever's in season. This doughy delight is mixed together to form a large ball, put in a cotton bag tied up with string, and placed on a wire mesh rack in a large pot with an inch of water. The steaming takes two hours. A double-bottomed pot may be used, or a double-boiler if you want to forego the bag, but since half the fun of a bagged pudding is the damn bag, why forego it? *Poutine en sac* can be served with sweet cream, brown-sugar sauce, or even slices of fried pork.

There are also Acadian poutines that resemble pies (*poutine à la mélasse*) and bread puddings (*poutine au pain*).

SOUPE À N'IMPORTE QUOI (IT-DOESN'T-MATTER-WHAT SOUP)

Soups have always been important in cooking as a means of keeping leftovers to a minimum, and Acadian cuisine takes full advantage of this soupy ploy with hundreds of recipes. I much like the name of this vegetable-and-meat soup with barley. It is often made on Saturday and served as a main course after Sunday mass, thus another of its names, *soupe du dimanche*. Other monikers include *soupe à la baillarge* (barley) and *soupe à toutes sortes de choses* (all-kinds-of-stuff soup).

With the self-mocking humour that still tickles the Acadian funnybone, a very thin broth used to be called *soupe à l'ombre* (shadow soup). The old tale goes that in times of great poverty, the same soup bone would be passed around to many neighbouring houses and tied over the boiling soup pot so that only a few drippings of bonefat would drip down into each pot, and the soup was prepared in the shadow (*ombre*) of the soup bone. Another homey name adorns a fresh vegetable-in-beef-broth pottage called *soupe de devant de porte* (right-beside-the-door soup), presumably because the crisp veggies would be picked fresh from the vegetable patch nearest the house. Around Chéticamp on Cape Breton Island in Nova Scotia, this hearty soup with potatoes added as thickener is called *soupe varte* (with the Acadian dialect spelling of *verte* 'green').

TAILLE (POTATO SLICE)

Tranche is the word for slice in standard French, but Acadian uses *taille*. These popular potato slices are baked in an oven pan until golden and crispy, then served with butter and salt, to accompany many other Acadian dishes. Tailles may also be fried.

TCHAUDE

A *chaude* or *tchaude* among Nova Scotian Acadians is a fish stew originally prepared in a big iron cauldron called a *chaudière*, the same word from which English by adaptation got the word *chowder*. Tchaude almost always contains potatoes and diced salt pork fat, along with the featured fish, such as cod or mackerel.

TÉTINES DE SOURIS

In Canadian English, sandfire greens refer to little succulent seashore and mud-flat plants, glassworts, called in botany *Salicornia* (salt-horn) *europaea*. The Acadians named them after mouse nipples because of the little, dotlike balls that cluster on the stem. They are harvested when the plants are young and are eaten fresh.

Both sandfire greens and false samphire are parts of an interesting etymological progression: *l'herbe de Saint-Pierre* > *sampierre* > *sampere* > samphire > sandfire. The last alteration, from samphire to sandfire, occurred not only from English ears mangling a French word while turning it into something comprehensible in English, but also because this little glasswort of beaches and shorelines turns red when it gets old and grows in the sand, hence sandfire.

True samphire is a different plant that does not grow wild in Canada, but is found on the European coast of the Atlantic Ocean. For the distinction between false and true samphire, see the entry for sandfire greens in the chapter on Nova Scotia foods. See also the entry in this chapter on *passe-pierre*.

CHAPTER 5

New Brunswick

*T*he first named group of humans to populate what is now New Brunswick were the Mi'kmaq people, followed by Acadian French, and then, in the 17th century, forced from their New England homelands, the Maliseet people came north. Note that the Maliseet call themselves *Wolastokwiyok* 'people of the Beautiful River,' referring to the Saint John River in New Brunswick. The term Maliseet, first applied around 1690, is actually a derogatory term said of them in derision by the Mi'kmaq. In the Mi'kmaq language *mali:sit* means 'speaks poorly,' a possible reference to the fact that, since both Mi'kmaq and Maliseet are Algonquian languages, there would have been some mutually understood words, but even words of the same root would have been embedded in two distinct languages and have developed forms that were for the most part not mutually comprehensible.

After the expulsion of the Acadians came an influx of Protestant New Englanders, Pennsylvanians, and Yorkshiremen. Then some Acadians returned from exile to find the best land in the hands of British usurpers. Soon afterward arrived Loyalist exiles from the war in America, and later, in the earlier part of the 19th century, the largest group of Scottish and Irish immigrants, although, of course, some Scots and Irish had come earlier.

By far the largest number of distinctive food words in New Brunswick are of Acadian origin, and the reader should look for them in my chapter devoted to culinary Acadiana, although a few Acadian dishes that are exclusive to New Brunswick are mentioned here.

Like other provinces of Canada, New Brunswick has several places evocatively named after food words. Samp Hill in Kings County west of Havelock is named after an aboriginal food which also saved many an early white settler. See the entry in this chapter.

The village, harbour, and river of Cocagne in New Brunswick were named for Cockaigne, a mythical paradise in medieval French literature, a kind of gourmand's Utopia where "houses were made of barley sugar cakes and streets were paved with pastry." It was named by Nicolas Denys (1598 – 1688), the great recruiter of settlers for Acadia, after he camped at the harbour mouth for a week, and noted the teeming wildfowl, the excellent fishing, and especially the local oysters and other shellfish. Denys is the author of an important early book on Acadia, *Description géographique et historique des costes de l'Amérique septentrionale* (Paris, 1672).

Dessert in Cocagne

This pastry heaven was a popular medieval concept in almost all languages of Europe, for example, in Spanish, *cucaña;* in Portuguese, *cucanha;* in Italian, *cuccagna;* all deriving from medieval Low German *kokenje,* a sweet little cake, being the diminutive of *koke,* cake. The root is a common Indo-European one, and *koke* is cognate with or borrowed from Latin *coquere* 'to cook.' But it has nothing to do with the addictive drug, cocaine, which has its origin in indigenous South American languages like Aymara and Quechua where *kuka* and *koka* are names of the shrub known to modern botany as *Erythroxylum coca,* from whose leaves the soul-destorying white paste and powder are made.

CANADA POTATO *or* JERUSALEM ARTICHOKE

There is some evidence that this edible tuber of one of the sunflowers was first collected in the wild and sent back to England from Halifax by a plant collector who had been searching for botanical specimen plants in what became southern New Brunswick. The Canada potato is the tuber of *Helianthus tuberosus,* whose specific makes clear that the plant possesses "many tubers," which is the meaning of the botanical Latin adjective *tuberosus.* On the other hand, the generic label *Helianthus* derives from the Greek *helios* 'sun' and the Greek *anthos* 'flower.' This genus contains about sixty species, most native to North America.

Early colonists observed the Mi'kmaq and Maliseet peoples harvesting these tubers during the winter. They are best after a few frosts have finished off the sunflower's top growth. But, because they keep well in the ground through the winter, they were dug up as needed rather than stored above ground. When the tubers and some sunflower seeds first reached England and then France and Italy, gourmets thought the tubers tasted a bit like artichokes. In Italian, the plant was called *girasole* 'turn-sun.' After all, it was a sunflower. But when the English first heard *girasole*, they could make nothing of the word, and so — as happens so frequently when words hop from one tongue to another — the English decided to call it: Jerusalem (girasole?) artichoke. In keeping with howlers among common names, this is neither an artichoke nor is it from Jerusalem.

Aboriginal peoples of North America cultivated the plant for its edible tubers, and white settlers learned to eat it. During the early 20th century, the Jerusalem artichoke declined in popularity, but lately it has been making a modest comeback in North American gardens and kitchens. It is a hardy sunflower, and quite easy to grow in any spot that sunflowers flourish. Just be warned that, if you leave a few tubers in the ground and do not harvest them, a new plant will grow even from the tiniest piece of a tuber hacked into pieces by a questing hoe. This tuberous sunflower is an invasive plant.

These "Canada potatoes" are sweeter and crunchier than ordinary potatoes. When the tubers are dug up in late autumn or through the winter, they should be washed off gently and then sliced raw into salads or steamed for a few minutes in boiling water. If you overcook them, Jerusalem artichokes turn to tasteless mush. So practise. And try them if you have not, for something Canadian and new to most modern tables.

FIDDLEHEADS

Fiddleheads are the spring-fresh fronds of the ostrich fern, plucked before they unravel to the forest sun, and consumed as a delicacy, often by steaming or boiling, and then buttering. Eat only the youngest, freshest fronds just as they begin to unfold. Learn to identify and collect only the fiddleheads of the ostrich fern, *Matteuccia struthiopteris*.

Either check the correct field identification marks in a plant manual, and, better yet, go fiddleheading with an experienced collector. Although the fronds of several other fern species are eaten, some are toxic. Medical literature reports ignorant gatherers plucking the young, fernlike leaves of poison hemlock by mistake. Fatal mistake. Never, of course, eat mature, unrolled fronds of any fern. Stay away in particular from the fiddleheads of the bracken fern which are carcinogenic in many animal species.

The tedium of washing fiddleheads thoroughly and cleaning the scales off these curly little crosiers detracts considerably from the joy of relishing eventually their buttered succulence — at least for this amateur botanizer. If you want to enjoy a harvest each spring, don't be a fiddlehead fool and pick all the unfurling fronds from one plant. If you do, it will die. Smart picking of fiddleheads will let you collect in the same ferny dell every year. New Brunswick packers ship frozen fiddleheads all across the country, and these can be savoured at any season.

Fiddleheads and their filigreed fronds even figure in the frolic of a potent Maritime home hootch, too much of which will render the imbiber "stewed as a fresh-boiled owl." It's called moose milk. Up north, moose milk is homebrew or rum and milk. But a more piquant potion is concocted in the Maritimes where one lollapalooza recipe for moose milk calls for emulsified fiddleheads and clam juice, liberally diluted with a budget wine. Perhaps Chateau Moncton? Two carafes will have you heading home but listing well to starboard. The snootier sommeliers whisper that last week was a fine vintage.

MADOUÈCE RÔTI (ROAST PORCUPINE)

Madawaska, the New Brunswick county and river name, derives from a local Aboriginal word for porcupine, *madawes* in the language of the Maliseet people, so that *madawes-ka* means 'porcupine place.' The present city of Edmunston in New Brunswick, say some authorities, was first called Madawaska by the Maliseet people. The Acadian dialect word for porcupine is *madouèce* or *madouesse,* while standard French is *porc-épic.* Both porcupine and *porc-épic* are related to medieval French *porc espic* and *porc espin* 'bristle pig,' itself from Old Italian *porcospino,* ultimately from Latin *porcus* 'pig' + *spina* 'prickle, bristle, spine.'

As one Acadian cookbook states, the Madawaska area is home to a recipe for roast porcupine in which, after skinning, cleaning, and washing, the porcupine "is occasionally pre-boiled to remove some of the woody taste." It then needs to be roasted for two and a half hours.

Residents of the Madawaska area have their own local nickname for themselves, *les Brayons.*

PLOYES (BUCKWHEAT PANCAKES)

Ployer is a dialect form of the standard French verb *plier* 'fold, bend.' These buckwheat pancakes served with butter and maple syrup are specialties of the Madawaska area in New Brunswick. *Ployes* are also called *plogues* there. In Québec, they are more formally known as *galettes de sarrazin.*

RAPPIE PIE or PÂTE À LA RÂPURE

Râpure is anything that has been grated; in the case of this familiar Acadian main course, it's grated raw potatoes. This is yet again a dish of necessity, for, in pioneer times, the grated raw potatoes were squeezed dry in a cotton bag, and the "potato water" was used as starch when the week's laundry was done. After removal of the "starch water," the potatoes were mashed in with whatever meat was being used, perhaps salt pork or chicken or seafood, plus onions, eggs, and seasonings like summer savory, coriander, salt and pepper. It goes by variant names, like *pâté râpé* or *chiard*, depending on which part of Acadia you're making it in. There are also several distinct methods of making rappie pie, another of which involves making a broth of the chicken or clams or mussels or rabbit, and as part of the preparation, scalding the squeezed potatoes in this broth.

Le pâté in Acadian is the traditional meat pie. The French word *pâté* has an interesting etymology. Before 1165, it was spelled *pasté*, stemming from Vulgar Latin *pasta*, itself from Greek *paste* 'flour sauce.' By the time of Late Latin, *pasta* meant 'dough' and 'flour adhesive' as well, and was the source both of the Italian word *pasta* and our modern English sticky word *paste*. Every region of Acadia has its local meat pie, and not just for supper. Some *pâtés* are served for breakfast or even as midnight, after-skating snacks. In some places in New Brunswick, variations consisting of miniature, folded *pâtés* (fifteen centimetres wide) are called *petits cochons* (piggywigs), little lunar crescents of golden-brown crust enclosing juicy bits of pork, chicken, potatoes, and onions. In Acadian and Québec French, *petits cochons* is also one of the common names for the bog-dwelling pitcher plant.

RESTIGOUCHE SALMON

The Restigouche River — world famous for its Atlantic salmon run discovered by Mi'kmaq fishermen — flows into Chaleur Bay and forms part of the northern border of New Brunswick with Québec. The Mi'kmaq source of its name, and for the town in Québec officially spelled Ristigouche, is *lustagooch* 'good (for canoeing) river.' Other Mi'kmaq interpreters have suggested the word could refer to the branches of the Restigouche and could mean: 'river divided like a hand,' 'five-finger river,' 'five-branches river,' or 'many-branched river.' The drainage area of the Restigouche is home to two sleek creatures now on New Brunswick's endangered species list: the elusive, furry-footed Canada lynx and that superb flying fisher, the osprey.

SAMP

Samp Hill in Kings County west of Havelock, New Brunswick, is named for a now lost incident involving Indian cornmeal mush. There were many variant spellings for this corn porridge including saupon, supawn, supon, and supporne. It appears to derive from a term widespread in many of the Algonquian languages, including Mi'kmaq. As early as 1643, Roger Williams, the founder and first governor of Rhode Island, writes in his *Key into the Language of America*: "nasaump . . . a kind of Meale pottage . . . the English samp is corn, beaten and boiled and eaten hot or cold with milk or butter." *Nasaump* is the name for this food in the Algonquian language called Narraganset. In the Massachusetts language it is *saupáum*. The root meaning is 'water-softened' (corn). In later American English, with the addition of wheat flour to the corn flour, a British phrase was borrowed and samp was called hasty pudding, later giving a title to the famous Harvard University students' club, The Hasty Pudding Theatrical Society. Along the Atlantic seaboard, in early America and the Canadas, samp was sweetened with maple sugar or molasses.

A bay, a cape, an island, a river, a town, and a delicately fleshed, two-valved mollusc bear the name *Shediac*, from the Mi'kmaq place name *Esedeiik* 'running inland,' a reference to the indented coastline of the area where pleasant summer resorts now laze along the shore of Northumberland Strait.

SHEDIAC OYSTER

Singin' Johnny, from northern New Brunswick and the Gaspé is homebrew made by putting ripe black currants and sugar into a liquor bottle in July, filling it with gin, and letting it ferment until Christmas, when it was served to holiday visitors.

SINGIN' JOHNNY

Singin' Johnny takes a brief, subtabular interval of repose.

SPRUCE TEA

Spruce Tea was hailed in one 19th-century advertisement for natural remedies as "The Great Antiscorbutic Elixir of the Canadas, Most Easily Made and Necessary To Be Had by All Persons There Resident." Here's one blurb by a snake oil peddler that turns out to be true. Scurvy was a vitamin C deficiency disease that was rampant among the first European immigrants to the New World. Many a spindly scorbutic wretch was snatched from the Grim Reaper's clutch by a humble mug of spruce tea, whose recipe was passed to whites by different tribes of First Peoples.

One recipe is given here with the caution that you make certain which fir twigs you have collected. Yew, for example, is poisonous. Also, quaff not quarts of spruce or any other evergreen tea. Try a modest cup for interest. If you have scurvy (unlikely), see a doctor and chew vitamin C tablets on the way to the appointment. Don't pick White Spruce twigs to make tea. Its resin is too overpowering. If you are botanizing in eastern British Columbia or western Alberta, avoid Engelmann spruce. Its resin really stinks. Try Black Spruce, while remembering that some other conifers make pleasanter-smelling teas. Maritimers claim their native Red Spruce, *Picea rubens*, makes the most palatable infusion.

Recipe for Spruce Tea

Collect twig tips of fresh, young growth in late spring. Put a fistful of twigs in a warm pot. Fill pot with water heated to a rolling boil. Steep about five minutes. Sweeten with honey or maple syrup. Spice with a dust of cinnamon, a zest of orange peel, a nail or two of cloves, or bob dried blueberries in this fragrant tea.

In olden days, molasses was added to the steeped tea and it was left for days to ferment into a spruce beer with a very high vitamin C content. This type of tea was the famous antiscorbutic brew that saved Cartier and his men, and many other intrepid adventurers, from death by scurvy. But different Aboriginal peoples used different fir trees. For example, Cartier and his men were rescued by an infusion made from twigs of Eastern White Cedar.

TOGUE

Togue was once abundant in the larger lakes of New Brunswick. The popular name of a tasty lake trout, also seen as 'og,' illustrates one of the trade-offs people make in using common names — since togue can refer both to a freshwater fish (also called gray lake trout, mackinaw trout, mountain trout, and salmon trout) and also to a saltwater fish, an Atlantic wrasse, the tautog (*Tautoga onitis*). Tog and togue all stem from an eastern Algonkian plural *tautauog* 'black fishes' which gives an American common name for the saltwater species 'blackfish.'

WHITE EYE *or WHISKY-BLANC*

White eye or *whisky-blanc* was illegal liquor smuggled from the French islands of Saint-Pierre and Miquelon. The grain alcohol was manufactured in France and smuggled through the islands to the New Brunswick and Gaspé coast where locals might get "boary-eyed drunk on white-eye." Not every local partook, of course. Some did not wish *se mouiller le canayen* 'to wet their whistle.' Those who did hanker for a jar of the pellucid distillate naturally confined their intake to such times of high festivity as were deemed fitting and appropriate through the counsel of wise elders.

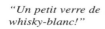

"Un petit verre de whisky-blanc!"

CHAPTER 6

Québec

Menum menum! That's "Yummy!" in Québec. And it's my reaction to the food words and the word lore of *la cuisine Québécoise*. The province's food words were baked in many linguistic ovens. The Québécois language may have begun as a colonial dialect of European French, but many — although not most linguists — would argue that it is today too different and too vigorous to be dismissed with a cozy label like dialect. Québec French bubbles with a rich stew of unique vocabulary drawn in the beginning from the 17th-century vernacular speech of the first immigrants who came to *La Nouvelle France* from the northwestern provinces of old France, with additions from English and the languages of our First

Peoples, later from the zesty slang of *joual*, and from its own coining of words like *acériculture*.

Acériculture denotes maple sugar production. *Acer* is the word for maple in Latin, and also its botanical genus. Incidentally, Latin *acer* is one of the verbal building blocks that make up the French word for maple *érable*, which descends — after shuffling off an unstressed initial syllable and several final unstressed vowels — from a medieval Latin form *acerabulus* 'maple tree.' One of the terms coined in Québec French denoted our North American sugar maple, *érable à sucre*. Also indigenous is *érablière* 'sugar bush,' any maple syrup operation on a farm.

Anticlerical humour, a fixture of popular Québec speech from inception, finds its shocking way into food words of the province, for example, *oreilles de crisse*, which are little slices of salt pork grilled or fried, but which mean literally 'Christ's ears,' so-called from the way the little slices curl up when grilled.

Standard French culinary terms developed new meanings in the new world of New France. For example, in older continental French *un réchaud* was a portable warming oven, from *réchauffer* to reheat, to warm up again. But early voyageurs and coureurs de bois venturing across North America to what would become the Canadian Prairies, began to use *réchaud* to denote pemmican mixed with flour and veggies and warmed over an open camp fire. With variants like *richeau*, this term for a staple trail food was widely used among French and English-speaking trappers and settlers.

New words were needed for new food sources, especially plant and animal species unique to North America. Thus, many words from Aboriginal languages entered early Québec French, like the Cree and Ojibwa word for a fish, a bass, *achigan*, occasionally found in early Canadian English as well, and still used in Québec. *Achigan* in Algonkian languages means 'struggler, splasher, fighter.' Other loans were more direct, like *banique* from Gaelic *bannock*, probably through English and Gaelic in our Maritimes.

Many terms in English were borrowed and spelled to accommodate French speakers; for example, beans baked in salt pork fat could be *les binnes*, *les bines*, or *les fèves au lard*.

Food and kitchen references enter provincial folk sayings. Out in the countryside of rural Québec, a slangy way to say "She is stuck up" or "She is very snooty" is: *È se mouche pas avec des pelures d'oignons*. 'She doesn't blow her nose with onion peels.' The inference is that some down-to-earth *habitante de pure laine* might have done so in days long past.

This chapter discusses food terms that are used generally across the whole province, and some that are strictly regional dishes. At the end of the chapter I have listed separately some Gaspé terms including — to no one's surprise I trust — some distinct food terms from the Canadian English spoken in the Gaspé and in northern New Brunswick.

ACHIGAN

This word, unique to Québécois French, denotes two related species of freshwater fish, one a small-mouthed bass, the other a large-mouthed bass, both feisty faves of sport fishermen. The word was borrowed early into Canadian English and French from the Algonkian languages, Cree and Ojibwa, where *achigan* means 'struggler, splasher, fighter.' North of Montréal flows the Rivière de l'Achigan 'Bass River,' which counts among the pleasant hamlets along its meandering course Saint-Roch-de-l'Achigan. The river begins at Lac de l'Achigan.

BABOCHE
BAGLOSSE
BAGOSSE
PETIT BLANC
ROBINE

All these colourful Quebecisms refer variously to homebrew, moonshine whisky, and hootch, with the implication in the words that the distillate under discussion is not of the highest quality. In other words, these are pretty good translations of "rotgut." Like all tongues, *la langue Québécoise* has a lively hoard of booze words and phrases. To wet one's whistle can be translated *se mouiller le canayen*. To be a female on the wagon is *être Jeanne d'Arc*. To be a male who has given up ruinous drinking habits is *être Lacordaire*. If one falls off the wagon, one is likely to have *mal aux cheveux*, a hangover, but literally "a hair-ache." So don't go on a bender, that is, *partez pas sur une balloune*.

The last word on the above list of hootch terms is *robine*, borrowed from that poisonous tipple of impoverished alcoholics called in English *rubbing* alcohol, and incidentally the source of the Canadian disparagement, rubbie. A rubbie or wino or sodden bum in Québec can be called *un robineux*.

BAJOTTE

This is the distinct Québec word for a pork jowl, an old dialect form that has disappeared from modern French where the standard term for jowl is *bajoue*. The suffixes *-ot* and *-otte* were originally diminutive endings, popular add-ons in the vernaculars of most Romance languages. *Bajottes* could be baked or grilled by themselves or ground up along with every other part of the pig except the squeal to make pork sausages. *Bajoue* was first a compound, in Medieval French *bas joue* 'low(er) cheek.'

BEURRÉE

In Québec, this is a slice of bread generously buttered. The standard European French word for a piece of buttered bread is *tartine*. One might add jam, or on *une beurrée de miel*, honey. Even more redolent of *la cuisine Québécoise* would be *beurrée de sucre d'érable*, a stout cut of home baked whole-wheat bread, slathered with sweet Lactantia™ butter, and sprinkled with maple sugar.

LES BINNES *or* FÈVRES AU LARD

It's pork and beans, sweetened not with molasses and brown sugar tonight, but with ambrosial rills of maple syrup. Diced salt pork makes up the meaty bits. Stirred in will be a hefty spoon of fiery dried mustard. As we slip the large casserole into the oven for its five-or-six-hour baking, we may place a tender chicken breast in the beany midst of the dish.

And never, never shall the meat consist of some quick, slipshod, make-do protein like sliced hot dogs. *Tabarnac!* Why, such sausageoid abominations might contain the curly tails of hapless piggywigs, the noble ears of once proud steeds, the very genitalia of innocent lambkins who lately bleated their bliss on hillsides green. The legal ingredients in hot dogs in Canada — believe it or not — also permit a certain amount of "mouse droppings and insect parts." That quote is from the Agriculture Canada regulations. For a bracing corrective, I recommend some eventide a close reading of what is permitted in processed meat in Canada. Read it a considerable time after supper.

Va aux bines! is a provincial slang expression equivalent to "buzz off!" in English.

Les deux cochons

BLÉ D'INDE

This North American French term for corn first appeared in print in 1603. A variant was *blé indien*. Both mean 'Indian corn.' The French in North America called it *blé d'Inde* because some Aboriginal peoples encountered by early Europeans told them that the cultivation of corn occurred first in the islands *des Indes Occidentales* 'of the West Indies.' In fact, the Taino, the Caribs, and other island peoples brought knowledge of corn growing with them from the mainland. The earliest corn remnants found by paleobotanists and archaeologists at Tehuacán in Mexico have been carbon-dated as being 7,500 years old. Corn's cultivation had spread southward and northward long before Europeans arrived in the "New" World. Explorer Jacques Cartier found it being grown plentifully along the St. Lawrence in 1535.

Although *blé* means 'wheat' in modern French, earlier it referred to corn in the sense of seeds of any cereal crop. Corn still has this meaning in British English. The word *blé* appears in French manuscripts as early as 1080, with subforms like *blet*, derived from the language of the ancient Franks where *blad* meant 'something harvested from the earth.' The ultimate Indo-European root of *blé* is * *bhle-* 'flower, leaf, plant part.' The asterisk preceding an IE root citation labels the form as hypothetical, a root based on comparative research and conjecture as opposed to printed proof. Since the earliest speakers of Indo-European were pre-alphabetic, no inscriptions survive.

In standard French, corn is *maïs*, as it is maize in Great Britain, both derived from Spanish *maíz*. Spanish conquerors first encountered corn on the island of Hispaniola being grown by the Taino people. The Taino lived on several other Caribbean island groups such as the Greater Antilles and the Bahamas. They and their Arawakan language are now extinct. Corn in Taino was *mahiz*.

BOUILLON D'HABITANT

In ancient France, *bouillon* was the broth or stock rendered from boiling (*bouiller* 'to boil') vegetables or meat, and many a humble kitchen kept a stock pot ready to simmer in a permanent place on the stove. In classic French cuisine, *bouillon* is the liquid part of a *pot-au-feu*. But among the first French settlers and explorers of what became Canada, a bouillon came to refer to a hearty stew of whatever vegetables and meat or fish were readily to hand. So pervasive was its use that the word passed into Canadian English. Various recipes and local adaptations of *bouillon d'habitant* 'farmer's stew' were carried across the country right to the Pacific and into our North by French traders, trappers, and much later by *bûcherons* 'lumberjacks.' One writer about the rolling lands of our Dominion was Stewart E. White who sings the delights of this stew in *The Forest* published in 1903: "[trout] mingled in the famous North Country *bouillon*, whose other ingredients are partridges, and tomatoes, and potatoes, and onions, and salt pork, and flour in combination delicious beyond belief."

From the same verb *bouiller* 'to boil' comes another common food noun, *bouilli*, which in France, as still in Québec today, is a boiled dinner.

A Note on Habitant

A few words are of interest here concerning the people who brought the old recipes to Québec and who through the centuries have grown so much of its food. At different times in the history of Québec, this familiar word has had different meanings. Habitant began as a legal term in the "new" feudalism of New France. A habitant was a free proprietor who held land in tenure within the seigneurial system. This system, in legal force from 1627 until 1854, was a way to distribute and occupy land in a new colony. Seigneuries were large tracts of land granted to the richest colonists of New France, often sons of French nobles. In return for their provision of teaching and medical services, convents and other religious bodies could also be seigneuries. These large tracts of land were also granted to high military officers and certain civil administrators. In turn, the seigneur divided his land grant into parcels, and leased these smaller farms by contract to tenants, called *censitaires* or *habitants*. The habitant was obliged to put the land into fertile production as soon as possible, to grow enough food to sustain his family, and to be productive enough to have some crops or money left over to pay his tenant's rent to the seigneur. This fee was the famous *cens et rente*, the *cens* being a small feudal tithe, the rent being money or its equivalent in produce. The habitant also had to pay a grain tax called *les banalités*.

The seigneur was given other rights pertaining to his land. A seigneur could set up a court of law, a mill, a commune, and sell licences to hunt, to fish, and to cut wood on his land. The habitant was under legal obligation to grind grain at the mill of his seigneur. As well, the seigneur could demand a certain number of days of free work from each tenant. This required labour was *une corvée*. As the *corvée* was technically illegal, it generated resentment, and was eventually suppressed. By the 1850s, *corvée* gained a new meaning and denoted the volunteer work that local people performed to help build a barn, a new silo, or a church.

As the 19th century dawned, almost 80 percent of Québecers lived as habitants, and another system of land distribution, the township system — still familiar to us — began to grow alongside the seigneurial holdings. Tenured land favoured the wealthy seigneurs, and prevented economic and industrial progress, so, as the century reached midpoint, a bitter struggle to end the seigneuries ensued. Finally, in 1854, it was abolished and habitants could claim farmlands as their own.

By the end of the 18th century, a growing number of people held no land even in tenure. They worked as farmhands for landed peasants, and they, too, came to be called *habitants* in North American French. Eventually in Québécois, *habitant* meant simply any 'farmer.' In modern Québec French, it also carries a subsidiary meaning reeking of classist put-down. For example, *un habitant* can mean 'a person with boorish manners.' *Faites pas l'habitant icette* could be translated: 'Don't try that country hick act around here.' In the 19th and early 20th centuries, habitant in English referred to anyone from rural Québec, not always in a pejorative sense.

CALVABEC

Here is a modern, spritely portmanteau word that combines **calva**dos and Qué**bec** to name an eau-de-vie or brandy distilled from apple cider. Calvados is a department of Normandy in northern France noted for its apple brandy, also called calvados. In France, the short form is widely used when ordering in restaurants: *"Garçon, un calva, s'il vous plaît."* So it was natural to name a local apple brandy *un calva de Québec* or *un calvabec*.

PLUS JE BOIS
MIEUX JE CHANTE!

CHIARD

It means 'ground meat' in Québec, and also has the more general slang sense of 'grub.' Chiard also names a tasty fried hash: hamburger or leftover meat chopped up and fried with potatoes and onions, seasoned with the most popular herb in *la belle province*, savory. Diced salt pork was once a favourite ingredient of *chiard* or *chiards blancs* (white hash because of the potatoes). Once fried, this "grub" would keep for a day or two, and could be packed as a meal for a fisherman, hunter, or trapper going out on a short trip. In fact, it has variant names like *chiard de goélette* 'fishing-boat hash' and *chiard du pêcheur* 'fisherman's hash.'

Extended figurative meanings occur as well, where *un chiard* is 'a mess,' 'a large crowd of people,' and 'a small fight, a scrap.' "*Quel beau chiard!*" "What a major-league screw-up!"

Some authorities — those few who deign to speculate on the origins of French slang — suggest that the prime meaning of *chiard* is 'mess,' and that it begins as a popular cradle word for a child, and stems from the vulgar French verb *chier* 'to shit,' ultimately from Latin *cacare.* Thus, *chiard* has the verbal stem *chi-* and adds the common French pejorative and agent suffix *-ard*, so that its literal meaning is 'shitter,' but in its use as a French nursery term, *chiard* is playfully applied and means 'little shitter' as an endearment. In the slang of present-day France, *chiard* is still used this way. So, could it have once named a fecal-brown hash? Seems quite likely. The *Petit Robert*, a well-known French dictionary, states that *chiard* to describe a child is a coinage of the mid-20th century. I suggest, first, that we know the verb *chier* has been in French since the 13th century, and, second, that *chiard* was coined hundreds of years before the mid-20th century, and carried by immigrants from northern France to the new world as a humorous tag for a peasant hash.

CIPAILLE

Here is a word for a layered meat pie familiar to all who love Québec cookery. Not so well known is the delightful linguistic dispute attached to this term. Both French and English claim its origin. According to most recent etymological probings, Québec's *cipaille* is just the English phrase *sea pie* wearing French spelling. Borrowed from British nautical slang — where it named leftovers of meat and vegetables layered in a big pot since at least 1751 — sea pie now is a deep-dish meat pie made by layering assorted uncooked, cubed meats inside a pastry-lined Dutch oven. Herbs, onions, potatoes are added, then bouillon, and perhaps wine. Nineteenth-century British sailors spoke of two- or three-decker sea pies.

But one alternative source is warmly embraced by French etymologists who state that *cipaille* derives ultimately from Latin *caepa* 'onion' because both the dish and the bulb have many layers. To arrive at the French form *cipaille*, one might posit an intermediary diminutive or affectionate form like **cepallus* 'little onion.' **Cepallus* is a hypothetical construct — that's what some linguists call an informed guess, and that's what the asterisk means. However, *caepulla* 'onion bed' is an attested form in a farming handbook written in postclassical Latin in a manuscript dated around AD 350. Latin *caepulla* is the source of the modern Italian word for onion, *cipolla*. In fact, the Italian could be the transmission form into French, through one of the southern French dialects, in a chain that might look like this: *cipollo > cipallo > cipaillo > cipaille*.

Which origin is correct? Well, the British sea pie is the earliest in print, by 1751. But that is no proof that French borrowed it from English. We must await printed or written evidence that *cipaille* appears earlier than sea pie. Then perhaps we can begin to sift such evidence.

On every list of traditional Québec foods, *cipaille* was and is a particular favourite at *Réveillon*, the Christmas feast after Midnight Mass on Christmas Eve. Throughout the province there are many regional variations of *cipaille*, and in some places the food is called *tourtière* (see entry in this chapter), although that term usually describes a shallow-dished, thinner-crusted, unlayered meat pie. The Aboriginal Montagnais people of Québec adapted wheat flour, which arrived with white settlers, to create their own distinctive version of *cipaille* where the meat is a selection of wild game. In their earliest recipe, the dish was cooked in an earthenware pot and the dough pastry was put only on top of the pot contents near the end of the cooking. A big sea pie is still the favoured provender of a high feast among the Montagnais and may simmer for six hours, with each vast pot feeding twenty-five feasters.

Traditional meats in a *cipaille* included venison, pheasant, hare, or duck. After imported spices had been made regularly available in the province, the sweet pungency of cloves became *de rigueur* in the *cipaille* of some districts of Québec. Nowadays, the ubiquity of these wizened little flowerheads of the tropical clove tree have made cooks blasé about their inclusion. Often, today, spicing of *cipaille* consists of salt and pepper and a trite mélange of cloves, nutmeg, cinnamon, and allspice.

CIPÂTE

In some Québec places, *cipâte* is a synonym for *cipaille* to name a layered meat pie. There is even a local variant, *cipâre*. The Gaspé region boasts a salmon *cipâte*. French folk etymology suggests that *cipâte* is a shortened form of *six-pâtes* 'six pastries,' alluding to the numerous layers.

CLENNEDAK

This is a children's candy in the form of a cone of taffy. The name of this candy kiss is derived from a brand name, Klondyke, after the gold rush locality of the Klondike. The candy is also referred to in spoken Québécois as *kiss* or *tire*.

CRETONS

This, the favourite potted meat dish in the whole province, is a coarse *pâté de champagne* of medieval origin, made of ground pork and pork fat flavoured with cinnamon and cloves. The pâté is made from parts like pork shoulder and kidney put through a meat grinder and then into a saucepan with onions, garlic, salt and pepper. Add water; heat to a boil; simmer for two hours. The mixture is put into cold bowls or moulds (thus "potted"), and let stand to cool. Then it goes into the fridge to "mature" for one or two days.

In Old French, *creton* or *criton* designated a piece of pork fat fried in a pan. But *creton* has virtually disappeared from modern European French. The dish called *cretons* in Québec is similar to *pot de rillettes*, a potted mince of pork which is one of the specialties of Tours. Other European synonyms are *rillons* or *rillettes* by itself, both from 15th-century French *rille* 'a strip of lard.'

CROQUIGNOLE

In Québec, a *croquignole* is a homemade doughnut fried in lard. In France, it's a small, dry, crunchy biscuit, its name derived from *croquer* 'to crunch (between the teeth).'

ÉPLUCHETTE

Here's a Québec coinage, in print from 1862, to name a social and working occasion, a corn-husking bee, a shuckfest as it's called in Iowa. Although these pleasant get-togethers have vanished with the advent of automatic husking machines, another use has sprung up, in the current phrase, *épluchette de blé d'Inde* 'corn-roast,' held as a party, part of a family reunion, or to raise money for charitable purposes. *Éplucher* 'to peel' is ultimately from Latin *ex* 'off, out' + *pilus* 'hair, skin, fur.' Latin *pilare* 'to deprive of hair or skin' is the source of our English verb, to peel. Latin *pilus* also gives us the pile of a carpet (its 'hair').

ERMITE

This is a sharp, salty blue cheese made by monks of the Benedictine monastery at St.-Benoît-du-Lac in the eastern townships of Québec and named 'the hermit' or *l'ermite* because the place is a well-known Roman Catholic retreat. The Saint Benoît in the name of the locality is, of course, Saint Benedict of Norcia, founder of the Benedictine Order. The lake is the nearby and wonderfully named Memphremagog, which is a slight mangling of its first name in the Abenaki language, *mamhlawbagak* 'wide stretch of water,' referring to the forty-four-kilometre length of the body of water.

GALETTE DES ROIS (TWELFTH NIGHT COOKIE)

Three Kings' Biscuit is a treat baked on the church feast of Epiphany, January 6, commemorating the coming of the three wisemen or Magi to worship the baby Jesus. The feast of Epiphany is also called Twelfth Night in English. Roman Catholic immigrants to North America brought this traditional confection from France. Each little cookie usually contains one bean, *la fève des Rois*, the bean of the Magi.

The word *galette* has been in continental French from the 13th century to denote a flat round cake, derived from an older but still extant word *galet* 'a flat beach pebble polished by wave action.' *Galet* is a diminutive form of *gal* 'rock, stone' from Gaulish *gallos* 'stone.'

An older bit of comic dismissal in *joual*, the lively slang of Québec, is: *baise ma galette!* or buzz off! Literally, of course, it means 'kiss my cookie.' In old nautical French, galette was the word for hard tack biscuit, and it was used among French-speaking travellers across early Canada to refer to bannock bread done over a campfire or shanty cookstove. As well, galette is used to denote certain crêpes. In Québec and in some old regional dialects of France, *une galette de sarrasin* is a buckwheat pancake, while flat cornmeal cakes are *galettes de blé d'Inde*.

Other Uses of the Word *Galette*

This is french fries, cheese curds, sliced chicken, peas, and coleslaw, sometimes slathered with chicken gravy. The name of this homey slop arises from a vernacular French verb, *galvauder* 'to bum around,' with other connotations like 'misuse,' and 'desecrate,' especially with reference to words or names. So it might be said that this dish *galvaude(s)* the good name of poutine, of which this is really a culinary variation. See the *poutine* entry later in this chapter. *Galvauder* can also mean 'to chew food noisily,' 'to mess up something,' and 'to rummage around (in a drawer or closet),' therefore, as a recipe name, it might be translated playfully as 'sloshy slop.'

GALVAUDE

Gateau Jos. Louis is Québec's favourite packaged little cake invented by the Vachon family in the town of Sainte-Marie-de-la-Beauce. I grew up in southern Ontario and gobbled myriad Jos. Louis

GATEAU JOS. LOUIS

as a kid, to the undelight of parents and dentists. La Beauce, south of Québec City, home of vast maple stands, is one of the prettiest of Québec regions. The nickname of residents there, *les Beaucerons*, is *les jarrets noirs* 'the black hocks' referring to the black hocks of horses' feet that pulled farmers' wagons hauling produce to town along the muddy roads in days of yore. Among the local culinary features of la Beauce are *viande boucanée*, salt pork smoked in the rafters of a maple sugar shack, and an *omelette beauceronne* stuffed with lardons, tomatoes, and the mild *cheddar de la Beauce*.

GAUDRIOLE

A word coined in France to mean 'dirty joke' or 'trifling thing,' *gaudriole* in Québec referred to a mixture of oats, peas, and sometimes buckwheat, ground to a flour or rough meal and used to fatten pigs. Although it usually fed livestock, this mélange was eaten by humans in dire straits, according to the diaries of several early Québec settlers.

GIBELOTTE

Gibelotte de Sorel is a catfish or perch stew from les Îles de Sorel, islands off the little city of Sorel in the Côte du Sud region on the south shore of the

St. Lawrence, and east of Québec City. Every July there is a Gibelotte festival in Sorel, the fourth oldest city in Canada.

In popular speech of the province *gibelotte* has extensions of meaning like 'grub,' 'messy affair,' and the less common connotation of 'twaddle' or 'gibberish.' As a food term of France, *gibelotte*'s oldest meaning (1617) refers to a method of preparing fish. Then it came to name a *fricassée*, a stew of rabbit or fowl. *Gibelotte* is a variant of the earlier *gibelet* 'a dish of bird's flesh' from Old French *gibier* 'to hunt fowl.' Middle English borrowed *gibelet* to give giblets, the edible viscera of birds.

GORLOT

A French dialectic variant of *grelot*, whose original meaning was a bell tied to an animal's neck, *gorlot* referred in Québec first to sleigh bells on a cutter or on a horse's neck. By later analogy, *gorlot* denoted a very small, round, "new" potato. A juicy bit of provincial slang arose using this word as well, when gorlot acquired the slang meaning of 'mouth' or 'voice.' *"Ferme ton gorlot"* equalled "Shut up!" or literally 'stop your sleigh bell, shut your mouth.'

In some regional dialects of Québec, the original French form *grelots* 'sleigh bells' has the vulgar meaning of 'balls' or 'testicles,' while its metathetical form *gorlot* can mean 'dumbbell' or 'practical joker.' A busy pair of wordlets, this *grelot-gorlot* duo.

GOUDILLE
or GUÉDILLES

Un goudille is a heap of mayonnaise-gooped coleslaw served on a hot dog bun, a sort of very deprived and forlorn submarine sandwich. One slightly improbable source of this Québecism has been suggested, namely, the English vernacular term, *goody* 'something good to eat, a treat, a tasty food.' A particularly notable regional variation from the Gaspé is *guadielle* or pieces of boiled lobster in butter presented on a toasted hot dog bun.

GOURGANE

Gourgane is one of the most popular of Québec beans, a large green bean with red stripes, especially popular in cookery of the Charlevoix region and in the Saguenay where *soupe aux gourganes* is a local delight. The *gourgane* is a variety of the *fève des Marais,* a French bog-bean from the famous area around Paris brought to *la Nouvelle France* by the earliest colonists. Farms in the Lac-Saint-Jean area grow billions of gourganes for export every season.

GRAND-PÈRE

Standard French for grandfather, in Québec this is a dumpling boiled in water, soup, or broth, and eaten with maple syrup.

HERBES SÂLÉES

Herbes sâlées were the result of a special way that cooks in New France preserved herbs through the long winter. They mixed fresh herbs and vegetables in alternating layers in thick brine, bottled it, and used spoonfuls of *herbes sâlées* 'salted herbs' to flavour winter soups and stews. Many chefs both at home and in restaurant kitchens declare that no pea soup 'soupe aux pois' can be pronounced authentically *Québécoise* unless it be flavoured with *herbes sâlées.* Especially zingy bottles of *herbes sâlées* are often available in gourmet food shops throughout Québec, the best being *Herbes sâlées du bas du fleuve* made by J.Y. Roy at Ste.-Flavie, gateway to the Gaspé region, or as its promotional literature reads *"la Porte de la Gaspésie."*

LARDON

Lardons begin and accompany many traditional recipes of Québec. They are what the British call streaky bacon, that is, salt pork strips fried to make browning fat or eaten crispy as a side dish, much like fat back or Newfie scrunchins. Salt pork *lardons* often join cod and other fish in a gently heated frying pan. Fine-cut *lardon* slices are also part of some omelettes.

MECHOUI

Popularized by some of Montréal's 125,000 Lebanese people and others from the Middle East, this is the Arabic word for barbecue, usually a whole side of wild boar or venison or bison (!) rotated on a motorized spit, slowly, at a family reunion, company picnic, or wherever food for a large party is needed. Arabic *mechoui* is literally 'skewered,' hence 'barbecued.'

OKA

The most renowned of Québec cheeses, Oka gains its unique flavour during a special curing process in which the semihard cheese rounds are painted with brine, originally by Trappist monks at their Abbey of Notre-Dame-du-Lac, called *La Trappe*, just west of Montréal and still one of the largest Cistercian monasteries in the world. Much in the news is the nearby Kanesatake reserve where more than 800 Mohawk people live. Oka takes its name from a former Algonquian tribe who named themselves after their totemic animal, the *okow*, called the dory or golden pickerel in Canadian English, a golden-coloured, sweet-tasting fish still said to frolic in nearby waters and known commonly in Québec as *poisson doré*.

OUANANICHE

This prize eating fish of Lac-Saint-Jean, Lac Mégantic, and certain other lakes in Ontario and Québec is now very scarce and was never plentiful. It is a small, landlocked, fresh-water salmon of the

Atlantic salmon family, whose zoological tag is *Salmo salar ouananiche.* The word was borrowed directly in Canadian French from the Montagnais language where *wananish* means 'little salmon,' *-ish* being a common diminutive ending in this Algonquian tongue. Excessive sport fishing and industrial pollution sealed the fate of this delicate-fleshed creature. Near the town of Roberval there still flows the Rivière Ouananiche, but few 'little salmon' leap upstream to spawn now.

PAIN

There are several interesting expressions unique to provincial French that contain the word for 'bread,' among them *pain-fesses*, a double bread-loaf shaped like human buttocks. After all, English has its 'buns.' *Être né pour un petit pain* is 'to be born into the underclass,' to be a second-class citizen by birth and to be assured of only bread scraps. Homemade bread in Québec is *pain d'habitant.* French toast is *pain doré. Perdre un pain de sa fournée* is literally 'to lose a loaf in the oven' but means 'to be very disappointed' or 'to have cold water thrown on one.' *Ambitionner sur le pain bénit* means 'to go way overboard,' 'to take outrageous advantage of a situation,' *le pain bénit* being the consecrated bread of Holy Communion.

My favourite bread term from old Québec is *pain Jack*, a square loaf of a French bread said to derive from *pain Jacobin*, which might have been bread baked by Dominicans at their first convent in Paris situated on the Rue St. Jacques near an old Parisian entrance route, St. James' Gate, which was *porta Jacobina* in monkish medieval Latin. Or *pain Jack* might recall a loaf popular with the later Jacobins, the ruthless terrorists of the French Revolution.

PÂTÉ CHINOIS

Pâté chinois is basically shepherd's pie, called Chinese pie in Québec. Julian Armstrong, in her excellent recipe book, *A Taste of Quebec*, gives the following origin: "The name has been traced by Quebec food historian Claude Poirier to a town in the state of Maine called China. In the late 19th century, thousands of Quebecers migrated to the northeastern United States to work in the mills. Those who settled in the town of China returned eventually to Quebec with a recipe for shepherd's pie which they called *pâté chinois*."

PINTADINE

Although this is the standard French word for guinea hen, used in France and Québec, *pintadine* here is a large guinea hen specially bred as gourmet fowl on the Île d'Orléans. One of the scrumptious local recipes for it is *pintadine de L'Île d'Orléans aux groseilles or* guinea hen in a red currant sauce. Pintadine is a French expansion (1819) of *pintade*, a word for the African guinea fowl borrowed in French around 1643 from Portuguese *pintada* 'painted [bird].'

The Québec nickname for people born on the Île d'Orléans is *les Poireaux* or "Leeks" since les Orléannois put leeks instead of onions in their quiches, and also in their pea soups.

PLORINE

This is a type of Québec pork pie made of seasoned, chopped pork topped with a cap of pastry dough and fried. *Plorine* means 'old horse,' 'nag,' or 'ugly woman.'

PONCE

Among Acadiens and speakers of Québec French, this is a hot toddy given by mothers to children with colds and — with more alcohol added — a traditional drink to warm an adult after a winter outing. Hot water, alcohol, honey, and lemon are the common ingredients of this toddy. Dozens of variations exist using cognac, gin, rum, and spices like nutmeg or cinnamon sticks.

Ponce is a northern French dialect form of *ponche*, itself a variant of *punch*, borrowed into French as early as 1673. Later French writers, especially Voltaire and Rousseau, popularized the spelling *punch*. Punch had entered English by

1632, brought back from India by returning officers of the East India Company who had enjoyed a mixed drink there made with five traditional ingredients: rum, water, lemon, sugar, and spice. *Panch* is the Hindi word for the numeral five. In Persian, five is *panj*; in Sanskrit, a classical language of ancient India, five is *panchan*. These are all Indo-European languages distantly related to English, German, Latin, and even to Greek where the word for five is the similar *pente*, as in our terms *pentagram* and *pentagon*.

Another putative origin lies in a British naval word for a big barrel used on board sailing vessels to store rum, a puncheon, a large cask from which sailors were offered drinks.

POULAMON *or* PETIT POISSON DES CHENAUX (TOMMYCOD)

Tommycod, once abundant in the St. Lawrence, have been much reduced by pollution. But there is still an annual ice fishing derby for these *petits poissons des chenaux* held every January and February at Ste-Anne-de-la-Pérade. Tommycod come out of the St. Lawrence in midwinter, swimming into smaller streams to spawn. Then the Saint Anne River is crowded with hundreds of heated fishing cabins put on the thick ice. Tommycod is fished through holes in the ice inside the little cabins. Lit up at night, the windows of these *cabanes* give wintry twinklings to the frozen stretch of river which seems suspended in light between white snow and black star-flecked sky.

Poulamon was borrowed into early North American French in our Maritimes where it is the word for tommycod in the language of the Mi'kmaq people. To ichthyologists, tommycod is *Microgadus tomcod*. For more about the etymology of the word *cod*, see its main entry in the chapter on Newfoundland food words.

POUTINE

This word named many kinds of food in Québec and Acadia. Here we discuss only the modern Québec dish and provincial uses of the word. For details on Acadian use as in *poutines râpées* and *poutine au pain*, please see the *poutine* entry under Acadian food words.

Now pronounced [poo-TSIN] in Canadian French, the word stems ultimately from the English word *pudding*. Fascinatingly, it has been borrowed at least four different times into French. *Le pudding* was in French print by 1678 to denote a pudding steamed in a cloth bag. This acquired several variants including *le pouding* and, in northern France, *poudin*. Then again in 1753 French geologists borrowed an English phrase, pudding stone, that named a certain kind of conglomerate of pebbles embedded in a finer matrix. This went into French geology as *la poudingue*. The third borrowing happened along the shores of the Mediterranean. Pudding had been borrowed into Italian by *i nizzardi*, natives of the city of Nice and surrounding territory. In the dialect of Nice, pudding became *la poutina*, but it named a mess of fried sardines and anchovies done in lemon and oil and used to accompany a soup or even to fill an omelette. In the south of France, maritime cooks borrowed the Italian word and named this fishy Italian fry *poutine*. Finally, northern French people immigrating to North America, to become eventually Acadians, reborrowed pudding as *poutine* and began the evolution of its present pronunciation [poo-TSIN].

The most recent reincarnation — or should we say re-empuddingment — of poutine happened in Québec in the fall of 1957, and made poutine the most familiar Québec food word in North America, to the chagrin of Quebecers proud of the gourmet delights of their provincial cookery. Why, they wonder, does poutine get all the fanfare while truly exquisite and scrumptious recipes like *pintadine de L'Île d'Orléans aux groseilles* do not receive the attention they deserve? Perhaps more people like junk food than appreciate guinea hen in a red currant sauce?

Today's poutine is a serving of thick-cut French fries, topped with fresh cheese curds and hot gravy poured on top of the curds before serving or, by some cooks, served in a little gravy dish on the side so the fries do not get soggy. Two men claim to have invented this poutine in the fall of 1957 in a region of the province's Eastern Townships called Bois-Francs "hardwoods" just south of the St. Lawrence. In Warwick, Québec, near Victoriaville, halfway between Montréal and Québec City, Fernand Lachance, *"le père de la poutine,"* and his wife Germaine operated the Café Ideal. One of the *piliers du café* 'regulars' was truck driver Eddy Lainesse. Now the region of Bois-Francs is dairy country, famous for its fresh cheese curds, and M. Lachance sold little boxes of the fresh curd in his eatery. One autumn day, Eddy Lainesse suggested mixing the cheese curds with fries. *Et voilà!* The gravy was not beef gravy at first, but Germaine Lachance's special recipe of brown sugar, ketchup, and a plop or two of Worchestershire sauce. After interviewing these three innovators for the October 9, 1997, edition of the *Globe and Mail*, reporter Tu Thanh Ha points out just how popular this poutine is in the province: "Burger King's decision to add it to the menu in 1992 generated an extra $2-million in curds business for Warwick's Fromagerie Côté." Wherever Quebecers travel in numbers, from Alberta to New England, they like to see on distant menus some home dish; for some residents especially that *mets à la maison* is poutine. I've eaten it in a Manhattan restaurant — but the cheese curds had been stored in a refrigerator too long and were rubbery. Restaurants in Florida that cater to vacationing snowbirds from Québec actually fly in fresh curds by air freight.

RÉGALE

The special Canadian, now obsolescent use of this medieval French word for festive celebration involved the canniness of the superintendent factors of the North West Company, and later the Hudson's Bay Company. Drinking on post property was discouraged. But when trappers were setting out on a long, possibly hazardous canoe journey, probably returning to tend distant traplines, they were issued a pint of rum, with the understanding that said spirits should be drunk well away from the fort or trading post. A rum régale might be passed out to men coming in after a lengthy trip too, as long as they went off in the bush to drink it. A ration of liquor, usually a noggin of rum, given out on New Year's Eve or near Christmas, was also a régale. When whites and Aboriginal trappers had been given their rum ration and were getting ready to party, their wives and womenfolk, long before the preparation of festive foods, often took the initial precaution of hiding all the knifes, rifles, bows and arrows, and other objects that might become weaponry if party antics escalated to violence.

Distinct, modern Québec terms for what the British call "a right piss-up" or wild drinking party include *une buverie, une fringue, une ripe,* and *une soûlade.*

SMITH BROTHERS COUGH DROPS™

Smith Brothers cough drops are throat soothers invented by a restaurant owner in St. Armand, Québec, one James Smith. After his death, when his two sons, William and Andrew, took over the cough drop business, they put the engravings of their own bearded selves on the box as a trademark. Many suckers of cough drops thought the two hirsute worthies were inventions of an advertising artist, and that their names were Trade and Mark.

TARTE À LA FERLOUCHE

Tarte à la ferlouche is a yummy raisin-and-molasses pie. Several spelling variants exist, like *farlouche, ferluche* and *forlouche*. It is popular from the Outaouais region along the Ottawa River on the Québec side all the way east to Acadian country. The word may be of Aboriginal origin, but I have been unable to find an exact source. Anyone who knows the provenance of *ferlouche*, please write and tell me.

TARTE AU SUCRE

This familiar Québec brown-sugar pie has an addition when done *à la Gaspésienne*. Scottish-style rolled oats are mixed with the brown sugar — sometimes maple sugar or maple syrup is added — and spread over a pastry crust. A latticed pastry top covers the pie, and evaporated milk is poured through the pastry strips just before ovening. No calorie-counters should nibble even a small slice of *tarte au sucre*! In regional varieties of this pie, crunch is added to the filling by the inclusion of different kinds of nutmeats, while other cooks put fruit preserves in the sugar-and-oats mix.

TOURTIÈRE

A *tourtière* is a shallow meat pie with onions, often flavoured with the traditional French medieval spice combo of cinnamon and cloves. In kitchens along the majestic Saguenay River, a *tourtière* can be quite a production, consisting of cubed meat, potatoes, onions baked in many layers in a deep, pastry-lined casserole: in other words, what would have been called a *cipaille* or *pâté de famille* in older days is here a *tourtière de Saguenay*. In 1836 in Québec, a *tourtière* was a pork pie. One local *tourtière* became a favourite of Scottish and British soldiers posted to the citadel at Québec City who then stayed on, buying outskirt farms and growing oats. Thus, in one Québec City *tourtière* oatmeal thickens the ground pork filling instead of the traditional French potatoes.

The food *tourtière* took its name from the utensil in which it was baked. The original *tourtière*, in French print by 1573, was a pie pan for baking *tourtes*. In old French cookery, a *tourte* was a round pastry pie with a pastry top and filled either with meat and vegetables if it was a savoury or with fruit and cream if it was a dessert *tourte*. This word stems from the street Latin phrase *tortus panis* 'a round of bread.' The word *tourtière* also names the mould used to make these pastry *tourtes*. This *tourtière* has an expandable circumference, can be made of porcelain, clay, or glass, and can serve as a pie dish, a tart mould, or a flan ring.

GASPÉ FOOD TERMS

Gaspé derives from the Mi'kmaq word *gespeg* 'end of our land,' and indeed the peninsula is the traditional northern limit of Mi'kmaq territory. One nickname of Gaspé residents in Québec French, which local people do not always appreciate but which is nevertheless colourful, is *mangeurs de morue* 'cod-gobbers.' Residents must admit that cod is here THE fish. For example, *bouillabaisse gaspésienne* is a local version of the famous stew that naturally features codfish. There are English speakers in the Gaspé region, and they too have some distinctive food lingo which I present below along with French terms. It is said of the rare, bad cook in the Gaspé and northern New Brunswick: "That cook couldn't parboil shit for a tramp."

BREAD/*PAIN*

Bread from outdoor bake ovens in the Gaspé and New Brunswick can be flavoured depending on what kind of wood burns in the oven, thus one stills hears about birchbark bread, pine bread, and maple bread.

BUGGER-IN-A-BAG

Bugger-in-a-bag around Cascapedia Bay is a fresh-raspberry pudding in a cotton bag that has been oiled and floured to make it waterproof. The bugger is steamed for several hours and served with a sweet sauce.

CAKIN'

Cakin' around New Richmond on the Gaspé peninsula is visiting neighbours during the twelve days of Christmas, to receive a piece of Christmas cake. Receiving and eating twelve pieces of cake, each one made by a different neighbour, is said to bring good luck throughout the twelve months of the new year.

CARRY TOS

Carry tos to mean 'any form of social welfare' is used around Shigawake in the Gaspé. It's a bit of franglais or an anglicization of a word in ecclesiastical Latin, *caritas* 'Christian love of one's fellow humans,' and the origin, through French, of the word *charity*.

CHAUSSONS AUX POMMES

Chaussons aux pommes is a fancy Malbaie dessert in which a whole apple is sugared, cinnamoned, and wrapped up in pastry, then baked and presented with a gooey crown of maple syrup and whipped

cream. It originated in one of the France's best apple-growing areas of Normandy where it is still called *la pomme en cage*. Malbaie is near the famous Percé rock on an eastern tip of the Gaspé peninsula. It was named "bad bay" because numerous sandbars or *barachois* along the shore of the Gulf of St. Lawrence made putting ashore tricky or impossible for pilots of sea-going ships long ago.

Cipâte gaspésien is a layered, pastry-topped, salmon pie, cousin to the many *cipâtes québécois* whose layers contain no fish.

CIPÂTE GASPÉSIEN

Elbow cake is Mi'kmaq English, from the Maria Band in the Gaspé, to name a hot biscuit. The words for 'bread' and 'elbow' are phonetically similar in Mi'kmaq: *looskaneegan*. The surface of the hot biscuit vaguely resembles the skin pattern at the human elbow.

ELBOW CAKE

A humorous put-down happens here in the term *Gaspé steak*. It is always fried bologna, a staple of lumbercamp cooking.

GASPÉ STEAK

Horse beans are Windsor broad beans (*Vicia faba*), popular in the cold, wet soil of the Gaspé. Horse beans are shelled and boiled or baked. They can also be dried and stored for winter use.

HORSE BEAN

Laughin' potatoes are new, dry potatoes that burst their skins when cooked. And whether the split taties appear to be exploding with mirth, or whether it is the sound they make when they burst, their nickname is apt.

LAUGHIN' POTATOES

MOTHER OF VINEGAR

Mother of vinegar, also called "the old woman," is an acetobacillus culture allowed to grow at the bottom of the vinegar bottle, for use as a starter the next time vinegar is made.

PEDRIX AUX CHOUX

Perdrix aux choux from the Percé area of Gaspé is partridge with cabbage, and perhaps sausage, salt pork, carrots, and onions.

POUDING DU CHÔMEUR

Pouding du chômeur is a 'welfare pudding' in which cake batter is baked and then drenched with brown-sugar syrup. *La chômage* is unemployment insurance in Québec. *Un chômeur* is someone on the dole. In France, the French verb *chômer* from which *chômeur* and *chômage* sprang has less pejorative meanings. *Chômer* is 'to take off work during holidays,' and 'to be unemployed due to legitimate lack of work.'

Word Lore of *Chômer*

The root of the verb *chômer* is intriguing, because, tracing it, we can observe an ancient word rolling down through the millennia to its eventual place in the modern vocabulary of Romance languages. It begins with a term that appears almost 3,000 years ago in one of the founding masterpieces of western literature, *The Iliad* of Homer, where *kauma* means 'the burning heat of the sun.' The same Greek root, found in *kaiein* 'to burn,' gives the English *caustic* and *holocaust*. However, the Romans borrowed the word into late, postclassical Latin as *cauma* where it meant 'the hot part of the day, siesta-time.' For example, the word was used by St. Jerome about AD 384 – 404 when he was making a Latin translation of the Bible from its original Hebrew and Koine Greek, to establish a standard edition sanctioned by the early Catholic Church. The name of this translation of the Bible was *editio vulgata* 'common edition.' It is known in English as the Vulgate. St. Jerome used *cauma* in his translation of the Book of Job to render a Hebrew word that meant 'severe heat.'

In later Latin, a verb was formed and *caumare* meant 'to rest during the strong heat of midday, to take a siesta.' *Caumare* evolved into its early French form *chômer* by 1150 and developed meanings like 'to rest in the shade during the heat of the day' [at first said of cattle] and then 'to break off work during the heat.' More modern senses followed: 'to abstain from work during feast days' and then 'to be idle due to lack of work' and finally 'to be on welfare due to lack of work.'

The Late Latin verb *caumare* took one other little pathway into the Romance languages worth noticing. When it entered early Italian a letter *l* was infixed to produce *calmare*. This *l* just made the word easier to pronounce for the earliest speakers of Italian. Similarly, Late Latin *cauma* became *calma* in Italian. *Calma* was at first a nautical term in early Italian and meant 'absence of wind' at sea. This was quite a natural expansion of the original sense of *cauma* as the hottest part of the day, noontide, when the Mediterranean sun burned brightest, when beasts of the field rested, when the winds ceased and the warm air was still, and the very fields seemed *calm*. At such a time of day it was only natural that humans, too, would seek the sweet lassitude of repose, an interval of pleasant rest for aching muscles in the shade of trees. In Spain, people would call it a siesta.

SIESTA

Permit me a teeny digression here to explain the word *siesta*. It is Spanish, in full *la siesta hora* 'the sixth hour,' brought to ancient Hispania by Roman soldiers when they conquered the Iberian peninsula. The Spanish stems directly from Latin *sexta hora*. The Romans reckoned time by dividing the night into four watches and the day into twelve hours. A watch was *vigilium*, hence our vigil. The hours of the day *'horae dies'* were count-ed from sunrise to sunset. The *sexta hora* 'sixth hour' after dawn was midday, approximately noon, the warmest time. In Spain, *la siesta hora* was shortened to *siesta* and came to mean 'mid-day heat' and then an 'afternoon nap' taken to escape working when the sun was hottest. Along the northern littoral of the Mediterranean and later in the Spanish colonies of America, business was suspended during siesta and workers went home for a light meal, a sleep, and often the best sex of the day.

RID UP

In the northern parts of our Maritimes including the Gaspé, to rid up or red up is to clean the table after a meal and make it all tidy for the next meal, which is what we shall do now, as we abandon our *chômage* and move briskly on to the next chapter.

CHAPTER 7

Ontario

As the glaciers retreated about 10,000 years ago, during the last ice age, the first human beings migrated into northern Ontario as fishers and hunters. By about AD 100 the Algonquian and Iroquoian peoples had formed linguistically distinct tribal units, so there were Ojibwa, Cree, and Algonquin peoples to the north, and in the south Iroquois, Huron, Petun, Neutral, Erie, and Susquehannock peoples. A number of their food words eventually entered English and some are discussed in this chapter. The first significant settlement of Europeans in present-day Ontario was the Jesuit mission at Sainte Marie Among The Hurons, abandoned in 1649 because of dangers from the

Iroquois Wars. The next immigration of meaningful numbers was the influx of 6,000 to 10,000 Loyalists during and immediately after the American Revolution of 1776. More French speakers came as well, but larger groups from the British Isles later helped cement the Anglo-Saxon character of the province. Peoples from the West Indies and Asia have come more recently, especially to the Toronto area, along with immigrants from all over the world, making Toronto the focus of immigration to Canada. Thus, to discuss the plenitude of international cuisines that can be enjoyed, particularly in urban Ontario restaurants, and the riches of culinary vocabulary that accompany it, would take a thousand-page book in itself. So we must leave for another volume any all-inclusive feast of world food words, from Caribbean jerk chicken to the delicious Chinese lunch of plumply stuffed dumplings called dim sum — from Cantonese *dim sam* literally 'little bit-heart' but the phrase implies a little speck of goodness that gladdens your stomach and your heart. Here I give a lively sample of Ontario food words, one I hope will intrigue anyone who wants to begin exploring our teeming verbal larder.

BAKE-KETTLE BREAD

In a fascinating book about early 19th-century pioneering, *The Canadian Settlers' Guide* (1855) by Catherine Parr Traill, instructions are given for baking bread when no oven is available. Fill your well-greased bake-can half full of the kneaded dough, advises the author, cover the bake-can with a metal lid and set it at a moderate distance from the fire. When the dough has risen within a few inches of the top, place live coals (wood embers) from the fire below the pan and on top of the lid. Carefully turn the pan to ensure that the sides of the loaf brown, and, "when a crust is hard and bears pressure without sinking in, the bread is done."

The tail of Canada's largest and most symbolic rodent, *Castor canadensis*, is edible, in a dish called beavertail beans, for example, in which the tail is cut off and blistered over a fire until the skin loosens. After the skin is removed, the tail flesh is boiled in a large pot of beans.

But beaver tail also came to be applied to a recipe for quick-baked dough, especially in early 19th-century places where people might camp for one night and where there was no frying pan. The dough, with or without one of the "risings" (see entry in this chapter), was shaped into a long, narrow, flat loaf, vaguely resembling a beaver's tail, stuck on one or more sticks, and baked over an open fire.

BEAVER TAIL

One particular form of this "bread," adapted from a recipe in Renfrew County in Ontario, has become very popular at Winterlude, Ottawa's annual cold weather festival. Indeed Pam and Grant Hooker's Beavertails are the culinary hit of every winter carnival in Canada's capital city. The Hookers adapted an old family recipe, from a grandmother who lived near Medicine Hat, based on a German dish called *Küchl* or *Kökle* — 'little cake.' To make Hooker's Beavertails, a swatch of sweet, whole-wheat pastry dough is put through a roller and stretched out to a vaguely beavertail-like shape, then it is fried for a minute or two in hot vegetable oil. The fried dough is then painted with melted butter and various savoury toppings are applied. Among the Hooker's best-selling Beavertails are those bedecked with cinnamon and sugar. They have many franchise operations across Canada. A popular Beavertail at the British Columbia skiing resort of Whistler is one slathered with cream cheese and smoked Pacific salmon.

OTTAWA'S BEAVERTAILS

But, to repeat, there was a 19th-century dough item called a beaver tail. Here is a reference in print from 1896 in a book called *Explorations in the Far North* by Frank Russell: "If the traveler has no frying pan the bread is baked in a 'beaver tail.' Such a loaf is long and narrow and is exposed to the fire upon a stick, the lower end being set in the ground, two or three cross sticks, the size of an ordinary skewer, are required to prevent the loaf from breaking and falling as it breaks." A few years earlier, a Canadian author of outdoor books, Egerton Ryerson Young published *Stories from Indian Wigwams and Northern Campfires* in which he wrote: "When one side was down brown, it was turned over, and soon the 'beavers' tails' were ready for the hungry men."

BERRY CAKE

Aboriginal peoples from the Salish of Pacific shores to the Mi'kmaq of Atlantic coasts dried various berries and pressed them into small cakes as winter preserves. West Coast species such as purple salal-berries and ollalies (or salmonberries) were used, as well as more widely dispersed species like wild strawberries, blueberries, raspberries, and cranber-ries. The earliest white explorers learned to make berry-cake preserves from Aboriginal peoples.

BIRCH SYRUP

Yet another pioneer sweetener borrowed by whites from First Peoples is birch syrup, a sugary, purple-coloured treat made by boiling birchtree sap. Later experimenters trying to find new, fresh-tasting bev-erages to perk up the jaded palate used birch syrup as the basis for making birchsap ginger ale. Paper birch or canoe birch, *Betula papyrifera*, is wide-spread across much of Canada and provided these liquid delights, along with several of the other eight native species. Birch wine, an old continental cor-dial, is made from the thin, sugary sap of *Betula alba*, European white birch. The sap is collected in March, boiled down slightly with honey, cloves, and lemon peel, and then fermented with yeast. Birchwater tea, an infusion of the leaves, was once a specific for gout and rheumatism.

BOKKEPOOTJES

Bokkepootjes, 'goats' footsies,' are often available in Dutch bakeries in Canada, lovingly ovened for Canadians of Dutch descent. *Bokkepootjes* are pastries shaped like little hooves and dipped in chocolate. Medieval iconography associates the billy-goat with the devil. And *bokkepootjes* are devilishly tasty. In the Dutch term, you can see *bokke*, from the same root as the English word *buck* 'male goat.' *Pootjes* 'little feet (of an animal),' has the familiar and widespread Indo-European root for foot **ped* that appears as *pied* and *patte* in French, and in many Latin and Greek derivatives like pedal and podiatrist. Even English foot and Germanic *Fuss* are related — all one, big, wide, happy, foot family.

BOTZELBAUM PIE

In the Mennonite German dialect of Waterloo County, Ontario, this is a variant spelling and pronunciation of standard German *Purzelbaum* 'somesault.' The baked confection is thus a kind of upside-down pie, in which the dough is placed in the bottom of the pie tin, then the filling (made of flour, sugar, molasses, eggs, and water, spiced with cinnamon and cloves) is poured over the doughy bottom. While baking, the doughy part rises to the top. Any visiting *Topfgucker* will be delighted by the preparation of this dish. *Topfgucker* is a humorous noun heard in some German kitchens, literally a 'pot-peeper,' a nosy guest who peeks into every pot and saucepan to see what the cook is up to. The phenomenon is by no means confined to Teutonic cookrooms.

BROWN BISCUIT

This is hard tack made from wholewheat flour. Brown biscuit was taken by trappers going out on a line for several months, because it would keep all winter long. For an explanation of hard tack, its preparation and origin, see the *brewis* entry in the chapter on Newfoundland food words.

CALLALOO

Caribbean immigrants to Toronto brought the secrets of this lip-smacking stew or soup. Trinidad's callaloo is a hearty soup of greens like spinach fortified with crab, bacon, okra, and coconut milk. Many little variations of this soup exist, depending on which island developed the recipe. Callaloo as a word has been in Caribbean English since the middle of the 18th century. It is derived from American Spanish *calalú*, itself from an Aboriginal language of Central America where the calalu is a plant, an arum of the genus *Xanthosoma*, whose big, arrow-shaped, edible leaves were the original ingredient of the soup. The starchy tubers of some Xanthosoma species are also edible.

DREPSLEY SOUP

Many cultures have broth soups into whose boiling roil dumplings large or small are dropped, and this is a classic Mennonite version. The dialect form *drepsley* contains in its initial root a variant of the Germanic *Tropf* 'drop.' *Drepsley* might be a dialect form of one of those appositive compound nouns of which German is so fond, something like *Tropfshlich* in standard German, that is, Drop-Trick soup. When the chicken or beef stock reaches high boil, a runny batter made of flour, milk, and eggs is poured through a sieve or collander. Quickly put a lid on the pot of boiling broth, and turn the heat down. The little flour "dreps" are boiled at lower heat for four or five minutes, and the soup is served at once, so the "dreps" don't get too soggy with broth.

Fetschpatz is a German-Canadian dumpling treat you may find while grazing at the Kitchener Market in the heart of Ontario's Mennonite country. *Fetschpätzen* (one local spelling) are dumplings fried by dropping batter by the tablespoonful into hot fat and then dishing the dumplings up hot and slathered with maple syrup. The batter is often made of sour cream, flour, beaten eggs, baking soda, and *ein Fleck Salz* 'a little pinch of salt.'

Rather than an adjective + noun — *fett* (fat) + *Spatz* (sparrow) — the term is two nouns in apposition. *Fett* as a noun means 'lard.' This little dumpling, from its physical shape, is a lard-sparrow, *ein Fett-spatz.* The grease in which it was fried would have been originally lard.

FETSCHPATZ

GRAHAM GEMS

Reaching their highest popularity during the 1920s across Canada, a gem was a muffin baked in a fluted pan, a "gem" pan. Gems were often made from graham flour, a coarse wholewheat flour that is unsifted and was first processed by Sylvester Graham (1794 – 1851), an American food researcher who sought to improve longevity by reforming the eating habits of early 19th-century Americans. He died at the age of 57.

HAW EATERS

Haw eaters are Ontarians born and raised on Manitoulin Island. Their local word for themselves comes in three forms: run together as haweater, with a hyphen as haw-eater, and primly discrete as haw eater. They like hawberries, the dark-red fruit of a species of hawthorn common in northern Ontario. Haws can be lovingly ovened in pies, tarts, and strudels. Visitors to Manitoulin buy tasty haw jams too.

The word was brought to Canada by early immigrants from England and Scotland. One of the oldest berry names in English, haw pops up plump and ruddy in a glossary dated around AD 1000. Hawberry and hawthorn share an initial element which is cognate with Old High German *hag* 'enclosure.' The first meaning of haw in English was fence. Hawthorn bushes were early used to fence yards, hence hawthorn is fence-thorn. Our later word "hedge" is related to haw, and still hemming and hawing in some rural English dialects is church-haw for churchyard.

By the 14th century, 'enclosed yard' and 'pen for domestic animals' were common meanings for the word. Geoffrey Chaucer (1340 – 1400), the first great poet in English, used it that way, in "The Pardoner's Tale" from his *Canterbury Tales* written in Middle English: "Ther was a polcat in his hawe, That . . . hise capons hadde islawe." 'There was a polecat in his yard that his castrated roosters had slain [by pecking it to death].' A polecat is a smelly European weasel. Charming vignette. Chaucer used the word in its fruity sense in *The Former Age*: "They eten mast hawes and swyche pownage." 'They ate acorns and chestnuts (mast), hawthorn berries, and such pannage (pig food).'

A Dutch cousin of haw, Middle Dutch *hage* 'ground enclosed by a fence, park' gives both of the two names of the capital city of the Netherlands: *'s Gravenhage* 'The Count's Haw, or Park.' Modern English "The Hague" stems directly from the other name of the city in Dutch, *Den Haag* 'the hedge.' Both names refer to woods that were a royal hunting grounds surrounding a medieval palace. Such pleasant ripples in the pond of words waft us back to Ontario and a steaming mug of local tea described next.

HIGH HYSON

This was an early Ontario pioneer tea made from an infusion of fresh needles of the hemlock spruce, *Tsuga canadensis*, but named after a popular Victorian tea, the coarse, green Chinese tea *hyson*, dubbed like so many Chinese teas with a pleasant-sounding and auspicious name. Hyson is an Englishing of the Cantonese *hei-ch'un* 'bright spring.' It was also called hemlock tea, bush tea, and Yankee tea.

ICE CREAM SOCIALS

At the turn of the last century, an ice cream social was a festive get-together often sponsored by a church group to raise a few dollars for some charitable purpose. They were especially popular as outdoor gatherings on summer afternoons, perhaps on the parsonage lawn with entertainment provided by the local soprano essaying the intricacies of some Schubert *Lieder* followed by a recitation of lively

verse: "Next, Reverend Doalmer will brighten our modest fête with selected passages from Tennyson's 'In Memoriam.'" Nineteenth-century Canadians also flocked to strawberry socials, which remained popular well into the 20th century. The term *strawberry social* appears to have originated in Canada.

JAN IN DE ZAK

This means 'John in the Bag' in Dutch, and is Holland's version of the familiar European steamed pudding. Early Dutch immigrants to Ontario and our Prairies steamed the pudding in a rigorously cleaned pillowcase when no other cloth was available. *Jan in de zak* could include yeast if it were available, along with the usual pudding ingredients of flour, eggs, lukewarm scalded milk, and raisins, currants, and any fruit peel. After mixing the pudding contents in a large bowl, the pioneer cook covered the bowl and let the yeast rise in a warm place for just under an hour. The dough was then removed and rolled long to fit into a pillowcase. The open end was tied tightly and the pillowcase pudding was steamed for two or three hours. After being cut into slices with taut string, *Jan in de zak* was served with a brown-sugar-and-butter sauce, or, if that was not to hand, *stroopsaus* would do just fine. *Stroopsaus* was a Dutch molasses sauce. This was a highly esteemed pudding, much like Newfoundland's figgy duff. In fact, *Jan in de zak* may be the direct ancestor of that other steamed pudding of our Prairies, 'Son-of-a-Gun-in-a-Sack.'

LYED CORN

Tedious indeed was the early settlers' method of removing the skin from corn kernels to make corn mush and other dishes. The husked kernels had to be boiled in an alkali solution (hence lyed) until the kernels puffed up with water, the skins burst, and floated to the top to be skimmed off. Then the lyed corn had to be thoroughly washed and dried to remove all traces of the alkali. It was then ready to be made into several dishes, including corn mush or hominy, as American immigrants might have called it. Some English settlers called it corn frumenty. Corn mush, for example, required boiling again for two hours, with a little suet tossed in to make the corn split. Fur trappers' and voyageurs' provisions for large canoes usually included packs of lyed corn, to be made into mush over campfires along their routes.

MENOMINEE

Menominee is wild rice in the Ojibwa language (*meno* 'good' + *mini* 'grain, seed, berry'). This tall, gracefully swaying aquatic grass inhabits the shallows of some lakes and rivers in the Great Lakes region. *Zizania aquatica* was given its first European name by Jesuit missionaries in what became central Ontario. They called it *folle avoine* and English trappers later translated this to get the plant's earliest name in English, crazy oats. Called Canadian rice or Indian rice, it is now grown commercially, and many delight in its chewy texture and nutty flavour. The Ojibwa and other peoples harvested menominee by gliding a canoe into an undulant swatch of wild rice, bending each seed-heavy panicle over the canoe, and tapping the ripe panicles with a small stick, sending a shower of grain to the floor of the canoe.

MESS BEEF

Mess beef or mess pork was salt beef or pork imported in barrels made up of assorted cuts, as in this advertisement from the weekly *Quebec Gazette* of November 2, 1770: "Just imported from Cork . . . a few Barrels and Half Barrels of Irish Pork and Mess-Beef, and a few firkins of Hog's Lard."

MUSKIE

Muskie is a Canadian colloquial form of the name of this mighty, fighting sport fish of the Great Lakes, whose zoological name is *Esox masquinongy. Esox* is a Latin word for a European pike. Muskellunge is from the Ojibwa language where *mash kinonge* means 'great pike.' Prize muskies have been caught that weighed forty-five kilograms and reached a length of two and a half metres.

PABLUM

As the centre of food manufacturing in Canada, Ontario has coined many commercial brand names for various nutriments, and perhaps the most famous belonged to a baby food. Pablum! To think that a food so bland was invented by Canadians! Gosh, it's just not like us. Doctors Drake, Brown, and Tisdall, searching for a simple, nutritious breakfast for infants, spent many hours at Toronto's Hospital for Sick Children stirring vile gruels and loathsome porridges. Did they, like Macbeth's three witches, utter little rhymes as they whipped up their alimentary goo? In any case, Pablum first went on sale in 1930. Insipid it may be, but so wholesome! It contains wheat germ, alfalfa, oatmeal, cornmeal, wheatmeal, and other treats. When they came to christen their new product, the doctors or someone at the food company that was manufacturing the product did display a sense of humour. They found their name for the new cereal in Latin, where *pabulum* is the word for 'horse feed,' or 'animal fodder.' I like to think that the good doctors, in all their nurturant beneficence and tireless scientific inquisitiveness, nevertheless like all parents now and then, occasionally just wanted to stuff some kind of stodge into all those hungry, wailing mouths, and probably did think of their peckish little charges as livestock to be fed — wisely and lovingly, of course.

In northern Ontario around Finnish settlements, pulla is a braided Finnish bread spiced with cardamom and burnished with a glaze made from hot coffee and sugar.

PULLA

In pioneer days, before the appearance of storebought yeast, homemade leavening agents or starters had to be used during bread-making in the Ontario outback and in many other rural places across Canada. Emptyings or emptings were the prone-to-ferment lees left over after a substance had been processed. Among the leavens or risings used were the following:

RISINGS

Bran-rising – a leaven made from bran empty-ings soaked in water.

Hop-rising – a leaven used in what was called hop-yeast bread. Hop, *Humulus lupulus*, is a climb-ing plant of the hemp family whose dried female flowers have been used for thousands of years to flavour beer. English borrowed the practice and the word directly from Flanders where the Flemish word is *hoppe*.

Milk emptyings – fermented milk used as a leav-en. Susanna Moodie, in her 1852 journal of early Ontario homesteading, *Roughing It in the Bush*, men-tions her need to use milk emptyings.

Salt-rising – backwoodsmen and women often kept back a lump of sourdough to use as leaven in the next batch of bread and called this put-by leaven 'salt-rising.'

ROBIN RUN

The robin run in a Canadian sugarbush is the first flowing of maple sap, which is rich in sugar. After a robin run sap flow often diminishes or stops. Then follows the frog run, the secondary flowing of sap, not as sugary as the first, hence inferior for making maple syrup. Sugaring-off in the sugar bush in a sugar shanty has many terms not often met with elsewhere. One important word is spile. In a sugar bush the spile is the metal spout pound-ed into a maple tree to draw the sap. The word was brought to Canadian maple syrup production from Scottish dialects where a spile was a wooden peg, plug, or spigot.

SAGAMITÉ

Sagamité was, among the Huron people, a corn porridge or hominy. But much earlier it referred to a broth of boiled meat or fish among many Algonquin peoples. The word may have entered English directly first from the Ojibwa language where *kisagamite* means 'the broth is hot.' Compare also Cree *kisakumitew* 'it is a hot liquid.' Sagamité was one of the earliest Canadian food words to appear in print. For example, it is defined in 1633 in the *Relations des Jésuites* and a few years later, in 1665, is mentioned by the explorer Pierre Radisson. Aboriginal peoples, having made a thick broth of meat or fish, would also leave the broth to freeze solid in various waterproof birchbark containers called in Ojibwa *makak* or *onagan*, and thus have a 'portable' soup to take on winter journeys and heat up again quickly over a camp fire. Voyageurs called these containers *casseaux* or *cassots*.

SEA PIE

Borrowed from British nautical slang — where it has named leftovers layered in a big pot since at least 1751 — sea pie is an Ottawa Valley lumber-camp phrase for the Sunday meat dish, served with molasses and buns. Sea pie, or *cipaille* in Québec, is a deep-dish meat pie made by layering assorted uncooked meats inside a pastry-lined Dutch oven. Herbs, onions, and potatoes are added, then bouillon and perhaps wine. A big sea pie might be cooked for six hours and could feed twenty or thirty people. Québec's *cipaille* is just sea pie wearing French spelling. *Cipaille* was and is a particular favourite at *Reveillon*, the Christmas feast after Midnight Mass on Christmas Eve. For other details, see the entry for *cipaille* in the chapter on Québec food words.

CHAPTER 8

Manitoba

Although the Manitoba Act of 1870 created the province, its present boundaries were not set until 1912. The fur trade opened the area to European settlement. It had once been included in Rupert's Land, a huge territory granted to the Hudson's Bay Company in 1670. White explorers like Henry Hudson first visited the northern shores of Manitoba in 1619, searching for a northwest passage to the Orient. Instead, they found fur-bearing animals. The first settlement was Fort York, a trading post, established in 1612. Significant agricultural immigration took another two hundred years, and Lord Selkirk's Red River colony was established in 1812. The First Peoples spoke Cree in the north, along with Sioux and Chipewyan. Cree food words entered English and French at an early date and some, as you can read below, are still part of the Manitoba vocabulary that concerns food. Saulteaux-speaking First Peoples inhabited some of what became southern Manitoba. Later immigrants included British, French, German-speaking Mennonite farmers, Ukrainians, Poles, Icelanders, and many other ethnic strands.

Manitoba words, even some of the local food words, reflect the pluck and grit of those who homesteaded there. This courage still beats in the hearts of Manitoba people, as I discovered recently myself.

Two weeks before the Red River crested there last spring I was in Winnipeg, watching one of the most devastating floods in Manitoba history advance towards the city. My hosts had friends with a farm near Emerson on the Manitoba-United States border, so we drove down to help build sandbag dikes around their house and barns. On the highways going south we passed thundering convoys of military vehicles and police checkpoints. During two days at that farm I heard Manitoba sayings I will never forget. As we lugged and hoisted sandbags into low walls, my friend's friend looked out across one thousand hectares of prairie turned to farmland by the toil of three generations of his family. Most of it was under water. The diking was exhausting and wet. A miserably cold wind made hands and faces raw red. Riffing on the old prairie saw about a dry cold, he gazed across his flooded homeland and said, "At least, it's a dry flood." All day, as the dike slowly snaked around his house, he kept up this humour, to encourage us and himself. "And don't even think about climbing a tree. In this part of Manitoba, it's so flat, a gopher has to kneel down to eat." That farmer's stout heart in the face of emotional and financial loss stuck with me.

His gutsy humour prompted digging up other feisty words and phrases Manitobans have added to Canadian English. "Bodewash" warmed many an early Manitoba settler. This term for dried buffalo dung used as a fuel was borrowed from the Canadian French of fur trappers where it appeared — at first humorously — as *bois de vache* 'cow wood' and also in the more refined phrase *bois des prairies* 'prairie wood.' Buffalo chips or cow chips were both called *bodewash*, which is a direct Englishing of *bois de vache* that shows up in the Manitoba folk saying "squished flatter 'n a bodewash chip." Anyone who could find the chips of buffalo dung used them, since there was little wood available. Dried cattle burns with a heavy odour, while buffalo chips are relatively odourless and were in plentiful supply before the vast herds were slaughtered.

Ever chaw down on a "jambuster"? That's the unique Winnipeg term for a jelly doughnut. One might consume it at the Peg's famous windy crossroads of Portage and *Pain*. After traversing it, folks might raise a glass using an old western drinking toast, "Here's a Ho!" The exhorting word *Ho!* was used to begin the attack in community buffalo hunts of yore. Sodbusters and stubble-jumpers would toast that way to make sure no one mistook them for a bunch of high-falutin' *cigarette dudes* (old Prairie slang for a 'city slicker'). The interjection *ho* is widespread in Indo-European languages, appearing in Old Scandinavian as a shepherd's call to wandering sheep, in Old French as a command to stop, and in Middle English as an early spelling of whoa, a call to an animal to halt. It was also a common direction, as in westward-ho!

A verb I first heard in a Manitoba kitchen appears in this sentence: Mom came over to help us do down some saskatoons. A saskatoon is a prairie berry. To do down is to make preserves or jam of fruit or to can vegetables for winter use. Many Canadians use the opposite adverbial completion in phrases like "do up some jam." From turn-of-the-century railroad construction camps came "CPR strawberries," Canadian railway slang for prunes. My own favourite prairie term describes what settlers wore to protect themselves from the relentless blessing of the sun, a big straw hat, or, as they said, a cow's breakfast.

Some Manitoba place names have comic roots in food terms, too. Quite official are the following toponyms from the province's map: Pork and Bean Point, Brownie Bay, Sausage Lake, Weiner Hill, Sauerkraut Point, and in the extreme north of Manitoba, Fudge Lake.

Yes, there's humour and grit in the Manitoba soul, as well as the laughter of survivors. Its echoes ricochet off many a word and phrase Manitobans call their own, including some of the hearty food terms that follow.

BOUEAU

This Canadian French word named a rough stew of buffalo pemmican and potatoes. Its root lies in the standard French word for mud, *boue*. It was a synonym for another early Quebecism, *bouette* 'little mud,' Canadian French for pig slop or whey fed to other animals as food. In Acadian French, *bouette* also meant 'fish bait' or 'dry grain fed to chickens.' Standard French for wet fodder fed to domestic animals is *la buvée*. *Boueau* probably received its rural nickname from the muddy colour of the buffalo stew.

BUFFALO BEAN

This yellow-flowered prairie legume, *Astragalus crassicarpus*, is a wild pea whose fruits or "beans" were sometimes canned as a winter preserve in early prairie kitchens. This humble and not very palatable bean was also, in flights of prairie exaggeration and pioneer optimism, called "buffalo apple."

BUFFALO BERRY

This prairie shrub, *Shepherdia canadensis*, offers a profusion of red, currantlike berries that are acidic and very, very sour — until nipped by fall frosts, at which time they sweeten up and make a delicious addition to buffalo stew (hence their common name). Buffalo steaks and tongues, salted and smoked to preserve them, made a very dry meat and needed a juicy garnish, even if it was acidic. Buffalo berries often served as this garnish. White settlers learned from the Cree and other First Peoples of our plains to dry them as winter preserves. In 1851, explorer Sir John Richardson published an account of his search for the lost Franklin expedition under one of the long-winded titles popular with Victorian travellers. In *Arctic Searching Expedition: A Journal of a Boat-Voyage Through Rupert's Land and the Arctic Sea . . . With an appendix of The Physical Geography of North America*, Richardson mentions that buffalo berries make an excellent quick beer, fermenting in just twenty-four hours into a beverage "most agreeable in hot weather."

BUFFALO GREASE

Fur traders, early settlers, Métis people, and Aboriginal prairie-dwellers prized the marrow fat from buffalo bones as a frying and cooking grease. Europeans found it an acceptable substitute for butter. To obtain what was usually called buffalo grease, the bones of buffalo cows were preferred. They were broken and boiled. The marrow fat rose to the top of the kettle and was skimmed off and stored in buffalo bladders which could weigh almost six kilograms when full.

BUFFALO SUET

The hard, white fat around the kidneys and loins of the buffalo was used as a substitute shortening in many pioneer recipes. It was also ground up for use in steamed puddings, mincemeat, and some baked goods. Its deadly habit of sticking to and clogging human arteries was not then known. Buffalo suet and that from other animals could be rendered into tallow and used to make candles and soap, neither of which had pleasing aromas.

BURNT WHEAT

Wheat grains were roasted as a substitute for coffee. Like other once-wild grasses, the grains of most cereals have been used for millennia to make hot drinks. When wheat is just ripe, break off the heads as they turn brown and store them to dry. After extracting the grains and winnowing the chaff, roast them over a moderate campfire (or in an oven at 120° centigrade) until dark brown. Then grind to a powder and add to hot water. Sweeten to taste with honey or molasses or sugar. Some pioneers preferred coarse-ground wheat grains and percolated hot water through them. Don't get too frisky with field-escaped wild wheat until you learn to identify the poison fungus, ergot, which looks like hard black kernels and sits in the wheat heads precisely where healthy grains do, replacing them.

DOUGH GODS

This was once a common Western slang expression for the dumplings that are dropped into dozens of hot soups in the cuisines of many European and Asian peoples. Dough gods were a popular addition to chuckwagon chow for cowboys tending cattle out on the range.

FRIED-OUT PORK

This was a prairie method of preserving meat. Fresh pork slices were fried crisp, layered into a crockery pot and covered with their own hot fat. Jars of beef could be done the same way. Stored in a cold cellar, this fried-out meat would keep well for ten months.

GIN POLE

To preserve meat for a shorter time in our pioneer West, fresh beef or buffalo was cut up and stuffed into gunny sacks or clean flour bags that were tied to a pulley and hoisted to the top of a pole reaching nine to fifteen metres high. This gin pole held the meat above "the fly line" where blowflies could not deposit their eggs in the meat, and so the beef was prevented from turning maggotty. The cooling prairie breeze at such higher heights may also have helped preserve it temporarily. The name derives from a hoisting gin, a device usually consisting of three poles united at the top and used to raise heavy weights with an attached windlass, pulleys, and ropes. Gin here is a contraction of engine or its Old French form, *engin*.

HEARTS OF THISTLE

Cirsium arvense or Canada thistle was a common prairie weed used as an emergency food if famine struck. Hearts of thistle were the soft inner piths of the youngest stalks only, with the prickles and tough outer parts of the stalks removed. They were used as salad greens or boiled in salt water until tender. Another emergency food for those lost in the countryside and without provisions were the roots of the Scottish or bull thistle, *Cirsium vulgare*. The roots of young plants could provide some make-do starch when eaten raw, boiled, or roasted, although those forced to eat them said these roots were tough and had no taste.

KASHA

Ukrainian immigrants made this thick pudding or porridge from buckwheat groats, cornmeal, or millet. It required a lengthy preparation that included first browning the buckwheat in fat, then boiling it in water and salt until the groats had absorbed plenty of water, and then baking them tightly covered for another two-and-a-half hours. Groats are cereal grains which have their hulls removed.

LAKE WINNIPEG GOLDEYE

This tasty, freshwater fish has the most renown of Manitoba's finny legions. Although native to Lake Winnipeg, *Hiodon alosoides* swims in other waters of our Northwest as well. Algonkian-speaking First Peoples called it *nacaish*, which early French trappers and voyageurs heard as *la quesche* or *lacaiche* or *lacaishe*, the latter two still being its names in Canadian French. Cree people like to ponask or ponash goldeye, that is, clean and split the fish, attach it to green twigs and roast it over an open fire. See the *ponask* entry later in this chapter. Smoked Winnipeg goldeye was once a steady menu item on CPR dining cars. Goldeye was also frequently part of official dinners where an all-Canadian menu was thought appropriate, for example, at hoity-toity Ottawa feasts where our politicians might be feeding traditional Canuck fare to American lobbyists — perhaps as a second course after letting them consume most of our economy and patrimony.

MARQUIS WHEAT

"The wheat that changed the West," one journalist called it. Dominion cerealists and brothers, Percy and Charles Saunders began crossing and hybridizing spring wheats at the experimental station at Agassiz, Manitoba, as early as 1892. By 1907, they sent seeds of Marquis to prairie fields where the wheat matured much earlier than previous strains, thus greatly extending the area of prairie where wheat could be grown commercially. Marquis made good flour and kept its grains on the head even when stalks were buffetted by the constant wind of the plains. By 1911, Marquis wheat was being exported, and, as exports grew, this wheat improved the economy of our prairie provinces. Ninety percent of spring wheat grown in Western Canada during the early 1920s was Marquis, and more than half of the wheat crop south of the border was Marquis, as American farmers learned the advantages of this Canadian hybrid.

MEETSU(K)

Meetsu or *meetsuk* or *mitshim* was a general word for meal or mealtime in Algonquian languages including Cree. Compare, for example, Ojibwa *michit* 'he eats it.' " Thus "Meetsu! Meetsu!" was the common "dinner-is-served" cry of cooks in many a northern camp. Métis, First Peoples, and white trappers understood the common root *mich* 'eat' and English speakers thought it sounded like 'meat,' so for camps full of men of mixed heritage it was a more efficient call-to-table than "Grub's on!"

MOOSEBERRY

Here's a loan-translation into Canadian English of the Cree term *mongsoa-meena* 'moose-berry.' In Western Canada, mooseberry often refers to the low-bush cranberry. Elsewhere and among the Cree peoples who named it, this is *Viburnum opulus*, the high-bush cranberry, a favourite nibble of moose and humans. The scarlet-to-orange-coloured and pleasantly acidic berries were added to pemmican and used to make pioneer preserves, compotes, jams, and sauces for fowl and game. In *Flora of Manitoba*, Scoggan gives its accustomed sites as "woods, thickets, shores, and gravel ridges throughout the province." See also the *pembina* entry in this chapter. Explorer Samuel Hearne in *A Journey From Prince of Wales's Fort in Hudson's Bay To The Northern Ocean. In the Years 1769, 1770, 1771 & 1772* gives this report:

> Cranberries grow in great abundance near Churchill [site of Fort Prince of Wales, a Hudson's Bay Company trading post where Hearne was for a time governor], and are not confined to any particular situation, for they are as common on open bleak plains and high rocks as among the woods. When carefully gathered in the Fall, in dry weather, and as carefully packed in casks of moist sugar, they will keep for years, and are annually sent to England in considerable quantities as presents, where they are much esteemed. When the ships have remained in the Bay so late that the Cranberries are ripe, some of the Captains have carried them home in water with great success.

NETTLE SOUP

No, this is not some nightmare decoction from a masochist's kitchen. The old pioneer name "Indian spinach" suggests the use of only the young, tender, sprouting leaves of stinging nettle as a soup green. The plant is widespread over the northern hemisphere and, surprisingly, humans have eaten the boiled leaves for millennia. The botanical name is *Urtica dioica*, the genus name *urtica* having as its root the Latin verb *urere* 'to burn.' Both the stem and leaf surfaces bristle with tiny hairs that, triggered by the slightest touch, release a stinging oil rich in formic acid and histamines. Touching stinging nettles produces an intense burning sensation and often angry, red wheals. The medical phrase describing this skin reaction is contact urticaria. But the sting of the bristles is removed by boiling in water, which quickly dissolves and dilutes the histamines and acids. Outdoorsy adventurers who wish to try this wild food ought to wear rubber or thick leather gloves and should use a knife or scissors to harvest stinging nettle leaves.

The boiled leaves are a good source of vitamins A and C, and some minerals. To prepare nettle broth, plunge clean young leaves into rapidly boiling water for one full minute. After draining and rinsing the boiled leaves with cold water, boil a few cups of beef or vegetable broth, drop the boiled nettle leaves into the boiling broth and simmer for two minutes.

Although boiling removes the sting of nettles, drying the leaves does NOT do this, as an incident well known to botanists illustrates. During the bombing of Britain during the Second World War, various important specimen collections were vulnerable. The British government called for their protection if possible. One of these was the great herbarium of Linnaeus, the Swedish botanist who founded modern plant nomenclature. This herbarium was the prince of botanists' very own collection of dried herbs, purchased from his native Sweden by British interests. Its mounted specimens were almost two hundred years old. Gladys Brown, a British photographer, was asked to photograph each specimen lest the whole collection be destroyed by Nazi bombing. When she gently removed Linnaeus' stinging nettle specimen from its mounting, she was stung on the arm and a red blister raised — by a two-hundred-year-old nettle. Perhaps, after all, this nettle soup is a bit of culinary lore better tasted on history's page than on neophyte's tongue.

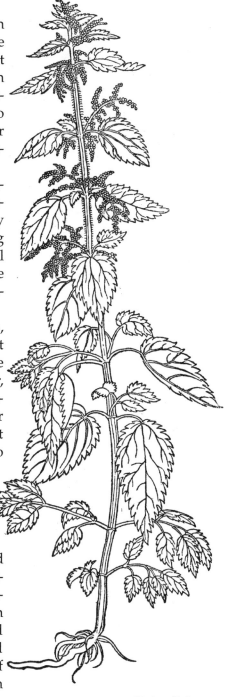

Urtica dioica,
the common nettle.

Stinging nettles have also been deliberately applied to the skin in northern folk medicine, both European and North American, as dubious remedies for rheumatism and arthritis. The skin surfaces of afflicted limbs were rubbed with nettle leaves in the unscientific belief that the pain caused by the nettle sting would relieve the deeper rheumatic or arthritic dolor. This was once called urtication, although the word is now used in medicine to refer to the burning sensation caused by nettlelike skin reactions and the subsequent development of urticaria — the painful red rash and swelling. When ancient Roman legions were marauding through Teutonic and Gallic tribal lands far from sunny Italy, imperial soldiers are reported to have rubbed stinging nettles on their exposed skin to warm themselves in the damp gloom of infidel forests. If such torture did not heat them up, it certainly would have been conducive to keeping alert those posted on watch.

PEMBINA BERRY

Pembina is a synonym for highbush cranberries, from the Cree phrase *nipi-minan* — literally 'summer berries.' The Cree words were heard by early French fur trappers and explorers as *pembina*. The word was much used as a place, river, and commercial name. The Pembina River is still an important waterway in southern Manitoba near the Pembina Mountains. There is the Pembina highway. Pembina was one of the settlements founded by Lord Selkirk, one that unfortunately did not endure. Alberta has a long and important Pembina River as well. Still heard in our West is pembina berries for highbush cranberries.

PINK TEA

A pink tea was a prairie social gathering attended mainly by women, each bringing homemade food and wearing something pink. Such teas were convened frequently for charitable purposes or to raise funds for a project at a local church.

PONASK

From the Cree language, westering travellers borrowed the cooking practice and the verb, to ponask, sometimes seen as ponash. Ponasking is splitting a fish or piece of game, sticking it on a spit and roasting it quickly over an open fire. While meat requiring much tenderizing was boiling in a pot hung over a roaring campfire, strips of more delicate flesh might have been impaled on ponasking sticks held by hand or stuck in the earth around the edge of the fire.

PONNUKOKUR

Icelandic palates around Gimli and other centres of Icelandic immigration in Manitoba delight in these traditional Christmas crêpes, often presented to revellers with hot chocolate on Christmas Eve. In *ponnukokur* (pancake) one can see something of the Icelandic language's relationship to tongues in the North Germanic or Scandinavian branch of the vast Indo-European proto-family, as well as its not-too-distant cousins, German and English. *Ponnu* is related to German *pfanne* and English *pan*, and *kokur* to German *kuchen*, English *cook*, and Latin *coquere*. These tasty little pancakes are made with sweet milk and sour cream or buttermilk, along with the usual eggs, flour, sugar, baking soda and baking powder, and spiced with cinnamon, salt, and vanilla.

PRAIRIE OYSTER

On the prairies this almost always refers to calves' testicles washed, skinned, soaked an hour in salt water, rinsed, breaded in seasoned flour, and then fried in hot fat. In other parts of Canada, and abroad, a prairie oyster is a hangover cure in the hair-of-the-dog category. It consists of a raw egg sprinkled with pepper and slurped down whole or plopped into a shot or two of brandy or whisky, and gulped quickly while invoking any hovering deity who may watch over the bibulous. Even Bacchus may haunt the occasional coulee and with proper invocation may deign to quell one's throbbing noggin.

RED RIVER BANNOCK

Red River bannock differed from true Scottish bannock because wheat flour eventually replaced oatmeal in the recipe. The Red River settlers' original recipe had no leavening agent and was a hard flour-and-water biscuit cooked in an exterior brick or mud oven or on a hearth. Where the Scottish recipe might call for beef drippings, later prairie bannock was likely to use buffalo fat.

The colony established by Lord Selkirk in the valley of the Red River in 1812 borrowed its name from the French name, Rivière Rouge, used as early as 1740. But that, in turn, was a loan-translation either from Cree *Miscousipi* 'red water river' or Ojibwa *Miskwa-gama-sipi* 'red water river,' both Aboriginal names deriving from the red silt frequently carried by the river's current.

Bannock was also called trail biscuit, bush bread, river cake, and galette. The word is Scots Gaelic, *bannach*, for a thin oatmeal cake, ultimately from an Old English word *bannuc* 'morsel, little bit.' As to its taste, it is perhaps best to recall Dr. Samuel Johnson's definition in his famous dictionary (1755) — "Oats, n. a grain which in England is fed to horses, but in Scotland supports the people." To the first Canadian settlers of the eastern seaboard, bannock was flour, lard, salt, and water, done over an outdoor fire in a frying pan if one was on the trail, and at home pan-fried at the hearth. This rough bread is remembered in the little town of Bannock, Saskatchewan.

SKYR

Skyr is a kind of Icelandic yogourt. A gallon of fresh skim milk is boiled, let cool to lukewarm, and then a cup of cultured buttermilk is stirred into the warm skim milk. The starter for the culture is often a couple of tablespoons of skyr from the last batch made. Sometimes a few drops of rennet are added to help the milk set. The mixture is then put aside to let the culture work at a slightly high room temperature, just above 21° centigrade being best. After letting the culture work for about fifteen hours, a big bowl is lined with cheesecloth and the mixture is poured in. The full cheesecloth is lifted to drain another half-day at warm room temperature. The skyr is beaten briskly and served. It can be kept chilled and will last for several weeks. Skyr was eaten by itself with cream or poured on porridge. Some Icelandic cooks added fruit flavours to their skyr, but traditionalists considered this act sacrilege.

VINEGAR PIE

Here is another of those substitution recipes from pioneer days or from war times when no fresh fruit like lemons or, worse, no eggs were readily to hand. In one of the recipes for vinegar pie, the filling was concocted of molasses, butter, bread crumbs, and flavoured with vinegar and cinnamon. Vinegar pie recipes from early prairie days were also just old-fashioned lemon pie recipes, topped with meringue, but substituting four or five tablespoons of vinegar with lemon extract mixed in, to replace lemons which, like oranges, were rarely available on isolated farms at the turn of the century, and well into the 20th century.

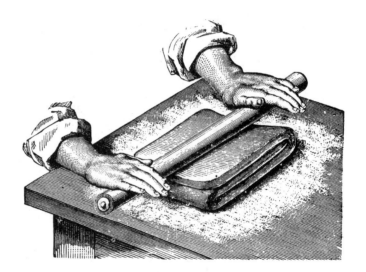

WAR BREAD & CAKE

War bread was common in Canada during the First World War, when the best wheat flour was shipped overseas, and brownish, poor quality flour was used to make domestic Canadian bread. Similarly, during the Second World War, amid ration coupons and scarcity, there was War Cake, a spicy, boiled, raisin cake made with no eggs, no butter, and no milk, much of which had gone overseas to the war effort.

WINNIPEG JAMBUSTER

This is a term for any jelly doughnut consumed in the vicinity of Portage and Main. On numerous field tests, your humble deponent, the author, has consumed coffee and jelly doughnuts in this very locale. While the repast was a pleasant interval of repose amidst the lip-flapping, book-flogging whirl of radio and television interviews, no discernible particularity of taste in the said jelly doughnuts was detected.

CHAPTER 9

Saskatchewan

*E*ven residents of Saskatchewan joke about the vivid landscape in the south of their province. Bald-headed prairie, the softly rolling plains with no trees, gave rise to this provincial folk saying: Parts of Saskatchewan are so flat you can watch your dog run away from home for a week. Why, a woodpecker here has to pack a box lunch. But I am fond of this description of southern Saskatchewan by our great prairie novelist, W.O. Mitchell, born at Weyburn, who opens his masterpiece *Who Has Seen the Wind* with these words: "Here was the least common denominator of nature, the skeleton requirements simply, of land and sky — Saskatchewan prairie. It lay wide around the town, stretching tan to the far line of the sky, clumped with low buck brush and wild rose bushes, shimmering under the late June sun and waiting for the unfailing visitation of wind, gentle at first, barely stroking the long grasses and giving them life . . . " Like many with their roots in the province, Mitchell loved the gently undulant plains of short-grass prairie and the broad, fertile wheat belt.

To a visiting botanist, prairie is a vastness of grasses, and of xerophytes, plants adapted to intermittent drought. To a homesteading newcomer in 1876, prairie might have meant "the first land anyone in my family ever owned." But who first applied the word *prairie* to the rolling grasslands in the middle of North America? Canoe-stiff French adventurers dubbed it, early in the 18th century. Rough explorers they were, greedy for beaver fur to supply felt hats for European city folk, voyageurs paddling the continental interior by unknown lakes and rivers. They had no exact French word to label the grassy plains whose immensity and reach had startled their sense of geographic proportion, based as it was on the populated density of their native Europe. But there was a French word for grazing land, sometimes used to describe dry scrub in the south of France. *Prairie* 'grassland' had entered Old French by 1180. Its first meaning in French was 'pasturage,' any field with plants that were suitable fodder for domestic animals.

La prairie may have arrived directly from a Late Latin phrase like *terra prataria* 'meadowland.' Compare such borrowing in other Romance languages where Italian has *prateria* and Spanish *pradera*. The classical Latin root was *pratum* 'meadow.' But *pratum* had come into French earlier as *pré* 'meadow' and so French *prairie* may simply be an extension of *pré* formed by adding to it *-erie* to produce *préerie*, which is actually one of the early spelling variants. The noun suffix *-erie* gave *préerie* the sense of 'a considerable area of meadowlike land suitable for pasturing cattle and sheep.'

Back home in Saskatchewan, where the buffalo roamed, later Canuck sodbusters were coining a variety of phrases for the plants, animals, and foods they used. The Prairie lily became the official floral emblem of Saskatchewan, *Lilium philadelphicum*, also called the red range-lily. The phrase "prairie squint" entered Canadian English first in Saskatchewan, an affliction arising from too many long days in the sun harvesting that yellow grain. Did you know that Estevan, Saskatchewan, has more hours of sunshine than any other city in Canada — 2,537 hours per annum, on average? Of course, there is a small town — Manyberries, Alberta — which also claims to be the sunniest spot in Canada. Only comparative visitation can settle such a dispute.

The province takes its name from the Saskatchewan River. The Cree people called it *ki-siskat-chewani-sipi* which means 'quick-flowing-river.' In the Cree phrase, one can hear the sonorous onomatopoeia that is a feature of most languages, including English, where we form some words to imitate sounds, for example, in terms like buzz, pop, moo. *Ki-siskat* is a quick word. *Chewani* flows. And *sipi* we recognize from many Aboriginal river names, particularly the Mississippi, which means 'big water.' Another English translation of the phrase *ki-siskat-chewani-sipi* gives a name to the city of Swift Current, Saskatchewan.

Food terms helped make several Saskatchewan place names. The name of the town of Moosomin in southeastern Saskatchewan is from the Cree term *mongsoa minan* 'mooseberries' or 'highbush cranberries,' which abounded in the area. In our western provinces, mooseberry can also be applied to lowbush cranberries. The town of Kalyna in Saskatchewan is named with the Ukrainian word for cranberry. More recent, official places in Saskatchewan include Pita Lake and the Buttermilk Lakes in the south.

This little gopher-scurry through Saskatchewan food terms takes some account of the many ethnic flavours that went into the tossing of the racial salad of present-day Saskatchewan. Ten thousand years ago, the First Peoples arrived in what became Saskatchewan, following migratory herds of caribou and bison, a gradual incoming that consisted of peoples speaking a variety of Aboriginal languages: Chipewyan, Amisk, Slavey, Cree, Blackfoot, Assininboine, and Gros Ventres. French and British came later, first to trade and trap for fur. Later still arrived Germans, Ukrainians, Scandinavians, Austrians, Russians, the Polish, the Dutch, and most recently peoples of Asian origin. Although all contributed their foodways to the province, our chapter will look at some of the older culinary terms and, because of the limitations put on the size of books, only a few of the newer ethnic food words.

APPALAT

To grill little strips of meat *en apala* was to skewer them and place them over a campfire, rather like ponasking meat (see entry under Manitoba food words). *Appalat* or *apoulard* both stem from early French slang *apala* 'tidbit, little piece.'

BACKFAT or DÉPOUILLE

Backfat was a choice cut of fat just above the muscles along the back of any well-fed animal, reaching its maximum weight late in the fall after the animal had put on its winter fat. Especially prized for melting to make pemmican was the tender backfat of buffalo, and, farther north, of caribou. An obsolete synonym for this *dépouille* (in standard French, 'skin' or 'hide'; in early Canadian French, 'backfat') was Indian bread. The verb *dépouiller* means 'to skin (an animal).' Buffalo hunters stripped long pieces of this fat from the shoulders back along the spine, then fried it in hot grease and smoked it. It was then used to make a kind of complete-meat sandwich. A leaner, drier piece of meat was put between, or wrapped with, a long piece of Indian bread.

BOSS RIBS

This was the anatomically incorrect slang for meat attached to bones from a buffalo's hump. This fine-grained flesh, supported by the spinous processes jutting up from the cervical vertebrae, was esteemed as one of the most delicate and tasty parts of the buffalo, along with the tongue and the backfat. Being a popular boiled food, the boss had several slangy synonyms in pioneer English and French, including the bunch, *grosse bosse*, the hunch, and the wig. The boss was nick-named the wig by British hunters because the buffalo's thick mane of neck hair flowed down over its hump, suggesting a bewigged head. Most exquisite in taste was the front part of the bison's hump, called *la petite bosse* by French hunters. It weighed about three pounds and was attached to the main boss above the neck.

CARIBOU

In Québec, the Algonkian word for the North American reindeer had a later playful extension of meaning when it came to refer to a drink composed of red wine and often homemade whisky, or wine mixed with pure grain alcohol. But among some French settlers who ventured westward, *caribou* referred to another local potable, namely dandelion wine mixed with gin.

By 1665, the name of the animal entered early Canadian French from one of the languages in the widespread Algonkian family, perhaps from Mi'kmaq *xalipu* 'pawer, scratcher.' The caribou uses its front hooves to scrape snow away to get to the grass and moss beneath the snowdrifts. The large reindeer was probably one of the first animals encountered and named during the waves of migration that brought North America's First Peoples across the Bering Strait 20,000 to 40,000 years ago. In Quinnipiac, one of the extinct Algonkian languages, once spoken in what is now Connecticut, the word was heard by a European listener to the language as *maccaribe*, showing its putative Proto-Algonquin compound origin in a form like *mekalixpowa*, made up of *mekal-* 'to scrape' + *-ixpo-* 'snow' + *-wa* 'animal agent.'

One of the 19th-century folk etymologies is amusing. Some French speakers respelled caribou as *carreboeuf* and suggested it might have derived from *carré boeuf* 'square ox.' It did not. However, one alternate spelling, Cariboo, did give its name to the famous region of British Columbia that enjoyed the gold rush in 1860, and to several derivative phrases like Cariboo fever and Caribooite, an historical bit of slang applied to placer miners who hit the Cariboo Trail during the gold rush.

COTTAGE ROLL

This term for a boned, rolled, cooked ham appears to have originated in Saskatchewan during the mid-fifties. Its earliest known appearance in print was in the pages of the *Cut Knife Grinder*, a weekly newspaper published in Cut Knife, Saskatchewan.

DENVER SANDWICH

What elsewhere in Canada is called a western is all over the Canadian west called a denver. This names a toasted, scrambled-egg sandwich or, more usually, a small omelette — usually diced ham, chopped green pepper, and onion — presented on a sandwich of toasted bread. Named after the capital city of the state of Colorado, this term is an obvious U.S. import.

KARTOSHNIK

This is a Doukhobor recipe from Saskatchewan based on a much older Russian version of potato cakes. Cooked potatoes are drained and mashed. Eggs and cream are whipped together with a pinch of salt and folded into the mashed potatoes. After a final brisk stirring, the mixture is spread on a greased pan and baked for half an hour. The potato cake is cut into squares and the kartoshni-ki are served immediately with butter.

About 7,000 Doukhobors, members of a pacifist Christian sect, came to Canada to Saskatchewan in 1899, after they were attacked in their native Russia for refusing to serve in the Russian army. Their pacifist protest in Russia included the public burning of large piles of military rifles. Their peaceful farming in Saskatchewan was interrupted when the provin-

cial government enforced certain laws, such as making Doukhobors swear allegiance to Canada and forcing them to enrol their children in public schools. Rather than succumb to these demands, some Doukhobors moved on in 1905, to the remote West Kootenays in British Columbia, where today perhaps 30,000 still live. A radical anarchist sect of the Doukhobors called themselves The Sons of Freedom. Canadians may remember their arson, bombings, and nude protest marches in British Columbia during the late 1940s and early 1950s. But most members of this religious group were and are peaceful.

The name *Doukhobor* began in Russia as an insult. In 1785, a Russian Orthodox archbishop, from the lofty summit of his archbishopric, denounced the sect by calling them Doukhobors. *Dukh* is Russian for 'spirit,' if capitalized for the Holy Spirit, if lowercased for any spirit or goblin. *Borets* means 'fighter' or 'wrestler.' Thus *Dukhoborets* can mean wrestler against the Holy Spirit, and without the capital letter *D*, in Russian slang, it is 'spirit-wrestler,' quite the equivalent of 'holy roller' in English. A double-whammy insult, indeed. Nevertheless, after being called this in Russia, the members of the persecuted sect decided to adopt the name, nullifying the insult, because *dukhoborets* can also mean 'fighter for the Holy Spirit.'

KUTIA

Kutia is a traditional Ukrainian treat served on Christmas Eve or during the winter holiday time. It's made of wheat, nuts, honey, and poppy seeds. It might be served with *kalach*, a ring bread.

-MIN & -MINAN

Here is the Cree root for 'berry' that appears in well-known prairie food words and place names, two in Saskatchewan. Saskatoon was originally named by

early settlers because the site had many saskatoon berry trees. The Cree word for these succulent
purple berries is *mi-sakwato-min* 'tree-of-many-
branches berries.' Unique among Canadian cities,
the pert metropolis of Saskatoon was founded as
the proposed capital of an alcohol-free country.
The teetotalers in question began in Ontario in
1882, and chartered themselves as The Temper-
ance Colonization Society. That same year they
bought 100,000 acres of land from the Dominion
Government in what is now the province of Saskatchewan. By 1883, a party of settlers was eager
to flee the gin-soaked inferno of Ontario. They
went west by train to Moose Jaw, then trekked
overland to a place the Cree Indians had named
because there were many saskatoon berry trees in
the vicinity.

The name of the town of Moosomin in southeastern Saskatchewan is from the Cree term *mongsoa minan* 'mooseberries' or 'highbush cranberries,' which abounded in the area. In our western
provinces, mooseberry can also be applied to low-
bush cranberries.

NACHYNKA

This is Ukrainian johnnycake, a quick cornmeal
spoon bread. Cornmeal, sugar, and seasonings are
sautéed in a frying pan, then scalded milk is
stirred in and the mixture is cooked until thick.
Three beaten eggs and a little light cream are folded into the cooked mixture and poured into a
casserole to bake until golden-brown.

PARFLÈCHE

This was the bag made of buffalo skin often used
to hold pemmican. In fact, the prepared pemmican fat was actually sewn tightly into the
parflèche. See *pemmican* entry in this chapter. This
was an extension of meaning for *parflèche*, which

first meant 'arrow shield' in Canadian French from *parer* 'to ward off a weapon or blow' + *flèche* 'arrow.'

PASKA BREAD & PYSANKY

A traditional Ukrainian Easter bread, paska is served in large braided wreaths of vanilla-and-lemon-scented pastry. Often eggs in the shell are pressed into the centre of each wreath to cook, then removed, coloured and decorated, and put back into the baked wreaths of sweet-smelling pastry. On a side dish, a pious Ukrainian cook would present a *maslo*, a cross formed of clove-studded butter.

Pysanky are the well-known Ukrainian Easter eggs (singular *pysanka*), decorated with traditional Ukrainian designs and folk motifs. There are also *krashanky* (singular *krashanka*), which are dipped in dye of one solid colour. *Krashanky* are hard boiled and can be eaten, unlike *pysanky*. The special pen used to decorate pysanky is called a *kistka*.

PEMMICAN

This is one of the most surprising of all the terms I studied in writing *Canadian Food Words*, suprising because verbal roots similar to the initial one in pemmican appear in languages all over the world, languages which are said to be unrelated. The very Canadian word *pemmican* thus becomes a small key to the possibility of the monogenesis of language. In other words, what if all our teachers have been wrong, what if there was indeed one single mother tongue from which all the languages of the world have evolved? In the word lore of pemmican, we can see a hint of this. Read on.

Pemmican is a Cree word compounded of *pimii* 'fat' + *kan* 'prepared.' Buffalo meat was dried and then braised over fire for several minutes. Spread out on buffalo robes laid on the ground, this scorched meat was beaten with a stone pemmican-pounder or with hardwood poles until it was tenderized and fine. At this stage it was called 'beat meat.' Then bags made of buffalo skin, called *taureaux* or *parflèches* by the earliest French trappers who watched them being manufactured, were half filled with beat meat. The best-quality tarrow or rendered buffalo fat was poured in, along with dried berries, often cranberries, and sometimes other plant parts. The contents of each bag was sloshed and mixed thoroughly and set aside to cool. To keep the fat from settling to the bottom, the bags were turned while the contents were cooling. Then the bag was sewn up tightly. Pemmican had a shelf life that would make any modern food-packaging company green with envy. It lasted forever and supplied iron and protein on the longest, remotest trips through the wilderness. Canada's fur trade, and hence the opening up of the country itself, was absolutely dependent on pemmican. Tight in its bag, pemmican would keep even if dumped overboard from a canoe.

There were, of course, variations in the ingredients, hence names like deer or moose pemmican. Kinds of pemmican used in Canada included sundry berry pemmicans, such as one that featured the meat, crushed berries, and leaves of wild peppermint. One berry preparation actually bore the name of bourgeois pemmican. In his autobiography, *Beyond the Palisades*, G.S. McTavish writes: "When the Plains Indians put up a specially prepared lot of pemmican by adding native berries, the product was classified as 'Bourgeois' pemmican, suitable only to the palates and supposedly refined tastes of the 'Ookimows' (chiefs) among the pale faces." Among the Inuit, inferior blubber could be made into dog pemmican, fit only for dogfood, but made and packed by the Inuit before long journeys by dogsled. Fish pemmican, sweet pemmican, and after the coming of whites, even sugar pemmican appear.

Other Aboriginal words with the pemmican root include the Canadian term *siskawet* for a Lake Superior lake trout < Québécois French *sisquoette* < Ojibwa *pemite-wiskawet* literally 'oily-flesh fish.'

Pemmican's World Relatives

The word *pemmican* is related to terms in farflung languages, its relationship surprising and seemingly inexplicable. Naturally, I wouldn't say that unless I had an explanation. And here it is.

Let's take a common English tree name, pine. The word *pine* has the Indo-European root **pi-* or **pa-* whose basic meaning was fat, lard, grease, then any thick, sticky substance like resin or gum. The IE root had extensions like **pit-*, **pin-*, and **pim-*. *Pitys* is the classical Greek word for pine tree. Pine then is the gummy tree, the resinous one. In Germanic languages the IE root gives forms like fat, *fett*, and fetid (originally the bad smell of rancid fat). Note that \p\ to \f\ and \p\ to \b\ transformations are a normal part of consonant evolution in many languages. In ancient Greek, *pion* was an adjective that meant fat and *pimele* was lard.

This *pa-/*pi- root for fat seems to predate even Proto-Indo-European. It is found all over the world with similar meanings in languages that modern scholarship states have no relationship whatsoever. But let's forget the nagging finger of disapproval wagged by tenured linguists at universities and look at a few of these words ourselves. North Americans might begin with the term *pemmican*, a word common among Algonkian-speaking peoples. Its roots in the Cree language are *pimii* 'fat' + *kan* 'prepared.' Cree *pimii* looks similar to that classical Greek word for lard or fat, *pimele*. Sorry, that can't be, say professorial guardians of linguistic orthodoxy. Yet there it is again in a sister word in Ojibwa, *bimide* 'grease, oil.' The Blackfoot word for dripping fat or lard is *pomis*, and among the Munsee Delaware, an Algonkian-speaking people, there is *pumuy* 'grease.' Chinese could have no relationship whatsoever with Cree or Classical Greek, now could it? Yet there is the *pa root nasalized in the second part of the Chinese word for fat, *jy-farng*, in a romanized transliteration. Mere coincidence! scream many linguists. They must be hoarse from the number of times in the last twenty years they have branded as coincidental the growing number of words recognized as related in widespread languages not in the same current language family.

Now this *p(f)(b)im- root for fat appears in dozens and dozens of languages descended from Proto-Amerind. Oops, I forgot. Proto-Amerind never existed either! Just ask vested-interest academics who study Aboriginal languages at the Smithsonian Institution, linguists who have publicly condemned the very concept of Proto-Amerind. And yet — drat these manifold coincidences — there are all those languages of North and South America with many words whose roots show correspondence and similarity, words that evolved from three language groups recently dubbed Proto-Amerind (first American Indian), a family of tongues brought to the Americas when the First Peoples crossed from Asia by the Bering land bridge.

PLACOTTE

This morsel of obsolete Canadian French was coined by voyageurs and trappers in the West, from then standard French *plats de côtes* for rib cutlets. Placotte entered pioneer western English too, to refer to buffalo cutlets.

PRAIRIE CHICKEN

The prairie chicken is becoming very scarce. Although we give a pioneer recipe, game wardens plead with prairie visitors not to kill these birds, but to enjoy them alive in their plains habitat.

Potting prairie chickens was only one way of preparing this wildfowl, but a popular method. Cleaned, plucked, drawn, and trussed birds were dusted with flour and browned in hot bacon fat. Five or six birds were then put in a large stew pot. Several cups of stock, a few onions, spices, and a drift of flour were added to the bacon fat in the fry pan and the mixture was boiled and poured over the prairie chickens. The pot was covered and baked for two hours.

The greater prairie chicken, a member of the grouse family, is native to our southern prairies, and goes by a welter of other names such as heath cock, pinnated grouse, prairie fowl, prairie hen, and squaretail. Zoologically, it is *Tympanuchus cupido*. The genus name, from Greek *tympanon* 'drum' + *ochos* 'possessing,' arises from the deep, hollow booming sound uttered by male prairie chickens during their spring courtship activity, when they gather at familiar grounds called leks for elaborate displays of feathers and the drumming mating calls typical of grouse. Male prairie chickens return every year to the same lek. One instance is recorded where a prairie farmhouse was built on ground used as a lek. The next spring, the male prairie chicken returned and did his mating display on the roof of the farmhouse.

The sharp-tailed grouse, *Pedioecetes phasianellus*, a different species that is also called prairie chicken, is the official animal emblem of the province of Saskatchewan.

In the humorous slang of British Columbia lumber camps during this century, anyone born on our Prairies who went west to work in the logging industry might be called "a prairie chicken." But a man so-called might reply, "When you say that, stranger, smile."

PRAIRIE TURNIP

The prairie turnip, *Psoralea esculenta*, also called biscuit-root, breadroot, buffalo root, Indian carrot, or prairie potato, is the starchy, foot-long root of a legume, a member of the pea family, pounded and used as a flour by First Peoples of the prairies and early white settlers. It was not esteemed for its flavour. The explorer Captain John Palliser, after whom the Palliser Triangle is named, travelled along part of the Saskatchewan River and wrote in his 1857 journal that "the root is very dry and almost tasteless, and even when boiled for a great length of time does not become soft, and is at best but insipid, unnutritious trash." Yikes! I wonder if Cap'n John was sufferin' a patch of canoe-chafing that day? Earlier, French Canadian voyageurs encountering the staple food had dubbed it *"pomme de prairie."*

ROBIN HOOD FLOUR™

In 1909, a miller on the banks of Thunder Creek at Moose Jaw, Saskatchewan, began to make an all-purpose, hard-wheat flour that he named after Robin Hood. It first came to market in 100-pound sacks marked "Absolute Satisfaction or Your Money Back Plus a 10% Premium."

RUBBABOO

Rubbaboo was a stew or soup made by chopping up pemmican and tossing it into boiling water. Any other available nutriments lurking in a saddlebag or camp larder might be thrown in as well: a handful of flour, a few wild onions, perhaps a few roots of prairie turnip, and a hunk of salt pork. Because it was a mixture of whatever was available, rubbaboo later came to refer to any miscellaneous collection of things. When settlers and trappers used a mixture of French, English, and Aboriginal words — as was often necessary — this mixed bag of words could be called a rubbaboo. There has even

been an anthology of Canadian stories and poems entitled *Rubbaboo.*

The etymology is complex and obscure. Rubbaboo seems to be a comic attempt at saying the name of another pioneer stew, ruhiggan burgoo. *Ruhiggan* was a word in Algonquian languages denoting 'beat meat,' the first preparatory stage of making pemmican. Burgoo was a word for stew used by many British immigrants, derived from 18th-century British naval slang where burgoo was oatmeal gruel eaten by sailors. Canadian and American English also grabbed the term from British traders who used burgoo to name any unappetizing food, especially a thick stew made from camp or kitchen scraps of meat and vegetables. For an extensive note on the origin of burgoo, see the *bargou* entry in the chapter on Acadian food.

But the form *rubbaboo* was also influenced by Ojibwa and Cree words for soup, namely, *nempup* and *apu*. One must remember the polyglot salad of words that might fly across a prairie campfire when French-speaking voyageurs met up with English-speaking trappers and perhaps with Cree-speaking Métis along with, say, Blackfoot people. It was indeed a verbal rubbaboo, out of which this word emerged.

As usual, the finicky and fastidious palates of some Europeans were appalled by what they had to eat on their travels across the North American continent. A Scottish poobah, one James Carnegie, Earl of Southesk, trekked through our West in 1859 – 60, and later published his reflections in *Saskatchewan and The Rocky Mountains: A Diary and Narrative of Travel . . .* Among useful comments, the good Earl also had this to say:

Pemmican is most endurable when uncooked. My men used to fry it with grease, sometimes stirring in flour, and making a flabby mess, called 'rubbaboo,' which I found almost uneatable. Carefully-made pemmican, such as that flavoured with the Saskootoom berries . . . or the sheep-pemmican given us by the Rocky Mountain hunters, is nearly good — but, in two senses, a little of it goes a long way.

SASKATOON-BERRY

The Cree word for these succulent purple berries is *mi-sakwato-min* 'tree-of-many-branches berries.' They are the fruit of a serviceberry tree, *Amelanchier alnifolia,* and the acidic sweetness of the berries helped cut the fatty taste of pemmican, so that saskatoons were frequently added to the buffalo fat in preparing pemmican. The fruit ripens across the prairies in June and July. First Peoples on their initial migrations into prairie regions more than 10,000 years ago would have seen bears eating the tart, juicy berries.

SWITCHEL

Haymakers' switchel was a homemade drink served to thirsty threshers and other farm labourers on hot summer afternoons. One recipe calls for a gallon of water, a cup of vinegar, a cup of molasses, two cups of brown sugar, and one teaspoon of ginger. All the ingredients are sloshed in a bucket or jug, which is then hung down a well to cool early in the morning before the harvest work begins. The word *switchel* is of North American origin and may have arisen from the fact that a stick or switch was used to mix the ingredients. In any case, switchel does appear to be the origin of swizzle stick, now used to stir more potent potables. Some of the other ingredients that have been used to make switchel include rum, honey, maple syrup, and vinegar.

A thresher arrives with a cool can
of switchel for the afternoon break.

CHAPTER 10

Alberta

I once asked an outdoors guide, "How's it going in Alberta these days?" "Slicker 'n a brookie!" he replied, expressing a sentiment that many proud Albertans share. Brookie is a Canadian diminutive for brook trout. I picked up an opposite folk saying from a reader in Vulcan, Alberta: "I feel like a dyin' calf in a hailstorm." A southern Alberta euphemism for death is "Gone to Sand Hills," the Sand Hills being the Happy Hunting Grounds for the Blood people of the sandy hill country south of Lethbridge. From Three Hills, Alberta, comes this dismissal: "He's lower than a snake's belly in a wagon rut." Consider too this Albertan put-down:

"He's so stupid he thinks Medicine Hat is a cure for head lice."

Alberta! Chinooks warm it, Alberta clippers (cold winds) freeze it. Eons ago, this land rumbled to the thud of monsters like the Albertosaurus, actual scientific name of a dinosaur whose bones were discovered near Drumheller. But what brought humans to these grasslands and parklands just east of the Rockies might be summed up in five words: bison, fur, cattle, grain, oil. Before the Europeans arrived, ancestors of the Blackfoot and other Aboriginal peoples came, nomadic hunters following the great herds of bison in their annual migrations across the vast prairie. Other First Peoples include the Amisk or Beaver people, the Slavey, the Tsuu T'ina (once called Sarcee), the Bloods, and Gros Ventre.

Occasionally in anthropology one finds that a people's method of preparing food actually gives them their name. This happened in the case of a Siouan people called the Assiniboine who once lived in southern Manitoba, but today are found in Alberta, Saskatchewan, and Montana. Their name is a French version of the Ojibwa *assini-pwan* 'stone Sioux.' The Ojibwa named these nomadic Sioux after their culinary habit of boiling certain foods by dropping hot stones into water kettles. Their name still dots the map of Canada in Mount Assiniboine and the Assiniboine River. Manitoba's famous Red River colony was in the District of Assiniboia granted to Lord Selkirk in 1811. One of the early divisions of our Northwest Territories in 1882, which later became southern Saskatchewan, was called Assiniboia.

Place names sometimes reflect sources of food, both from animals and plants. In Plains Cree the whitefish was called "caribou of the water" and this gives the name of a small settlement in Alberta named Atikameg, from Cree *atik* 'caribou' + *ameg* 'water.' Castor, Alberta, on the Beaverdam River bears the name of the animal in Latin. Kaleland, Alberta, was named by Scottish settlers after a type of cabbage. A common Scottish term for vegetable garden or cabbage patch is 'kale yard.' Lac La Biche is a French translation of Red Deer Lake. Many-berries, Alberta, east of Pakowki Lake, was a traditional site for harvesting saskatoon berries prior to making fall pemmican and is a translation of its original name in the Blackfoot language, Akonisk-way. Another Blackfoot locality name with the *-niskway* 'many' root was Akokiniskway 'many rose buds' which was translated into English to give Rosebud, Alberta, a village southeast of Drumheller. Namao, Alberta, is Cree for 'sturgeon,' and this little village north of Edmonton is on the Sturgeon River.

Significant white migration to Alberta did not really begin in numbers until after 1896. From then into the mid-years of the 20th century, settlers poured into Alberta. The non-native population in 1889 was 17,500. By 1921, it was almost 585,000. Many immigrants came from eastern Canada and Europe. Alberta became an official province in 1905, at the height of this population influx. By 1986, approximately 2,366,000 Albertans enjoyed the booming economy and independent flair of "wild rose country."

The food words peculiar to Alberta reflect, first of all, cowboy humour and chuckwagon grub. Take, for example, that prairie pudding, Son-of-a-Gun-in-a-Sack. In earlier times, when scarcity reared its scrawny head, settlers used wild plants as foods of necessity, and that too is reflected in some of these terms, along with a rough-and-tumble taste for spiritous liquors, more common in the past than now.

BAKED WIND PILLS

It's a cowboy slang phrase for beans, heated up in many a black pot over a rangeland campfire. "Beans, beans, the musical fruit. The more you eat, the more you toot." While French and Métis fur trappers tending line in what became central and northern Alberta might have longed for their staple *fèves au lard* (pork and beans), what in fact they and the earliest buffalo hunters often ate, when the supply of salt pork dwindled, was — rubbaboo and beans, in which chunks of pemmican were diced and tossed into the bean pot.

BALSAMROOT or SPRING SUNFLOWERS

This yellow-flowered perennial, a member of the daisy family, grows on sunny hillsides and flatlands from the foothills of Alberta into the southern interior of British Columbia. First Peoples, including the Interior Salish of B.C., dug the sweet taproots early in the spring and roasted them on hot rocks or in steaming pits. The roasted roots were eaten as a cooked vegetable, and also ground up and brewed in hot water as a drink sweetened with honey or berry juice. Early settlers sometimes used balsamroot as a coffee substitute. Balsamroot was translated into Greek-based botanical Latin to get the plant's scientific name of *Balsamorhiza sagittata*.

Sagitta is the Latin word for arrow, and the species name, *sagittata*, refers to this composite's arrow-shaped leaves. South of the border the plant is called Oregon sunflower, and many Aboriginal peoples of the Pacific Northwest also gathered the little seeds in midsummer in buckskin bags, which were then pounded until the seeds were reduced to a meal. This nutty-flavoured starch was added to native stews and soups and also blended with berries as a dessert.

BELLYBUSTERS

Sourdough biscuits and unleavened bannock made over a chuckwagon fire were both called bellybusters, betokening their hardness and frequent indigestibility.

CALGARY REDEYE

This simple brew is beer and tomato juice. Redeye was an earlier Canadian slang phrase for any cheap, homemade, often bootleg whisky, as were these terms, some imported to the frozen north by our American cousins: blaze-belly, bug juice, coffin varnish, embalming fluid, moose milk, pink-eye, prairie dew, rotgut, and snake poison. Imbibing too great a quantity of such booze often induced a temporary loss of certain male sexual functions, the general affliction bearing the all-Canadian name of — Brewers' Droop.

CANOLA

Canola could have been listed under any of the prairie provinces where more than two million hectares of this crop are grown annually, because it supplies seed, meal, and oil of high commercial value. In 1994 – 95 canola surpassed wheat as the largest cash crop in Canada. It used to be called turnip rape, from *rapum*, the Latin word for 'turnip.' But, let's face it, turnip rape conjures sexual shenanigans which might have befallen lonely tillers but are best left out of harvesting anecdotes. Even rapeseed as a term was tainted by the fact that it is spelled and pronounced exactly like sexual rape (from an entirely different Latin word *rapire* 'to seize and carry off'). And that, in spite of the fact that rapeseed has been a valuable source of nutritious vegetable oil for more than four thousand years in Asia.

Canadian farmers first grew the yellow flowers of this crop during WWII when rapeseed oil proved to be an effective lubricant for ship engines. After the war, Canadian scientists led by R.K. Downey hybridized rape to produce an oil high in monounsaturated fats and low in cholesterol. The euphemism *canola* was formed by compounding *Can* (Canadian) + *ola* (Latin, *oleum* 'oil'). Canola oil is used extensively in food processing, in margarines, salad dressings, soap manufacture, synthetic rubber, and as a fuel and lubricant.

CUSHION CACTUS FRUIT

This squidgy midget cactus hugs the slopes of dry coulee ridges in southern Alberta, with only its tiny but nasty spines protruding from the fingerlike mounds of the central fleshy mass of the cactus. Desert botanists sometimes call these little segments of cushion cactus, tubercules. But the plant taxonomist who named the species first thought these little mounds resembled nipples, hence the plant's genus *Mammillaria*, from Latin *mammilla* 'nipple.'

This Alberta cushion cactus was formerly labelled a mammillaria, but it now has the botanical name of *Coryphantha vivipara*. The genus name is made up of two Greek roots, *koryphe* 'hilltop, summit' and *anthos* 'flower,' and is so called because it bears flowers on the "hilltop" of its cushion. Latin *viviparus* 'bearing live young' as a species name in botany denotes that the plant bears little miniature plants on its leaves or in its flowers. Cushion cactus has striking, glowing dark-red flowers in June. The greenish-red fruit is harvested later, after first frost on the prairie, and has a delicate gooseberrylike flavour. Although the fruits do drop off the plant and ripen on the ground, care must be taken if picking them off the plant, since the fruit is often obscured by bristling spines.

DOLLY VARDEN TROUT

The Dolly Varden trout is a fish of our Pacific and western rivers and lakes, including some in central and northern Alberta. Not a trout, it's actually a char with gaudy orange speckles on a greenish skin. Dolly Varden is a character in Charles Dickens' novel *Barnaby Rudge.* The 1841 historical romance centres on the anti-Catholic riots in London in 1780. Dolly Varden is a buxom flirt, the daughter of a locksmith, who knows how, within her means, to dress flamboyantly enough to attract men and yet earn the approving comments of women. Dolly is a charming little coquette, and his prose makes it clear Charles Dickens approved most heartily of her. So did his Victorian readers. During the book's first printing Dolly Varden bonnets became all the rage in London. Thus it was quite natural, a century later, for some literary angler to name a vividly speckled Canadian fish after Dolly.

DOUGH GODS

In the cookhouses and around the chuckwagons of cattle-ranching operations in south and central Alberta, dough gods was a slang phrase for the flour dumplings often tossed into a big, black soup kettle. The nickname arose presumably from the lordly bobbing of the dumplings on or near the surface of the boiling broth.

ENGLISH MILK

In the speech of indigenous peoples trading with British trappers, English milk was a now obsolete synonym for rum. The phrase is noted in print as early as 1761. Some natives also called rum "milk" and "new milk."

FIREWATER

As early as 1743, both French and English translated an expression in Algonquian languages that denoted the cheap brandy or diluted whisky that white traders often bartered for furs with Aboriginal peoples. In the Cree tongue it was *iskotawapo* < Cree *iskota* fire + *wapo* water. In Ojibwa, firewater was *ishkodo-waaboo*. English traders also used the indigenous term in barter speech where *scuttaywabo* was frequently heard. The phrase suggests two things. High-proof alcoholic beverages like strong rum or whisky would ignite if tossed into a fire or if a lighted taper was brought close to a cup of booze.

It was firewater also because of the taste, feel, and effect of alcohol on someone drinking such potent spirits for the first time. But it was chiefly firewater to Aboriginal peoples because more sophisticated traders like the Blackfoot people soon realized, when trading with whites for whisky, that they had to test each batch of rotgut whisky by fire, because white traders diluted the alcohol to make it as weak as they could and still barter furs for it.

The term began in Canada. For example, James Isham wintering at Haye's River for the Hudson's Bay Company in 1747 lists, among his observations on local words, "brandy: scut ta wop pou." Although some of the most evil whisky traders were Americans along the border, both the British and Americans in the 19th century blamed the introduction of alcohol to native peoples on whites who came to the Canadas — and well they might have. Here's a taste of blame from James Fenimore Cooper's famous frontier novel of 1826, *The Last of The Mohicans*: "His Canada fathers . . . taught him to drink the fire-water, and he became a rascal." Forty years later the term had spread to standard British English, as here in 1861 in another popular novel, *Tom Brown at Oxford* by Thomas Hughes: "His father . . . had a horror . . . of the fire-water which is generally sold to undergraduates."

Perhaps the most notorious den of whisky-peddlers and frontier badmen was at Fort Whoop-Up, a whisky post set up in 1869 by two American thugs from Montana Territory named John Healey and Alf Hamilton. Fort Whoop-Up was established at the confluence of the Oldman and St. Mary Rivers near the site of present-day Lethbridge, Alberta. "Keg angels" and "whisky ranchers" were other names for these merchants of illicit alcohol. The going rate was one cup of whisky for one buffalo robe, that is, a buffalo hide dressed on both sides. The firewater they peddled to First Peoples was often — reports one source — diluted with swamp water. As it happens, one actual recipe survives in the archives at the Glenbow Alberta Institute, a holograph in the hand of John D. Higinbotham, a pioneer Lethbridge druggist, whose note I quote:

FORT WHOOP-UP

Fort Whoop-Up Recipe for the Liquor Traded to Indians:
Alcohol 1 qt.
Black Strap Chewing Tobacco - 1 lb.
Jamaica Ginger - 1 bottle
Black Molasses - 1 quart
Water - q.s.
The whole boiled until "ripe."
A cup of the above for one buffalo hide.

The abbreviation *q.s.* is pharmacist's Latin for *quantum satis* 'however much is enough,' that is, sufficient quantity to do the job. Some job. So wide and ill was the repute of this whisky fort that the whole area around the Alberta-Montana border came to be known as Whoop-up country. In 1874, the Northwest Mounted Police arrived, booted the whisky traders out, and took over the fort as a police outpost.

Whoop-up as a noun denoting a rousing western party had existed before the fort was named. Whoop as a verb and hunting interjection has been in our language since Middle English. Whoop-up and its American equivalent whoop-de-doo and whoopla and whoopee are in print by the middle of the 19th century.

GOLDEN CURRANT

The golden-yellow flowers of this shrub of southern Alberta found on streamsides and creek banks give it a common name, and *Ribes aureum* is its botanical tag. *Ribes*, the botanical Latin name for the goose-berry and currant genus, derives ultimately from Arabic or Persian *ribas* 'tart, acid-tasting,' and refers to many of the fruits in the genus. Gold currant has a blackish-purple berry with a strong but pleasant taste. Blackfoot people collected golden currant as part of their late-summer and early-autumn berry picking. Along with saskatoonberries and other prairie pickings, its tart taste helped pep up the greasy beat meat to which it was added to make pemmican.

HOT ROCKS

In western parlance, hot rocks were sourdough biscuits, named for their hardness and also perhaps for the fact that they could be baked on flat stones heated at the edge of a roaring camp fire.

INDIAN CELERY

Also called desert parsley and Indian consumption plant, *Lomatium naudicaule*, a perennial member of the celery family, prefers habitats like bluffs and dry meadows and woods. It grows in southern British Columbia and its range ends in southwestern Alberta. The young leaves of Indian celery were cooked as greens and used to flavour stocks, soups, and stews. A handful of young leaves was often boiled in water and allowed to steep to produce celery tea, which was drunk as a specific against sore throat and the common cold. As one of its names suggests — Indian consumption plant — the seeds of this celery were chewed because their juice was thought to assist those afflicted with tuberculosis. Indian celery seed is still used by those who grow herb gardens as a flavouring. A poultice of crushed seed was applied by Salish peoples of British Columbia to sores on the skin. Various lomatium species are grown for their sheer attractiveness as herb garden subjects.

INDIAN MUSTARD

Brassica juncea, Indian mustard or Chinese mustard, is a nasty annual weed of grain fields in much of western Canada. But young mustard leaves, rich in minerals and vitamin A, make delicious salad greens. They can be cooked in soups and casseroles, too. The seeds can be ground up and sharpened with a little vinegar to make a thick mustard similar to commercial preparations. Oil from Indian mustard is used in Russia, India, and central Africa much like olive oil in Europe and America.

JUNIPER TEA

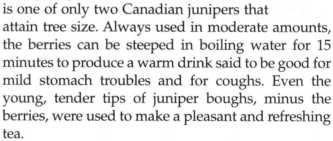

From southern Alberta's foothills to British Columbia's interior mountain ranges grows Rocky Mountain Juniper, *Juniperus scopulorum*, Latin 'of the rocky cliffs.' In spite of its specific, this conifer grows best in rich, well-drained, moist loam but can be seen clinging to a lofty precipice now and then. But it is one of only two Canadian junipers that attain tree size. Always used in moderate amounts, the berries can be steeped in boiling water for 15 minutes to produce a warm drink said to be good for mild stomach troubles and for coughs. Even the young, tender tips of juniper boughs, minus the berries, were used to make a pleasant and refreshing tea.

The ripe berries — really the cones — of several other juniper species are used as part of the flavouring of the French liqueur, Chartreuse, and, most famously, to flavour gin. Juniper berries begin green and take two to three years to ripen to a dark blue when they are harvested to add piney zest to pâtés and to game meats like venison and rabbit.

European immigrants found First Peoples burning juniper needles as incense and as an inhalant to cure coughing, as well as using the berries in herbal remedies. But note that raw, unprocessed berries and boughs of some juniper species can be toxic to livestock and are reported to have poisoned humans, although grouse, pheasants, and other birds bolt the berries with impunity. The teas made from juniper are for occasional, herbal use, and should not be taken daily.

MOUNTAIN OYSTER

In the slang of Alberta cowboys, mountain oysters are the fried testicles of a lamb or calf. Back east they are sometimes referred to as lamb fries or calf fries.

PRICKLY PEAR CACTUS

One of the cactus family native to Canada, *Opuntia polyacantha* (Botanical Latin < *polys* Greek, many + *acanthos* Greek, thorn, spine) has indeed many spines. On the dry banks of old coulees in southern Saskatchewan and Alberta, on the dry hills of British Columbia's interior, even on some dry islands in Georgia Strait, the prickly pear cactus blooms in early summer. Surprisingly, it also grows on Pelee Island in Lake Erie. Among the cat's cradle of prickly spines sit sensual cups of translucent yellow sepals, seemingly spun of buttery silk. These cactus flowers really do look like sexual organs, and of course they are, as they beckon insects into their vulval bowls with the promise of nectar, and send them on their way with a freight of pollen, male microspores eager to egg-on any friendly ovum in the area. But sweet as the flowers are, prickly pear spines penetrate shoe leather quick as steel needles. They also hide under snow and stiletto straight through a ski boot.

But you can eat the flesh of this cactus. If you skin the stubby leaves and carefully pluck out the spines, you can eat the leaves after roasting them in the bottom of a hot fire. If raw cactus leaves, peeled and despined, are too sticky, just wash them off in cold water. As a fresh vegetable, they can be served marinated in vinegar and lemon juice or raw in salads.

RATTLESNAKES

This is Alberta rangeland slang for rashers of bacon, just as "red lead" is chuckwagon ketchup, "tent pegs" are frozen strips of beef, and a fried hash that kept too many days in a trail cook's larder was called "yesterday, today, and tomorrow."

SON-OF-A-GUN-IN-A-SACK

Son-of-a-Gun-in-a-Sack is a chuckwagon "pudding." An empty sugar sack was dipped in water and dusted with flour. Pudding ingredients enough to feed twenty cowboys were spooned into the sack and the top sewn up. The pudding sack was plunged into a large cauldron of water and boiled for three hours. To serve, the sack was peeled off and the pudding cut into slices for eating. If it didn't turn out to be quite as toothsome a repast as the cook expected, those nibbling some times dubbed it "son-of-a-bitch-in-a-sack." At one roundup, the frowsy head of an unpopular and generally unclean cook was covered with an empty sugar bag and he was plunged into the water pot "to clean him off." Itinerant kitchen workers, take due note.

CHAPTER 11

The North

Modern humans first came to North America about 12,000 to 25,000 years ago. The archaeological record favours 12,000, while linguistic, genetic, and palaeodental studies agree that somewhere around that time, three waves of migration took place as the glaciers of the last ice age slowly retreated northward, permitting a crossing by the Bering land bridge. First came peoples speaking Proto-Amerind languages, and then, some time later those speaking Na-Dene languages, and last to migrate, the Inuit-Aleut peoples who migrated eventually as far as Greenland. As the first humans in the North they left their foodways and food words, some of which entered English to stay.

All newcomers to the North and Arctic following these First Peoples have been chided more or less gently about their parvenu status. On my own first visit to the Yukon, I was playfully labelled a real cheechako. Prospectors heading north to the Klondike gold rush of 1898 brought this Pacific coast word for 'greenhorn' or 'newcomer' with them. Cheechako is Chinook Jargon, *chee* 'new' + *chako* 'come.' Another definition of a cheechako was a prospector who had never seen the ice go out in the spring. Such tenderfoots were different than old gold-rush hands who called themselves sourdoughs, even if they had only been in the Yukon gold fields for a few months, even if they had not yet staked one claim. Sourdough was dough fermented with yeast; a portion of this leavened dough was saved to start the next batch of bread. Both terms were widely introduced into Canadian and American English by the popularity of Robert W. Service's books of frontier doggerel, especially by *Songs of a Sourdough* (1907) and *Ballads of a Cheechako* (1909). Do see the entry below for another term denoting a newcomer to the North, a porkeater or *mangeur de lard*. Sourdough is discussed elsewhere in this book, to leave room for other northern food words, a few of which are — I hope — new to you.

ALPINE BISTORT

This member of the knotweed family, a low-growing perennial herb of the tundra, is very widespread north of the tree line. *Polygonum viviparum* is also called serpent grass. *Viviparus* is a botanical Latin specific that means 'bearing live young' and in reference to this plant, it notes alpine bistort's habit of producing pinkish bulblets in the axils of its stem leaves. Autumn winds knock these little bulbs off the plant and they roll along the ground or are borne by high winds to new soil where they plop, send down roots, and establish new plants, hence the somewhat far-fetched species adjective *viviparum*. The pecan-sized roots of this bistort are cooked as a starch source and taste pleasantly of almonds. Many northern fanciers of wild plant food also eat the bulblets, which turn purplish-red as they ripen and can be plucked off the bistort plants to make a sweetish, almond-flavoured munch on a fall afternoon.

ATUNGAWIAT BEARBERRY KINNIKINNICK YUKON HOLLY

These terms all refer to the bearberry. *Atungawiat* is the plant's name in one of the dialects of Inuktitut, the many-dialected language of the Inuit. Other English terms are Bear's Grape and Indian Tobacco. And like many plants useful to humans, the bearberry has local names, too, such as Yukon holly. It's a member of the heath family of plants. Precisely, *atungawiat* is northern bearberry, the sweet dark fruit of *Arctostaphylos alpina*, a low shrub of the Barren Grounds; it is related to the more southerly kinnikinick (see below) but much sweeter, a true tundra treat. The tiny flowers look like white bells with pink rims, and the dense mats of leathery, evergreen leaves hug the northern ground, in some places like a green carpet. The red fruit of the bearberry is much munched by bears, hence its common name and the botanical label of the more southerly species: *Arctostaphylos uva-ursi*. *Arctostaphylos* means 'bear berry' in botanical Greek. *Uva ursi* means 'grapes of the bear' in Latin.

In all the northern climes of the world, humans have made tea from the dried leaves of bearberry, usually by a simple steeping for five minutes in boiled water. The red berries are also added crushed to tealike infusions. Early white fur trappers and prospectors often soaked the leaves of bearberry in whisky before steeping them to make tea. As a natural herbal remedy, the tea has been used for kidney and bladder troubles. Russians call the tea *kutai* and in their country it's widely used for various stomach disorders. Because the red berries are persistent through the long winter, *atungawiat* is an important emergency ration for those lost and hungry in the arctic barrens. Eaten raw, the berries are dry, floury, and tasteless, so they are mixed with other, sweeter wild foods, if possible.

Kinnikinick is another common name for this plant. The word means 'mixture' in Cree and Ojibwa, specifically a smoking mixture that might contain dried bearberry leaves, dried sumac leaves, red-osier dogwood bark, and tobacco. This very pungent Indian tobacco was smoked in a pipe.

Every native language seems to have a word to denote this widespread plant. Among the Chinook people, bearberry is *iss-salth*. The Cree call it *tchakoshe-pukk*; in the Chipewyan language it's *kleh*.

ARCTIC CHAR

One of the most esteemed freshwater food fish of northern Canada and still shipped south to Canadian restaurants and fish markets, this char is *Salvelinus alpinus*. Brook trout and lake trout are also Canadian chars. There are two varieties of arctic char, one landlocked and the other pelagic but going into fresh water to spawn.

Why, incidentally, does English call far northern realms "arctic" regions? The idea was borrowed into late Middle English from classical Greek, where *arktos* is the word for bear. The Greek adjective is *arktikos* 'pertaining to a bear.' But the Greeks used the terms to refer to one of the largest and brightest constellations in the northern skies, known to the Romans as Ursa Major 'The Great(er) Bear' and more familiarly known in English as The Big Dipper or The Plough. The Greeks thought of the distant, largely unknown lands lying under The Great Bear as dark, cold places perhaps devoid of human population. Hence our arctic, land under the constellation of the Great Bear. And, of course, opposite (Greek *anti* or *ant-*) the north pole is the land of the south pole, hence Antarctica.

In Greek myth, randy old Zeus, king of the gods and a major nymph-chaser, had a son out of divine wedlock by the nymph Calisto, who called her baby Arcas. Hera, queen of heaven and jealous wife of Zeus, was really ticked off, and seizing the opportunity to make a nasty pun (*Arcas-arktos*) caused Calisto's little bundle of joy to be turned into a large, revolting bear. But Zeus took pity on his now lumpish bastard son and set him up in the heavens to be forever with his papa in cloudland, and thus did The Great Bear come to adorn the northern night.

ARCTIC WILLOW TEA

There are dozens of species of ground-hugging dwarf willows in our north and they hybridize freely. Keeping low and clustered together is a protective strategy to keep out wind and freezing cold, and makes dwarf willows among the prostrate plant forms most common in subarctic and arctic regions. The bark of this scrawny, mat-forming shrub contains the antirheumatic chemical, salicin. Willow bark was imported into ancient Egypt to treat fevers and aches. More than 2,400 years ago, Greek physicians prescribed extract of white willow for gout. Many of the First Peoples of North America, including the Inuit, chewed its bark to alleviate toothache and, like the Montagnais of eastern Canada, also brewed a rich tea of arctic willow leaves and drank it to reduce headaches and for a warm pick-me-up.

Salix arctica takes its botanical name from Latin *salix* 'willow tree,' akin to the English word *sallow*, pale-yellow, in reference to the leaves or bark of several European species. In Middle English, a *sallow* was one of the broadleaved willows.

BEAR FOOT

This is a wooden, Aboriginal food-gathering device shaped like the claws of a bear and used to harvest blueberries. This little hand-sized rake can be used to gather other wild berries as well.

BEAR'S BUTTER

Also called bear's grease, this is the rendered white fat of a bear, used as food mixed with wild fruit like saskatoonberries, also used to fry food, to make medicine, as a cosmetic base, and smeared all over the body in emergencies to insulate the body from arctic cold. As a commodity, it came to the official attention of Hudson's Bay Company factors, appearing in the minutes of an HBC council meeting in 1824: ". . . that the Gentlemen in Charge of districts be directed to use every exertion to collect Bears' Grease as it is likely to become a valuable article of trade."

BLACKSKIN _or_ MUKTUK

Called _maktaaq_ in Inuktitut, usually spelled muk-tuk, blackskin is the tasty, edible skin of whales like the beluga, narwhal, and white whale, eaten fresh and raw by some Inuit, usually cooked by whites. "It tastes a little like coconut and shellfish," writes one culinary adventurer. "Not bad," reports another, "a bit like hazelnut." This protective outer covering is also called whale cork.

A narwhal whale

BOIL-UP & "A PIPE"

A boil-up is a stop for tea and a rest on northern trails, the term used as noun and verb: "We paused for a boil-up just past seven in the evening" and "We'll boil up at the next ridge." Boil-up places that were used frequently were marked as such on company or individual maps. Similar terms in the Canadian north are mug-up and smoke-up. Drink-up is saved for the return to town. Another early (1806) term for a rest-break was a "pipe." In the days of the fur trade and later, from voyageurs' French _une pipe,_ English picked up 'pipe' as a measure of distance. A pipe to explorers like Simon Fraser was the distance rowed or traversed between rest breaks. During such breaks but not usually en route, men would smoke a pipeful of tobacco.

BOISSON

Borrowed into Canadian English from early Québécois French _en boisson_ 'drunk,' a boisson was a booze-up or whisky feast at a trading fort when white trappers and First Peoples came to a post to trade.

BROCHET BANANA

Brochet banana is comic food parlance to denote a caribou tongue, still eaten as a delicacy in the Far North, and named after Lac du Brochet, itself named after the Québec French word for northern pike, *brochet*.

DEER'S TONGUE

Deer's tongue is a native plant, a liatris also called blazing star, whose leaves were used to flavour homemade tobacco mix.

ESKIMO ICE CREAM

Eskimo ice cream is a derogatory, obsolete, racist term for an Inuit pemmican — a dish of reindeer tallow, blueberries, and chunks of whitefish kneaded in the snow until frozen. It is on a disreputable par with "eskimo salad," a white insult phrase to denote half-digested moss found in a caribou's stomach and enjoyed as food by some Inuit.

Eskimo as Ethnic Slur & Other Racist Names of People

A note follows about the politically incorrect label, Eskimo. Eskimo is NOT an Inuit word, and is not liked or used by Inuit people except in jokes and ironical statements. French fur traders picked up the term *Esquimaux* from people speaking Algonkian languages. Eskimo means 'eaters of raw meat,' the insult implying they were so primitive they had not discovered the art of cooking meat. This misunderstanding would occur when a southern Aboriginal people wandering north saw Inuit eating certain parts of raw fish and mammals that had been freshly killed. Compare Cree *askimowew* 'he eats it raw' and Ojibwa *askkime* 'raw-flesh eater.'

The people call themselves Inuit. Inuit is the plural of *inuk*, a person. Inuit means 'the people.' And their language is Inuktitut, which encompasses meanings like 'the way of the people' or 'the Inuit way.'

Of course, racism abides in every people. The Inuit sometimes disliked southern Aboriginal peoples. Those whom frontier English called redskins and Indians, the Inuit often called *Irkrekret* 'lice.' European whites bore several insulting names in Inuktitut, among them *kablunet* 'people with big, hairy eyebrows,' that is, really ugly! A current word for whites in one of the eastern dialects of Inuktitut is *qallunaat* 'eyebrows and big stomach.'

More than 40 percent of all the world's tribal and national names contain a root that signifies 'the people.' For example, Inuit and Innu mean 'the people.' Dene, the correct name of the Athapaskan-speaking peoples, means 'the men' or 'human beings.' When people of different races speaking different languages meet in history, there is territorial animosity, war, and rarely peaceful cooperation. There is also name-calling, mutual mangling of tribal names, and odd labels for newly encountered groups.

When the people our history calls Algonquin or Algonkin met their first whitemen along the St. Lawrence and in the Ottawa valley, these Anishnabeg — correct name for the Algonquins — were startled by French priests with wooden crucifixes. So the Anishnabe word for the French is *wa-mit-ig-oshe* 'men who wave wood over their heads.'

White immigrants to North America were less kind in what they called First Peoples. The Huron people may have been given that name as an insult, from an Old French word for wild boar's head or lout. White invaders also had the clumsy habit of asking tribes what they called their enemies who lived near them. Farther west and north, another large group of Aboriginal peoples, the Athapaskans, never called themselves by that appellation, for the good reason that it means 'strangers' in Cree.

FIREWEED TEA

Some Aboriginal peoples of the North like the sugary pith of fireweed obtained by splitting a young stalk and scooping it out. Elk and deer browse in fireweed fields, and bees produce a dark, sweet-smelling honey which makes it worth putting beehives near fireweed. Beekeepers also plant fireweed close to northern apiaries because the honey produced is of superior taste. French-Canadian voyageurs called fireweed *l'herbe fret* and cooked it as greens. In Russia, fireweed leaves are brewed for kapporie or kapor tea. Other names for this wild plant, which is invasive on cleared or logged-off land, are mooseweed or willow herb. Its most common name signifies that fireweed is among the first plants to bloom on land after a burn-over. Campers in our North may brew up a refreshing backwoods tea by pouring hot water over the tender young leaves of fireweed. The tea is light green and sweetish. Just make sure you have correctly identified fireweed before teatime, so that there may be an after-teatime.

August 17 is Discovery Day in Yukon Territory, recalling the big strike of 1896 that began the Klondike gold rush. A sprig of fireweed often decorates posters and advertising concerning Discovery Day because the pink-blossomed fireweed, *Epilobium angustifolium*, is the official flower of the Yukon. When the pod dehisces after midsummer, it sends out delicate aerial flotillas of silky-winged seeds across thousands of northern acres. The specific adjective *angustifolium* means 'with narrow leaves.'

There is also a broad-leaved species, *Epilobium latifolium*, called mountain fireweed or river beauty, whose deep pink flowers are truly startling spread across a damp arctic-alpine meadow or scattered beside a northern streamside.

The young shoots and flower buds of fireweed and mountain fireweed have been eaten raw or cooked as emergency foods. *Coureurs de bois* and colonists learned from Aboriginal herbalists to make a poultice for skin sores from the ground-up root of fireweed.

GRUBSTAKE

Here's a term brought north to Canada by Yankee prospectors looking for Klondike gold. But once established in mining parlance, grubstake acquired several extensions of meaning in Canada. Grubstake, an American word from the California goldfields of the mid-19th century, developed out of earlier British slang. Grub meant first 'something dug up,' like the edible roots or tubers of a plant, then 'food,' and by 1821 it was a transitive verb meaning 'to supply someone with food.' And that's where grubstake steps in. The way it worked by the time of the Klondike gold rush was simple: a person with money financed a prospector's attempt to find gold by supplying the eager miner's food and equipment needs. In return for the risk involved in this early form of venture capital, the person staking the miner got half of any gold the sourdough might find. Of course, if things didn't pan out — things like gold nuggets — then the prospector had enjoyed a free trial dig. In Canada, grubstake could refer strictly to the money or provisions alone: "Where's my grubstake? Gone." A grubstake could also be the accumulated store of food and provisions needed to reach the goldfields and stake a claim. In Canada, grubstake also passed into wide usage in the fur trade to refer to an advance given by the Hudson's Bay Company to a trapper going out on traplines, this grubstake being an advance against the profit the trapper would make when he returned to the trading post to sell his furs.

HOOTCH

Hootch and hootchinoo are one-hundred-percent Canadian booze words. Hootch, now a term for homebrew or a popular synonym for any liquor, was first popularized in the Yukon during the days of the Klondike gold rush, and has now spread across Canada. Hootch is short for hootchinoo, a cheap, inferior whisky made during the gold rush. Hootchinoo is the mangled English form of a word in the Tlingit language, *khutsnuwu*, or Grizzly Bear Fort, the name of a people and their village on Admiralty Island, where hootch was first brewed from molasses, yeast, local berries, and other ingredients best left veiled from mortal knowledge.

Tlingit is a member of the Na-Dene family of northern languages. It is spoken by a people now inhabiting southern Alaska and some offshore islands. In 1981 approximately 1,500 people still spoke the language. Tlingit in Tlingit means 'the people.' As for the roots of the name Na-Dene: in Chipewyan and in Proto-Athapaskan, *dene* means 'person.' *Naa* in related languages like Haida and Tlingit has to do with roots meaning 'house,' 'living,' and 'tribe.' Thus, the semantic sense of Na-Dene is 'our people.'

INCONNU

This northern treat is one of the prize catches of the Yukon and arctic fishery. Devotees say the flesh tastes like rich cream. Its French tag, short for *poisson inconnu* 'unknown fish,' is used in English, but many other peoples have named this finny delight. Also known in English as a connie, coney, or cony, in Russian it's *nelma*; in Chipewyan, *shee*; and in zoology, *Stenodus mackenzii* because this freshwater food fish is native to the Mackenzie River and many other lakes and rivers of our Northwest Territories. Inconnu is a game fish often caught by jigging for it through holes in the ice during late autumn when its flesh is firmest and tastiest. Inconnu can be pan-fried or poached. It is said that explorer Alexander Mackenzie named it inconnu because it was unknown in southern Canadian waters.

LOCHE

The loche is a freshwater cod of northern lakes, *mathemek* or *methy* in Cree. While loche liver is a Dene delicacy, many others who had to eat the fish of necessity reported its flesh to be "coarse" and "muddy." Standard French *loche* is related to British *loach*, but like many words carried far from their points of origin, some fish terms like loche come to denote several, entirely different species of fish.

MANGEURS DE LARD or PORKEATERS

Mangeurs de lard, used in English and Canadian French, were, of course, literally porkeaters. Both terms were now-obsolete insults by established local residents and indigenes of any newcomers, any passing voyageurs who depended on pork fat rations carried in their canoes, with the implication that they could not live off the land like those who had already settled an area. Porkeaters served as a put-down among the grizzled old interior trappers of the Northwest Company. These tough veterans of lonely canoe routes through interior country scorned new employees of the company who had to paddle only the canoe routes between Montreal and Grand Prairie. These young beginners lived "high off the hog" on salt pork rations, unlike the interior hunters who ate rougher fare like pemmican. So voyageurs came in two classes: raw beginners were porkeaters, while seasoned veterans were winterers or *hivernants* in Canadian French.

In explorer John Franklin's 1823 *Narrative of a Journey to the Shores of the Polar Sea in the Years 1819, 1820, 1821, and 1822* is this little note: "There is a pride amongst 'Old Voyageurs' which makes them consider being frost-bitten as effeminate, and only excusable in a 'Pork-Eater,' or one newly come into the north country."

MASO or LICORICE ROOT

This arctic perennial, *Hedysarum alpinum*, has carrotlike tubers that are long, flexible, sweetish, crisp, and edible. The Inuit name is *maso* or *masu*. The plant's favourite habitats are arctic riverbanks and lake shores where the licorice-tasting tubers are dug in early spring to be eaten raw or cooked. The tubers become woody and insipid as the short arctic growing season advances. The roots can be dried, powdered, and boiled in water to produce an herbal diuretic.

MOOSE MUFFLE SOUP

A moose muffle or mouffle or moufle is the nose and the pendulous, overhanging upper lip of the moose eaten boiled, baked, or fried as a delicacy. It was particularly prized among the Cree who boiled it and cut the muzzle into very thin slices. In 1754, Anthony Henday, exploring for the Hudson's Bay Company, wrote in his diary: "I dressed a lame man's leg. He gave me a Moose nose, which is a delicate dish, for my trouble." Canadian English *moose muffle* was borrowed from Québec French *mufle*, itself from Standard French *mufle* 'any animal's muzzle.'

Several recipebooks of Aboriginal cooking tips warn of moose nose and lips being "an acquired taste." Beware of any nutriment for which the eater must acquire a taste. Such a phrase implies that the eater must acquire the taste because the food lacks it. Although highly esteemed of yore, the spectacle of a moose's nose and upper lip — from which the large bristles and hairs have been uprooted violently with a pair of giant pliers — does not inspire in the novice diner any great confidence. Ditto with moose muffle soup, although it has one advantage: the moose's muffle has been chopped and diced until it is no longer recognizable as the flappy-lipped snout of a large, spooky mammal.

NIPKO

Nipko or nipkoo or nipku is an Inuit staple food, being strips of sun-dried caribou meat. The Eastern Inuktitut term *nikku* 'dried meat,' can refer to narwhal jerky or beluga jerky, as well.

QUAWK

Quawk is uncooked frozen meat or fish that is eaten so, from Inuktitut *quaq* 'frozen meat.' For example, fresh-caught seal and sometimes caribou rump are consumed as quawk. Certain arctic fish are said to taste best as quawk. In northern English peppered with Inuktitut words, the term is used as an adjective as well: "He ate the seal *quaq* [frozen and raw]."

ROCK TRIPE *or* TRIPE DE ROCHE

Rock tripe is a translation of the Canadian French coinage *tripe de roche*, here meaning 'rock guts.' Aboriginal peoples first showed whitemen how to eat this emergency food, which they called *wakwund*. Voyageurs often scraped this edible lichen directly off the rocks from their canoes, and sometimes carved their initials in the blank rock wall so exposed. It is not highly nutritious but does fill the stomach of a starving wretch until he finds his fellows, his fate, or some real food.

Lichen is a symbiotic partnership between a fungus and an alga. The fungus supplies the outer form of the lichen, the alga supplies chlorophyll so photosynthesis can take place. The genera that make up rock tripe are *Gyrophora* and *Umbilicaria.*

Here is explorer Samuel Hearne on rock tripe in his *A Journey from Prince of Wales's Fort* (1795):

> There is a black, hard, crumply moss, that grows on the rocks and sometimes furnishes the natives with a temporary subsistence, when no animal food can be procured. This moss, when boiled, turns to a gummy consistence, and is more clammy in the mouth than sago; it may, by adding either moss or water, be made to almost any consistence. It is so palatable, that all who taste it generally grow fond of it. It is remarkably good and pleasing when used to thicken any kind of broth, but it is generally most esteemed when boiled in fish-liquor.

Tripe started life at the back of the butcher shop. It's tissue from a cow's first or second stomach used as food. Tripe came into the English word-stock from Norman French after 1066 and all that. The French borrowed it from Provençal *tripa* and cow-stomach-eating troubadours heard it first in Italy as *trippa*. English extensions of the sense followed, and tripes meant guts, then tripe was a worthless person, food, or thing.

SCURVY GRASS

This fleshy herb of the mustard family is widespread through our northern vastnesses. *Cochlearia officinalis* has tender, crisp leaves which are indeed high in vitamin C, of which scurvy is a deficiency disease. But it tastes much like watercress and is a delightful nibble raw in a northern salad or sprinkled as a fresh green on a meat sandwich.

USSUSAQ

This is the Inuit term for a plant with the ungainly English name of Woolly Lousewort, a perennial herb common throughout the arctic tundra regions. The roots of *ussusaq* are eaten raw, or boiled and served with butter, salt, and pepper. They have a savour of sweet, young carrots. In June some northern peoples also boil the flowering stems of this lousewort as dinner greens or use the stems raw in salads.

CHAPTER 12

British Columbia

*B*ritish Columbia joined Confederation on July 20 in 1871. Among the gifts she brought to the Dominion were colourful place names based on the prized food fish of West Coast waters. Salmon Arm and Salmo (the zoological genus of the fish and the Latin word for salmon) are obvious. Less so is Coquitlam, from a Salish tribe who call themselves Kawayquitlam after their totem animal which was the sockeye. The name means 'small, red salmon.' Qualicum Beach, Vancouver Island, means 'place of dog salmon.' Whonnock, B.C. means 'humpback salmon place,' while the Similkameen means 'salmon river.' One authority does say Similkameen means 'swimming river.' Finally, in considering important fish, we must not forget that prize catch, former B.C. Premier William Van-der Zalm, whose surname means 'of the salmon' in Dutch. The name Vander Zalm recalls, to most who know the language of the Netherlands, a familiar Dutch figure of speech, *het neusje van de zalm* 'the snout of the salmon,' considered a delicacy in Holland. The phrase means the pick of the lot, the choicest piece. Some of us who remember Vander Zalm's time in office might find the connection quite fanciful.

Many other playful but official place names in British Columbia refer to food. Consider only Chili Creek, Coffee Crater, Fried Egg Lake, Mount Cold-ham, Orange Juice Creek on Vancouver Island, and Pancake Glacier near the border of the province with central Alberta. Sockeye salmon was named here, as was the Nanaimo bar, and, perhaps less known but no less worth trying, soapollallie "ice cream" and gooeyducks.

AMOTE *or* AMUTE

Amote was the term in Chinook Jargon for the wild strawberry of our Pacific coast. Chinook jargon was a lingua franca, a trading language based on the speech of the Chinook Indians, with words from French, English, Salish, Nootka, and other local tongues thrown in as needed. From it, West Coast English borrowed several food terms, as you will see below. Chinook jargon was used for over a hundred years until the turn of the century by Aboriginal peoples and the white traders who plied the Pacific coast.

Alexander Ross in *The Fur Hunters of the Far West*, published in 1855, described a good feed of local grub one day near the head waters of the Columbia River in what would become southeast-ern British Columbia. He spoke of an eater with "his bark platter filled top heavy with the most delicious melange of bear's grease, dog's flesh, wappatoes, olellies, amutes, and a profusion of other viands, roots, and berries." See the *soapolallie* and *wapatoo* entries below.

CAMAS

Salish people taught early white visitors, including explorer David Thompson, to eat and to make root bread from the sweet, starchy bulbs of this plant which are found two to six inches below ground in their preferred habitat of wet meadows. Other common names: Camas, camass, commas, kamass, or quamash — there are more spellings for this once staple food bulb of western Canada than you can shake a digging stick at. Camas was the name in Chinook Jargon which in turn borrowed it from the Nootka language where *camas* means 'sweet,' in reference to the edible bulbs. The original Nootka name for the place that became Victoria on Vancouver Island was *Camosun*, 'place where we gather camas.' Once Pacific coast peoples used to harvest the bulbs of this blue-flowered member of the lily family and bake them immediately in ground ovens. They could be eaten hot or could be dried and stored for winter rations. Another name for the plant was bear grass, because black bears would grub for the tasty bulbs in the summer. Humans, however, harvested them in the plump-bulbed autumn.

There is one fly in the paradisal ointment here — isn't there always? — and that is death camas, a nasty little plant that sometimes grows with camas and has bulbs similar in appearance, but it never has a blue flower. Death camas blooms a sickly white. *Zygadenus venenosus* is highly toxic to humans and other animals. Care had always to be taken at harvest. Indeed native peoples usually weeded out death camas when it flowered from among the food camas. In 1878 there was a camas war when the U.S. Army fought the Nez Percé people, after white settlers had let their pigs loose in the camas prairies that Nez Percé had used for centuries as natural gardens.

Several species including *Camassia cusickii* and the Canadian *Camassia quamash* make good garden subjects, planted like tulips in the fall and left undisturbed until overcrowding occurs. In its natural setting in British Columbia, camas likes mountain meadows that are wet in the spring and that dry up well by midsummer.

Camas were noticed by the 19th-century Canadian painter Paul Kane on his sketching tours of 1845 – 48. Kane published his field notes in 1859 as *Wanderings of an Artist* and wrote this of camas: "They are found in immense quantities in the vicinity of Fort Vancouver, and in the spring of the year present a most curious and beautiful appearance, the whole surface presenting an uninterrupted sheet of bright ultra-marine blue, from the innumerable blossoms of these plants."

CANDLEFISH *or* OOLICHAN

The oolichan, a very greasy little Pacific smelt, was an important source of oil for natives and settlers of our West Coast. Oolichan oil had medicinal properties, contained vitamins A and D, and was more pleasant to the palate than cod liver oil. A writer named Molyneux St. John offered one explanation of the common English name, in a book entitled *The Sea of Mountains — An Account of Lord Dufferin's Tour Through British Columbia in 1876*: ". . . candle fish; so full of oil that it can be lighted at one end and used as a candle."

GEODUCK *or* GOOEYDUCK

Gooeyduck is the wonderfully slurpy slang word for a tasty clam of Canada's west coast, one that inhabits the saltwater tidelands of our Pacific waters. It was not named because the glistening innards reminded someone of a duck pressed into a goo. One may dine on that in Paris. Another spelling is geoduck. The word is from the Nisqually language, from which it was taken into Chinook Jargon, the old trading language of southern British Columbia. The gooeyduck is the largest burrowing bivalve in the world, and that habit caused the Nisqually tribe to call it *go-duk* or dig-deep. Its very deep burrows make it a tricky clam to harvest. The geoduck (pronounced GOOee-duck) can attain a mature weight of more than seven kilograms and have a neck as big as a fire hydrant. There is already a black market trade in these clams which are illegally shipped to Hong Kong and Japan where a single gooeyduck sells for more than sixty Canadian dollars. Japanese prize them especially in geoduck sashimi, an example of a traditional Japanese dish (bite-size slices of raw geoduck) now made with this Canadian clam. Maybe we could induce our transPacific world-mates to put little leashes on the giant clams and trundle them around in wheeled aquaria? Perhaps they could bow to the gooeyducks throughout the day, instead of gobbling them up with such gusto? If you think wolfing down geoducks is cruel, do keep in mind that there is still a brisk market in the isles of paradise for Hawaiian broiled puppy.

GOW

Gow is a legal Canadian export, worth more than one million dollars a year, that you may not know. Gow is a rough Englishing of a Japanese word that signifies 'little eggs.' Gow is a delicacy in the cuisine of Japan. It is herring roe (fish eggs) spawned on a small piece of seaweed. Some B.C. fisheries actually plant severed fronds of algal seaweed within schools of spawning herring, and harvest the result for immediate air freighting across the Pacific. The delicacy was known to B.C. native peoples, whose ancestors may have brought the discovery with them eons ago when they first crossed the Bering Strait to enter North America.

HIGH MUCKAMUCK

Now referring to a pompous official, high mucka-muck once meant merely someone with plenty of food to eat. High muckamuck is a term I remember my father using as a way to describe any arrogant S.O.B. of an official. As he was a school principal, it sprang up often when he spoke of school boards. The term, first in Canadian, then borrowed into American English, was taken, with a touch of folk etymology, from Chinook Jargon, the West Coast trading language of the last century. *Hyiu* meant 'much' and came into the catch-all trading language from the Nootka tongue of Vancouver Island where *ih* means big. *Muckamuck* was food in Coast Salish. In the days when food gathering took much time and skill, anyone who had lots of food was an important and successful person, hence a high muckamuck. Its mucky sound in English made it appropriate as a deflator of ballooning egos. Muck-a-muck was borrowed into West Coast English very early as a synonym for food. Even a verb, to muck-a-muck 'to eat heartily,' appears in pioneer journals and diaries.

LINGCOD

While a number of different species of marine food fish are called ling by Canadian fishers, this lingcod is a large, edible denizen of our north Pacific waters. Sometimes it is considered as two words, ling cod. *Ophiodon elongatus* (literally 'snake-toothed [fish] with elongated body') is one of the favourite quarries of the spear-fisherman.

The word *ling* is simply a vowel gradation of Old English *lang* 'long,' referring to the animal's length.

MINER'S LETTUCE

In sandy soil of shaded northwest woodlands from California through British Columbia right up to Alaska, grows two species of miner's lettuce. Either one of the two species of this succulent member of the purslane family have provided vitamin-rich greens for Pacific-based First Peoples and for early white settlers, including the gold rush prospectors and miners of both California and the Klondike. *Montia perfoliata* and *Montia sibirica*, Siberian miner's lettuce, are the two species. Once seen, Montia is an easy plant to identify, and its specific adjective reminds us of its best field mark, perfoliate stem leaves. Perfoliate indicates that the stem seems to grow 'through the leaf' or in Latin *per folium.* In fact, the stem leaf clasps the stem near its top as a single, cup-shaped disc. It is from each of these clasping disc-leaves that the plant sends forth its little cluster of white flowers. Like many purslanes and portulacas, the plants develop a protective reddish coloration in locations where they receive full sun or where they grow in poor soil. The young leaves can be picked and eaten raw as a salad green, or cooked in salted, boiling water for several minutes, after which they taste like spinach. Miner's lettuce is still a staple green for many northern First Peoples.

MOWICH or MOWITCH

The Chinook Jargon word for deer or deer meat derived from Nootka *muwich* or from the language of the Chinook people *mow-wich*, both meaning 'deer.' It was fairly common in British Columbia rural English for years after Chinook

Jargon ceased to be widely spoken. Outdoors writer, R.D. Symons, as late as 1963 in his book *Many Trails* speaks of a "good breakfast of fried mowitch and bannock." Or consider this headline from a 1964 B.C. newspaper, the *Penticton Herald*: "Mowich on Road Cause of Mishap."

Nanaimo bar is a baked treat popular all across Canada, often as little cut squares of biscuit alternating with a sweet cream filling and covered with chocolate. They may have been first concocted in the city of Nanaimo on Vancouver Island. A number of local native bands amalgamated in the mid-19th century, calling their union *sne-ny-mo*, or 'big, strong tribe.' Something sweet about this island place has entered Canadian English, so the appearance of something slightly sour in a Canadian folk saying may balance the scales. If you boat in B.C. waters, you may someday hear this scrap of dialogue:

> Rich bully on big yacht: Did you see what that trash was wearing, Phyllis?
> Wife of rich bully tipping the scales at a pixie-like 150 kilos: Yeah, Full Nanaimo.

Are B.C. recreational boaters and yachtsmen a trifle snooty? They seem to pay finicky attention to how their fellow mariners dress. "Full Nanaimo" is an insult that applies to a chintzy outfit worn by a boating parvenu. Whitebuck shoes, white belt, polyester pants, and a blue blazer with a spurious yachting crest brand the wearer as a floating yutz of the first water. A similar chop is FDAM, pronounced to rhyme with ram. The acronym stands for First Day At the Marina.

NANAIMO BAR

Several species of the bulbous fritillary are native to western Canada and one of them provided food from its curiously shaped bulbs. *Fritillaria Camschatcensis* (botanical Latin 'of the Kamchatka peninsula,' located at the extreme eastern end of Russia, between the Bering Sea and the Sea of Ohkotsk) is also found on the other side of the Pacific Ocean, from Alaska, down through coastal British Columbia, with abundant stands on the Queen Charlotte Islands, to the limit of their south-

NORTHERN RICE-ROOT

ern range in the state of Washington. The curious bulbs look like a bunch of grains of cooked rice, hence one common name, northern rice-root. The flowers hang like dark-purple bells, hence another common name, black lily. Southern Inuit and many First Peoples of the Pacific coast dug the starchy bulbs in the autumn, dried them, and powdered them to use as a winter flour.

POTLATCH

The potlatch was an important ceremony of many Pacific coast and Interior peoples in which magnificent gifts were given and sometimes exchanged, chieftains invested with power, names bestowed on young persons, spirits propitiated, dances performed, and feasts enjoyed. The word came into English from Chinook Jargon from the Nootka word *patshatl* 'a giving, a gift.' But white busybodies did not always understand the complexity of the potlatch and how its sociological strands were woven tightly into band and clan life. Rivalry between clans of one people made obsessive potlatching reach alarming proportions toward the end of the 19th century, with heads of clans ordering the extravagant gifting and subsequent destruction of food and property merely to enhance the prestige of the clan-head giving the potlatch. Massive debts were incurred by clans, sometimes resulting in total poverty and actual starvation. Gifts in potlatch required the giving of a gift in return. Some clan chiefs set out deliberately to impoverish rival clans. Finally, the Canadian federal government outlawed the full ceremony in its 1884 Potlatch Law. By the time the ban was repealed in 1951 during revision of the Indian Act, serious clan disruption had resulted, permanently skewing tribal identities, ranks, and statuses.

Potlatch acquired many secondary and figurative meanings in Canadian English. It came to refer to a free handout or to any winter festivity including the watered-down "give-away dances" that replaced ethnic potlatches after they were outlawed. Informal use saw potlatch synonymous with party or celebration. During the 1940s and 1950s in British Columbia English a potlatch also named a carnival or fair held by Aboriginal peoples and featuring canoe races and games, sponsored to raise money for local and charitable causes.

SALAL

This member of the wintergreen genus is a little evergreen shrub native to our Pacific coast. British Columbians who enjoy wild foods pick the purplish salalberries in late summer or early autumn to make jams. Tart salal jelly makes a grease-cutting accompaniment to servings of game. Aboriginal peoples of our Pacific coast cooked salalberries into a jam between red-hot rocks in ground-ovens. Salal leaves and berries, containing methyl salicylate, the chemical that gives oil of wintergreen its distinctive smell and some of its properties, should not be fed to children who are hypersensitive to aspirin, the common analgesic that is related chemically to methyl salicylate. Otherwise salalberries or young, fresh leaves make a pleasant, fragrant tea. And the glossy, reasonably long-lasting leaves of salal are a favourite of West Coast florists' bouquets.

Salal's botanical name is *Gaultheria shallon*. The genus is named after a botanist who spent most of his life in 18th-century Québec City. Jean-François Gaulthier was a royal physician, amateur botanist, and friend to the Swedish explorer of North America, Peter Kalm, who in turn was a supplier of specimen plants to the great Swedish founder of botanical nomenclature, Linnaeus. Thus, after Kalm returned to Sweden with samples of wintergreen collected near Québec by Gaulthier, Linnaeus gladly named the wintergreen genus in honour of the

French doctor. The specific *shallon* and the common name *salal* both derive from the name of this plant in Chinook Jargon, the early trading language of our Pacific coast, which in turn drew it from the wordstock of the Chinook language where the berry is *sálal*.

SALMONBERRY *or* OLALLIE

Salmonberry is also known by its common name in Chinook Jargon, olallie, although olallie strictly denotes any berry. For example, among several Aboriginal peoples of British Columbia, homemade berry wine is olalliechuk, from Chinook Jargon *olallie* 'berry' + *chuck* 'water.' Salmonberry is *Rubus spectabilis*, a showy shrub of the raspberry family with pretty red flowers and salmon-coloured berries. The specific, *spectabilis*, means showy. There was a Canadian movie starring Alberta's k.d. lang entitled *Salmonberries*. In *Salmonberries* the frisky warbler of pop songs played a provocative but beguiling role. So too did the sweet red berries of this shrub that belongs to the huge rose family of plants. Its juicy fruits look like big raspberries and are eaten ripe or made into a delicious jam. The common name was used first along the banks of the Columbia River where native peoples had a favourite dish that consisted of the very young, tasty shoots of the plant eaten with dried salmon roe. Indeed, salmonberry's home range is the Pacific coast, and it thrives west of the Rockies. At one of the best dinners he has ever eaten in Canada, a private and delightful affair served at a table overlooking tidal pools on Vancouver Island's west coast, the author has tasted salmonberry charlotte, a dessert that combines sweetness, sin, and regional appropriateness in equal portions.

SIWASH

Siwash entered English from Chinook Jargon. But siwash began its verbal life as an insulting voyageurs' term for a native person, and it is still an insult. It is a slurry jumbling up in Chinook Jargon of *savage*, the voyageurs' French term for any member of an Aboriginal people, equivalent to savage or wildman, and based on standard French, *sauvage*.

Although siwash is vile and derogatory, or perhaps just because of its swinish bigotry, it gained wide use. Siwash tongue was a synonym for Chinook Jargon. To siwash once meant to travel quickly, deftly, and lightly, making use of natural shelters on the trail, or sleeping in the open as a First Nations person might do. Siwash wind is a Pacific Coast localism for any fresh gale that blows up briskly. A Siwash blanket is low cloud cover that portends weather warmer than if the ceiling were higher. In his 1963 book, R.D. Symons says that "most ranchers in the interior [of B.C.] loosely refer to all Indians as Siwashes." A synonym for a beachcomber in B.C. is a Siwash logger.

And so it was natural that several foods were tagged with the adjective too. Siwash pudding was made from dried saskatoons by boiling the dried berries, then adding a little flour and sugar. Siwash rhubarb is a wild plant also called Indian rhubarb. It is prepared by skinning the hollow stalk, cutting it like garden rhubarb into pieces, and boiling it in salted water. Then serve like any potherb with butter, salt, and pepper. For siwash waptoo, see below in the entry for *wapatoo*.

SKIL

Skil is a delicious, deep-water, food fish of the northern Pacific coast, the word derived from its Haida name, *squil*. Also called skilfish or sablefish, it is caught and smoked, and often sold under the name *black cod*. Giant specimens can attain a weight of ninety kilograms.

SLUMGULLION

In the United States where this word was coined to denote thick, runny mud, it was used in mining vocabulary where in certain kinds of excavation work, such guck often impedes tunnelling. During the gold rushes that brought prospectors to what would become northern British Columbia and the Yukon, and among those building the CPR railway, slum was any treacherous, slippery mud encountered as a barrier to progress. Cariboo slum was a term for the slithery muck prospectors often found in the creek valleys of the B.C. interior. Later in Canada, slumgullion named any catch-as-catch-can stew, any liquid-based slop a cook might confect from nutritious kitchen scraps.

SOAPOLALLIE SOAPBERRY or HOOSHUM

Best known is soapolallie "ice cream," which is soapberries whisked with water to froth up and with other wild berries like wild raspberry added, along with sugar, to sweeten the naturally slightly bitter soapberry. Earlier in West Coast history, this berry was also called brue, from voyageurs' French *broue*, the old Québec word for the froth on beer. Soapolallie ice cream is a foamy British Columbia treat made by picking ripe soapberries and macerating them with sugar. Then take a broad wooden spoon and whip them briskly until they foam and froth into what is also called Indian ice cream. The word is Chinook Jargon. Soap means soap, because they froth up so. *Olallie* is Chinook for 'berry.' The root shows up in the word for a potent homebrew of our West Coast called olalliechuk, which is a berry wine. *Chuck* is Chinook Jargon for water. Compare the common B.C. term for the ocean, the saltchuck, from Chinook Jargon *chuck* 'water.' Tribes of the southern Pacific coast also made a berry bread called olallie sapolel. Farther north, Athapascan-speaking peoples called soapberry *hooshum*.

Soapberry is a shrub, *Shepherdia canadensis*, whose berries were often dried into flat cakes by First Peoples of our Pacific coast, and packed as rations for travel. The cakes could be whipped into a foamy trailside drink after being soaked in water. A related *Shepherdia* of our prairies has the popular name, buffaloberry.

Once upon a time I was camping near Pacific Rim National Park on Vancouver Island. One morning as I hunched over a tidal rockpool to observe a starfish lazily lunching on a hapless mollusc, an elderly gentleman (of a type I seem to encounter in every natural setting) approached. Let's just call him the World's Foremost Living Expert — on pretty well every topic known to human conversation. We exchanged a bit of amiable lip-flap, and in the course of his jawin', the grizzled old salt asked me if I knew that the sockeye salmon received its name when hearty fishermen of olden days waded into the water and took the fish by belting it in the face. "It's an urge that could overtake any of us," I said, adding that I didn't see how the S.P.C.A. could permit such enormities.

Then, humbly, I suggested there might be another explanation, having to do with a local Aboriginal language; but by then the World's Foremost Living Expert was a hundred feet up the beach where I perceived that he had waylaid another innocent and was busily explaining why Ontario Premier Mike Harris is not the ravening beast he appears to be. "Why, with gentle stroking, he will take meat right out of your hand," reported the oldster, cheerfully gesturing with one hand whose digits were a token of the marvellous advances in recent prosthetics.

Back to sockeye salmon and the Coast Salish language. The Salish are a people who live, among

SOCKEYE SALMON

other places, on the southern part of Vancouver Island and some surrounding islets. Sockeye is the English version of the Coast Salish *suk-kegh* 'red fish,' an apt name for this frisky Pacific salmon.

VICTORIA SANDWICH

This is a local comic name on Vancouver Island for an elaborate sponge layer-cake that might bring afternoon tea beside the Pacific to a most toothsome conclusion.

WAPATOO

Wapatoo tubers grow in the muddy guck of shallow streams and marshes across Canada, where wild geese, ducks, beavers, and muskrats chomp them with gusto. Observing the animals feasting on tubers, native peoples found wapatoo could provide good food even in the winter. Adult Aboriginal peoples used digging sticks to harvest arrowhead tubers, but children jumped into the streams and found tubers by squishing them between toes in the warm muck and yanking them loose. Wapatoo is then boiled or roasted in hot ashes. *Wapatoo* is Chinook Jargon, borrowed from an Algonkin language where *wap* or *wab* is the stem for 'white.' Wapatoo means 'white root.'

Other common names for this plant include arrowhead, duck potato, *flèche d'eau*, and tule. Leaves shaped like an arrowhead give this plant its name in botanical Latin, *Sagittaria*. The Roman word for arrow, *sagitta*, also hits the target in Sagittarius, the sign of the zodiac that means 'the archer' in Latin, referring originally to the constellation. The two common species in Canada are the more southerly *Sagittaria latifolia* with its *lata folia* or broad leaves, and the more northerly *Sagittaria cuneata* with cuneate or wedge-shaped leaves.

Closing
the Menu

"*Cenabis bene apud me*" wrote the scallywag Roman satirist Martial, in one of the few witty poems in Latin about dining. "You will dine well at my house," Martial advised, if you remember, dear guest, to bring all the food, comfortable cushions, handsome slaves of your own, a few dancing girls handy with fans and the smoothing-on of perfumed unguents, and bring along also many bottles of good Falernian wine. As I finish this grand tour through the history of Canadian comestibles and the words we have created to name our foods, I feel similar to Martial in this sense: you will enjoy the modest menu of verbal delights that I have put before you, only if you bring your own experience with hearty Canuck fare to the table with you, and if you keep your word-finding palate perked up and on the *qui vive* for new Canadian terms. I have here concentrated on culinary terms of prime and historical importance. Every day in this country, it seems, enterprising cooks ransack larders of the past looking for old recipes that can be made new. Consider the Ottawa cooks who revived and re-invented the dish called Beavertails, whose story I recount in the chapter on Ontario food words. I believe our historical cuisine can be raided by other chefs and kitchen-dwellers who seek fresh items for cliché-stained menus. That is one of the reasons I wrote this little volume. The other chief one was to share my delight in the origin of food words, and that extends even to the very word *food*.

Food is one of the blunt, stark Saxon words that strike like monosyllabic hammers on the metal of an English sentence. It was *foda* in Old English or Anglo-Saxon, akin to the verb *fedan*. Food for animals, fodder, comes from the same root. So too does foster, a frequentative form whose prime and sensuous meaning is to feed frequently, hence to nourish, to rear. It finally gives us words like fosterchild. By the way, the same Indo-European root **pa* that shows up in Germanic languages as food and *Futter* gives the Latin *pabulum* for animal fodder or feed, akin to the Latin word for bread, *panis*, and to other English words borrowed from Latin like pastor, pasture, and repast, which have nourishment as their basic idea. As we learned here, Pablum, a well-known Canadian baby food, was named after Roman horse feed, as a joke. In other books I have collected Canadian folk expressions; some of the funniest have to do with food and eating. I heard a farmer near Morrisburg, Ontario, scolding a young hired hand who had made an error operating a tractor. He said, "I swear, boy, I've seen more brains in a sucked egg." The practice of sticking a finger through the top of a fresh egg and sucking out the yolk and the white has largely disappeared from rural Canadian eating habits. But the expression still makes a potent comic insult. So does this old grabber: His cooking is so bad, the flies are taking up a collection to mend the screen door!

And so I conclude with an egregious pun and a wish. As your samplings of our national foods continue, may you dine on Canadian fare well.

A Short List of Books
Containing Recipes
for Canadian Foods

Armstrong, Julian. *A Taste of Quebec*. Toronto: Macmillan, 1990.

Barss, Beulah M. *The Pioneer Cook: A Historical View of Canadian Prairie Food*. Calgary: Detselig Enterprises, 1980.

Canadian Mennonite ookbook. Toronto: Stoddart, 1989.

Cormier-Boudreau, Marielle, and Melvin Gallant. *A Taste of Acadie*. Trans. Ernest Bauer. Fredericton, NB: Goose Lane Editions, 1991.

_____. *La Cuisine traditionnelle en Acadie*. Moncton: Les Éditions d'Acadie, 1978.

Dunton, Hope. *From the Hearth: Recipes from the World of 18th-Century Louisbourg*. Sydney, NS: University College of Cape Breton Press, 1986.

Fat-back and Molasses: A Collection of Favourite Old Recipes from Newfoundland and Labrador. Ed. Ivan F. Jesperson. St. John's, NF: I.F. Jesperson, 1977.

Margaret, Len. *Fish & Brewis, Toutens & Tales: Recipes and Recollections from St. Leonard's, Nfld*. St. John's, NF: Breakwater, 1980.

Nightingale, Marie. *Out of Old Nova Scotia Kitchens*. Halifax, NS: Nimbus Publishing, 1989.

Northern Bounty: A Celebration of Canadian Cuisine. Ed. Joe Marie Powers and Anita Stewart. Toronto: Random House of Canada, 1995.

Pioneer Kitchens: Our Heritage from Many Lands. [Collected by an organization called Southern Alberta Pioneers and Their Descendants]. Regina, SK: Centax Books, 1995.

Recipes of Newfoundland. [Prepared by the Newfoundland 4-H Staff]. St. John's, NF: 4-H Clubs, 1969.

Sharp, James Jack. *Flavours of Newfoundland & Labrador.* St. John's, NF: Breakwater, 1981.

Spalding, Andrea, and David Spalding. *The Flavours of Victoria.* Victoria, BC: Orca Books, 1994.

Staebler, Edna. *Food That Really Schmecks: Mennonite Country Cooking.* 25th anniversary edition. Toronto: McGraw-Hill Ryerson, 1994.

Thomson, Eleanor. *A Loving Legacy: Recipes and Memories from Yesterday and Today, for Tomorrow.* Westport, ON: Butternut Press, 1987.

Watson, Julie. *Favourite Recipes of Old Prince Edward Island.* Halifax, NS: Nimbus Publishing, 1996.

Selected Bibliography

Note
It is not the done thing to list well-known reference books and dictionaries in a bibliography. However, in a book with extensive etymologies and wisps and filigrees of word lore, I hope it will be useful to readers to know some of the volumes I consulted, the better to test my own corrections and expansions of received etymologies, but also to provide signposts, should readers new to word study wish to test the trail. I can assure all who begin such a journey: the vista at trail's end is worth every page-turning step.

Apicius. *Cookery and Dining in Imperial Rome*. Ed. and trans. Joseph Dommers Vehling. New York: Dover, 1977.

Avis, Walter S., C. Crate, P. Drysdale, D. Leechman, M.H. Scargill, C.J. Lovell, eds. *A Dictionary of Canadianisms on Historical Principles*. Toronto: Gage, 1967.

Ayto, John. *The Diner's Dictionary: Food and Drink from A to Z*. Oxford: Oxford University Press, 1993.

Barney, Stephen A., with Ellen Wertheimer and David Stevens. *Word-Hoard: An Introduction to Old English Vocabulary*. New Haven, CT: Yale University Press, 1977.

Bélisle, Louis-Alexandre. *Dictionnaire nord-américain de la langue française*. Reprint of 1979 edition. Laval, QC: Éditions Beauchemin, 1989.

Bergeron, Léandre. *The Québécois Dictionary*. Toronto: Lorimer, 1982.

Brillat-Savarin, Jean-Anthelme. *The Physiology of Taste*. Trans. Anne Drayton. Harmondsworth, UK: Penguin, 1970.

Campbell, Art. *Mots and Phrases of the Gaspé*. Grand Cascapedia, QC: privately printed, 1995.

Canadian Encyclopedia. 4 vols. Edmonton: Hurtig, 1988.

286

Canadian Oxford Dictionary. Ed. Katherine Barber. Toronto: Oxford University Press, 1998.

Collie, Michael. *New Brunswick*. In the series *The Traveller's Canada*. Toronto: Macmillan, 1974.

The Concise Oxford Dictionary of Botany. Michael Allaby, ed. Oxford, UK: Oxford University Press, 1992.

Dalby, Andrew. *Siren Feasts: A History of Food and Gastronomy in Greece*. London, UK: Routledge, 1996.

Dictionnaire historique de la langue française. 2nd ed. Alain Rey, ed. Paris: Dictionnaires Le Robert, 1994.

Encyclopedia of Newfoundland and Labrador. Editor-in-chief: Joseph R. Smallwood. St. John's, NF: Newfoundland Book Publishers (1967) Limited, 1984.

Fisher, M.F.K. *The Art of Eating*. New York: Macmillan, 1990.

Gage Canadian Dictionary. Rev. ed. Toronto: Gage, 1997.

Grieve, Mrs. M. *A Modern Herbal*. Ed. C.F. Leyel. London: Penguin, 1977.

Hamilton, William B. *Place Names of Atlantic Canada*. Toronto: University of Toronto Press, 1996.

Horwood, Harold. *Newfoundland*. Toronto: Macmillan of Canada, 1969.

ITP Nelson Canadian Dictionary of the English Language. Toronto: Nelson, 1997.

Kuijt, Job. *Common Coulee Plants of Southern Alberta*. Lethbridge, AL: University of Lethbridge Production Services, 1972.

Larousse Gastronomique. English translation of 1984 French edition. London: Paul Hamlyn, 1988.

Lewis, Charlton T., and Charles Short. *A Latin Dictionary: Founded on Andrew's Edition of Freund's Latin Dictionary.* Impression of 1st ed. 1879. Oxford: Oxford University Press, 1958.

Liddell, Henry George, and Robert Scott. *A Greek-English Lexicon.* 9th ed. Oxford: Oxford University Press, 1953.

A Literary and Linguistic History of New Brunswick. Reavley Gair, ed. Fredericton, NB: Goose Lane Editions, 1985.

Mac Mathúna, Séamus, and Ailbhe Ó Corráin, eds. *Collins Gem Irish Dictionary.* Glasgow: HarperCollins, 1995.

Maillet, Antonine. *Pélagie-La-Charette.* Montréal: Grasset et Leméac, 1979.
_____. *Pélagie: The Return to a Homeland.* Trans. Philip Stratford. Toronto: Doubleday, 1982.
_____. *La Sagouine: pièce pour une femme seule.* Montréal: Leméac, 1971.
_____. *La Sagouine.* Trans. Luis de Céspedes. Toronto: Simon & Pierre, 1979.

Morton, Mark. *Cupboard Love: A Dictionary of Culinary Curiosities.* Winnipeg, MB: Bain & Cox, 1996.

The New Shorter Oxford English Dictionary. Oxford: Oxford University Press, 1993.

Noms et lieux du Québec: Dictionnaire illustré. 2nd ed. Sainte-Foy, QC: Publications du Québec, 1996.

O'Grady, William, and Michael Dobrovolsky. *Contemporary Linguistic Analysis: An Introduction.* 3rd ed. Copp Clark, 1996.

Oxford English Dictionary. James A.H. Murray et al., eds. Oxford: Oxford University Press, 1884 – 1928; corrected reissue, 1933.

Oxford English Dictionary. 2nd ed. R.W. Burchfield et al., eds. Oxford: Oxford University Press, 1989.

Partridge, Eric. *A Dictionary of Slang and Unconventional English.* London: Routledge, 1984.

_____. *Origins: A Short Etymological Dictionary of Modern English.* 4th ed. London: Routledge and Kegan Paul, 1966.

Poirier, Pascal. *Le Glossaire acadien.* Rev. ed. Ed. Pierre M. Gérin. Moncton, NB: Éditions d'Acadie, 1995.

Rayburn, Alan. *Dictionary of Canadian Place Names.* Toronto: Oxford University Press, 1997.

Robinson, Sinclair, and Donald Smith. *Dictionary of Canadian French/ Dictionnaire du français canadien.* Toronto: Stoddart, 1990.

Shipley, Joseph T. *The Origins of English Words: Discursive Dictionary of Indo-European Roots.* Baltimore, MD: Johns Hopkins University Press, 1984.

Stearn, William T. *Botanical Latin.* New ed. Toronto: Fitzhenry & Whiteside, 1983.

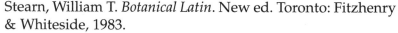_____. *Stearn's Dictionary of Plant Names for Gardeners: A Handbook on the Origin and Meaning of the Botanical Names of Some Cultivated Plants.* London: Cassell, 1992.

Sturtevant, E. Lewis. *Sturtevant's Edible Plants of the World.* Ed. U.P. Hedrick. 1919. Reprint, New York: Dover, 1972.

Story, G.M., W.J. Kirwin, and J.D.A. Widdowson, eds. *Dictionary of Newfoundland English.* 2nd ed. Toronto: University of Toronto Press, 1990.

Szczawinski, Adam F., and Nancy J. Turner. *Edible Garden Weeds of Canada.* In the *Edible Wild Plants of Canada* series. Ottawa: National Museums of Canada, 1978.

_____. *Wild Green Vegetables of Canada*. In the *Edible Wild Plants of Canada* series. Ottawa: National Museums of Canada, 1980.

Toussaint-Samat, Maguelonne. *History of Food*. Trans. Anthea Bell. Oxford: Blackwell, 1992.

Turner, Nancy J., and Adam F. Szczawinski. *Wild Coffee and Tea Substitutes of Canada*. In the *Edible Wild Plants of Canada* series. Ottawa: National Museums of Canada, 1978.

Vaughan, J.G., and C.A. Geissler. *The New Oxford Book of Food Plants*. Oxford: Oxford University Press, 1997.

Webster's Third New International Dictionary of the English Language. Springfield, MA: G. and C. Merriam, 1976.

Illustration Credits

pp. iii, vii, viii, ix, 1, 31, 62, 66, 69, 73, 115, 117, 124, 128, 134, 135, 137, 138-139, 143, 163, 181, 184, 187, 206, 215, 217, 279-281, 292, 294, 297, 300, 305 307, 311, Jim Harter, *Food and Drink: A Pictorial Archive from Nineteenth-Century Sources*, Dover Publications

pp. vii, xi, 57, 58, 78, 102, 105, 139, 147, 149, 154, 158, 159, 168, 190-191, 208-209, 282, Carol Belanger Grafton, *3,800 Early Advertising Cuts: Deberny Type Foundry*, Dover Publications

pp. 2, 54, 63, 98, 126-127, Carol Belanger Grafton, *Old-Fashioned Nautical Illustrations*, Dover Publications

pp. 5, 7, 15, 43, 83, 87, 93, 113, 166, 224, 227, 228-229, 255, 257, Carol Belanger Grafton, *Trades and Occupations: A Pictorial Archive from Early Sources*, Dover Publications

pp. 10, 109, Jim Harter, *Men: A Pictorial Archive from Nineteenth-Century Sources*, Dover Publications

pp. 18, 36, Carol Belanger Grafton, *Old-Fashioned Illustrations of Children*, Dover Publications

pp. 25, 33, 39, 51, 52-53, 60, 70-71, 76, 170, 174-175, 177, 195, 196, 222, 244, 251, 259, 270, Jim Harter, *Animals: A Pictorial Archive from Nineteenth-Century Sources*, Dover Publications

pg. 29, Jim Harter, *Women: A Pictorial Archive from Nineteenth-Century Sources*, Dover Publications

pg. 77, Harold Hart, *Dining and Drinking: Hart Picture Archives*, Hart Publishing Company pp. 74, 84, 131, 201, 240, Richard G. Hatton, *1001 Plant and Floral Illustrations from Early Herbals*, Dover Publications

pp. 99, 248, Jim Harter, *Transportation: A Pictorial Archive from Nineteenth-Century Sources*, Dover Publications

pg. 283, 284, 286, 287, 288, Carol Belanger Grafton, *Old Fashioned Illustrations of Books, Reading & Writing*, Dover Publications

pg. 120, Jim Harter, *The Ultimate Angel Book*, Gramercy Books

pg. 172, Carol Belanger Grafton, *Children: A Pictorial Archive from Nineteenth-Century Sources*, Dover Publications

pg. 189, Carol Belanger Grafton, *Old-Fashioned Christmas Illustrations*, Dover Publications

pg. 196, Carol Belanger Grafton, *Victorian Spot Illustrations, Alphabets & Ornaments*, Dover Publications

pp. 204, 208-209, 211, 212, 218, 219, 228-229, 231, 236, 238, 241, 243, 262-263, Carol Belanger Grafton, *Old West Cuts*, Dover Publications

All additional illustrations have been digitally prepared by the book's designer.

Index

A–Z

A

B

D

E

F

G

P

Q

R

S

U

V

W

Y

Z